HUMAN NATURE

An Introduction to Cultural Anthropology

HUMAN NATURE

An Introduction to Cultural Anthropology

James F. Downs

Professor of Anthropology,
University of Hawaii, Hilo College
and
Chairman,
Cross-Cultural Training Unit,
University of Hawaii Center for Cross-
Cultural Training and Research

GLENCOE PRESS

A division of Benziger Bruce & Glencoe, Inc.
New York • Beverly Hills
Collier-Macmillan Limited, London

Glencoe Press
A division of Benziger Bruce & Glencoe, Inc.
8701 Wilshire Boulevard
Beverly Hills, California 90211
Collier-Macmillan Canada, Ltd., Toronto, Canada

Library of Congress catalog card number: 72-86791

First printing, 1973

Dedicated in gratitude
to
Saint George,
who brought the Princess Sabra out of Egypt.

PREFACE

An anthropology textbook can take one of two forms: it can be a book of data and conclusions, or a book of theory. *Human Nature* falls into the second category. It is in no sense a complete and detailed survey of the entire field. Many subjects are omitted—a fact that will disturb some anthropologists, though I hope none of my omissions will disturb all anthropologists.

However, the book was not written for anthropologists. It was prepared for the student who knows little or nothing of the field, but wishes to begin his explorations of it. Some texts attempt to tell such students "everything," on the premise that anthropology may never get another shot at them. Such an approach, in my experience, almost guarantees that the student will leave his first course in anthropology determined to make it his last. He will have memorized much, been exposed to a veritable landslide of information about a lot of strange people to whom he cannot relate, and learned very little about himself and the people with whom he must deal every day.

The organization and content of the book are based on the questions students have reasonably brought to anthropology over the past fifteen years or so of my teaching. My goal has been to organize answers to those questions into a theory that illustrates the scope and approach of anthropology. The method is essentially traditional—that is, comparing various peoples (including our own) in the ways in which they deal with universal problems. But I have attempted to introduce the subject without belaboring the technical language of the field, and to relate the discipline to the life of the student. In the final analysis, it is the student who will decide whether the attempt has been successful.

—J. F. D.
January, 1973

CONTENTS

PART THREE—DEFINING AND STUDYING CULTURE

INTRODUCTION

Three thousand million years ago, or perhaps longer—a truly unthinkable period of time—by some process not yet completely understood, life appeared on the earth. Two and a half million years ago—a period still beyond imagining—one form of life, the product of an interminably slow process of evolution, developed into what would become the ancestor of the most dominant life form ever to have evolved: man. This mammal possessed the physical and mental potential for the development of culture.

Culture, in this sense, means the ability to adjust and adapt behavior through other than genetic or biological processes—and, most importantly, to pass these solutions on, in a social context, to succeeding generations. While other life forms remained to be ruled by the laws of biology, to evolve or die according to genetic codes and natural selection, man's subsequent history has been dominated by his special quality—the quality of culture. He has not escaped the network of biology but has been able to extend himself and build a wall between himself and his environment—a wall of social relationships, symbols, and technology that obeys laws of its own and has evolved, or developed if you prefer, into the institutions of modern humanity.

Since his earliest beginnings, certainly in all the time for which we have any record, man has been concerned with himself: with the proper modes of action and with the similarities and differences between himself and other men. Within the last century the speculations of wise men, philosophers, and theologians about the nature of man have been augmented by a scientific study of humanity in all its aspects and variations. This study is called anthropology, from the Greek *anthropos,* man, and *logos,* study.

Many attempts, none totally satisfactory, have been made to classify all the activities of anthropologists into "schools" or sub-disciplines. Departments of anthropology in the United States generally require courses in four fields to qualify for the B.A. or M.A. degree. These are **physical anthropology, cultural anthropology** (sometimes called ethnology or social anthropology), **prehistory** (or archaeology), and **linguistics.**

In Europe "anthropology" most frequently refers to physical anthropology; cultural anthropology is known as ethnology. In England, a sharp distinction is drawn between cultural and social anthropology, the latter being emphasized there.

The aims of the anthropologist are simple when stated but complex, sometimes seemingly hopeless, in practice: to understand the history and nature of man. To achieve these goals, anthropologists study man as a totality. Using a holistic approach to the subject matter, they study man as a physical being, a product of evolution and a part of nature. They also study him as a cultural being whose life style in each instance represents one form of cultural life as it has developed in these past two and a half million years.

To the anthropologist, any human activity or product may be relevant to a final understanding of the nature of man: religion, hunting techniques, personal decorations, music, house-building styles, sexual behavior, or means of social organization. Today no single anthropologist attempts to study all the conceivable elements of human behavior that may be significant. Each of us in a sense becomes a specialist in one or more areas of the world and one or more aspects of humanity. But as a discipline, anthropology studies the total man.

In order for many different specialists to continue to communicate and share their findings in a meaningful way, there must be some common assumptions upon which they all base their work. The purpose of an introduction to cultural anthropology is to discuss these assumptions and to illustrate how they have served us to establish at least some tentative generalizations about the nature of man. We say tentative because man is such an immensely complex subject, almost infinitely adaptable.

So diverse are the observable expressions of humanity that at one stage in the development of anthropology many responsible and respected anthropologists held the opinion that generalizations were impossible. Perhaps more as a matter of faith than of empirical reality, this opinion is no longer widely held and anthropologists do attempt, and sometimes achieve, generalizations. In part, a major part, this is due to the dedication to a particular method of research that has led men and women of the anthropological calling into the remotest areas of the world to study in detail the lives of unknown people.

In this way there has been a gradual accumulation of data about how the many varieties of human life are actually lived, relatively free from the romantic tendency to stress shocking or amusing oddities at the expense of accurate perspective on daily life. Thus there is an increasingly useful corpus of information on which to base analyses, tentative conclusions, and plans for further investigation.

The question that motivates anthropological research can be phrased in several ways: What is the essence of man? What is human nature? What is common to all men at all times? This book will discuss some of the conclusions that form the basis from which investigation continues.

FOUNDATIONS OF CULTURE

Part One

INTRODUCTION TO PART ONE:
ORIGINS OF ANTHROPOLOGY

Europe, after the fall of Rome, passed through a time of introspection and social disintegration often called the Dark Ages. The population was politically divided into myriad semi-independent feudal enclaves; communication and transport were primitive and became worse as the centuries passed. The aristocracy was involved in more or less constant internal warfare over feudal holdings, alliances, and obligations, relieved only slightly by the extension of these quarrels into the Near East during the Crusades. Although there were men and families that claimed the inheritance of Rome, no one actually held any overall power. Even Rome itself, the home of the Pope and of the Holy Roman Church (which was the only church), became part of the turmoil of feudal politics. The intellectual achievements of the Classical World, Greece and Rome, were all but forgotten.

During these centuries, the activities of European scholars were dominated by the church, which provided them with their only niche in the social structure. But the viewpoint of the ecclesiastical scholar was narrow and influenced by the need to serve religious doctrine. The early centuries of the Dark Ages were dominated by the belief that the world would end in A.D. 1000, and worldly things were considered of little importance. Non-Christians were beyond the pale of consideration and their achievements made small impression on the intellectual life of Europe.

Figure 1. In medieval Europe, scholarship was quite separate from technology. Scholars were churchmen who devoted their lives to serving religion. Artisans often served the church—as in the construction of cathedrals—but their technical skills remained separate from the activities of scholars. Thus, technology developed and expanded, but science did not.

A curious combination of events led Europe out of this period of insularity and incuriosity. One of the most important developments occurred in the remote corner of Europe that is today Portugal. Here, a feudal prince, newly freed from the presence of the Moors who had ruled much of Iberia for centuries, began to probe the secrets of transport. Far removed from the traditional sources of trade on the eastern shores of the Mediterranean, and unable to compete with the monopoly held by the great trading centers of Italy, Prince Henry of Portugal (1394–1460) began to dream of bypassing existing routes of trade and going directly to the sources of wealth, the almost legendary Indies and China.

Henry's plans were based on a combination of technical devices and techniques. A method of determining longitude by taking sights of the sun had been developed. This, combined with the use of the compass (a device used in Asia for centuries), permitted navigators to chart courses independent of the land. A method of making square-sailed ships move against the direction of the wind freed them from the slavery of the tradewinds. Now Portuguese seamen went scudding

Figure 2. The Portuguese were the first Europeans to develop a maritime technology that permitted them to sail against the wind and navigate out of sight of land. Thus, they led in the exploration of the world by Europeans.

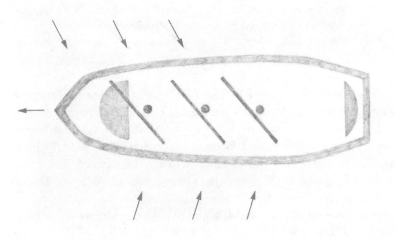

By revolving square sails on the mast, ships could sail across and against the wind, rather than depending on oars.

west into the Atlantic. In their wakes came the Spanish, who stumbled over two entire continents previously unknown to European men. Behind them came the British and the Dutch and the French, all scrambling for a share of the world which they, with characteristic European egocentrism, claimed to have "discovered."

These explorations were only one manifestation of the times. The Roman Church gradually lost its monopoly on the minds and souls of Europeans, and the old landed aristocracy no longer controlled all the sources of power. Trade and commerce provided new means of acquiring wealth and thus, power. Intellectual and artistic achievements began to flower, the works of the ancients were rediscovered, and the accomplishments of the Arab civilizations of the Near East began to be appreciated. Above all, an insatiable demand for knowledge about the rest of the world developed. Sea captains, merchants, adventuring semi-pirates, soldiers, and missionaries returned to Europe with tales of China and India, of the civilizations of western Africa, the remote peoples of inner Asia, and the "Indians" of the New World.

Members of the Church of Jesus Christ of the Latter Day Saints and the Reorganized Church of the Latter Day Saints, commonly known as Mormons and Josephites, believe American Indians are descendants of ancient Hebrews who came to the New World. They base this belief on the Book of Mormon, revealed in the early nineteenth century to Joseph Smith, whom both churches claim as prophet and founder.

The fabulous peoples of the Old World—Chinese, Japanese, Mongol, African, and Hindu—were indeed fascinating, but they were not altogether unknown to Europeans. Alexander had once conquered northern India, and Grecian states had flourished in inner Asia. China had been known since at least the days of Rome and described in detail by Marco Polo. The nomads of Asia had probed into Europe for nearly a millennium and Europeans had visited the courts of Genghis Khan and Tamerlane. Even Africa had a place (misty and distorted) in European knowledge. With relatively little trouble, the known peoples of the Old World could be related to the Bible. Africans were understood to be the sons of Ham. In Asia, it was believed, reigned a fabulous Christian king, Prester John.

Figure 3. The Maya and other Indian civilizations of North and South
America dazzled and amazed Europeans.

Attila was the Antichrist himself and after him came Genghis Khan
and his descendants.

The New World, however, presented Europe with new conceptual problems. The first accounts of the elaborate civilizations of
Mexico and Peru stunned the Europeans. The appearance and customs of New World peoples were often strange, seemingly unrelated to the familiar patterns of the Old World. How, the Europeans
asked, could Christ have died for people about whom no one knew
a thing? How could they exist as descendants of Adam if they were
separated from the Old World? Did they have souls? Were they
indeed human? If they were, where had they come from? Along with
the gold and silver of the New World which flowed into Europe
and upset the balance of the economy came many basic questions
about humanity that upset the balance of the European mind.

For the first time, Europeans were confronted with savage societies from the mountains of Mexico, the jungles of the Amazon, the forests of the American Southeast, and the deserts of the Southwest—men who often went nude or wore few clothes, who used stone tools and painted their faces, who practiced customs unknown to Europeans, or sometimes customs unknown save in the Bible. Were they animals, devils, humans; Atlantans, Greeks, Hebrews, Asians, Welshmen, Irishmen, Vikings? The question of their origin remained unsolved until after 1900. For some people, the explanations now offered by science are not yet accepted.

The variety of life styles of New World peoples deeply impressed European intellectuals for the next three hundred years. The philosopher Rosseau depicted them as idealized Noble Savages, and built a theory of the development of man and society on this base. Others considered them brutes, and offered countertheories. Shakespeare included them in his plays. Novelists, scholars, dramatists, and theologians pondered over them. For the European, man had developed a new dimension that threatened to tear asunder the entire structure of previous thought about human nature.

See John H. Rowe, "The Renaissance Foundations of Anthropology," *American Anthropologist* 67 (February 1966).

Professor John Howland Rowe has demonstrated that the European response to the discovery of new lands and peoples was not simply a matter of new information becoming available and people wanting to find out about it. The collection of information about strange peoples and their customs, he points out, was entirely foreign to Medieval Europe—and to Classical antiquity, too. Although Persians and Arabs had always recognized and appreciated cultural differences, the practices of barbarians had been considered unimportant by the civilizations of Greece and Rome. Greece produced only two writers who devoted any time at all to describing foreign peoples, and the most famous of these, Herodotus, was thought a liar and his cultural observations ignored. Rome produced but a single writer interested enough in foreigners to write about them: Tacitus, who described the tribes of Germany. In medieval Europe there was some interest in religious differences—but primarily with regard to their suppression. It was Italian scholars of the fifteenth century who introduced the idea of recording cultural differences between peoples. The Italians of the Renaissance, unlike Europeans of the Middle Ages, saw that their world was very unlike that of the ancient Greeks and Romans; they became interested in the contrast, and subsequently also developed an appreciation of contemporary cultural differences. The Italian style of scholarship was carried to Spain and Portugal, and it was from there that explorations began. Most of the early accounts of foreign peoples, in fact, were written by Italians sailing under a number of flags.

Perhaps the threat of this new knowledge would not have been so great had it not come at a time when Europeans were questioning many long-cherished truths. Copernicus (died, 1543) probed the movements of the heavens, and the elaborate and ancient astronomical theories of Ptolemy collapsed. Galileo (d. 1642) proved that heavy bodies do not fall faster than light ones, and suggested that the earth moves around the sun instead of being the center of the universe. Newton (d. 1727) considered the movement of objects and developed a new theory of physics. Lyell (d. 1875) explored the structure of the earth and gave birth to geology, challenging the dogma that the world was only six thousand years old.

Luther (d. 1546) questioned the Roman church and in his wake sprang up a thousand doubters, each asking different questions and offering different answers. The authority of the Bible was questioned, and the existence of God. Theories about the nature of man and the divinity of kings were reexamined and rejected. Political movements arose from religious ideology. New methods of production made obsolete skills cherished through generations. The modern sciences of biology, medicine, geology, physics, chemistry freed themselves from the dogmatic chains of their mystical or theological past and began to lay the foundation for future discoveries.

Above all, men began to ask the unaskable question: *Is today's world the way the world has always been?* And increasingly, they began to answer, no. The idea of evolution—the gradual development of the earth, of the life forms which inhabit it, and of man himself—began to develop. Almost imperceptibly, the intellectual community of Europe began to address itself to the problem of the nature of man.

No longer did they speak in terms of what man ought to be, striving to understand his nature by developing "natural laws" based on speculations about what was right or wrong. Instead, they began to look at man himself in his as-yet-bewildering variety and ask how, by observing the empirical facts, they might arrive at laws of nature concerning human behavior that were valid for all mankind.

The accounts of travelers from the far Pacific, from China and Tibet and New Mexico and the Arctic and the extremes of Africa, and the teeming cities of India provided for the first time a body of data that could be examined and analyzed. The adventures of Napoleon encouraged the exploration of the past of Egypt and helped set the stage for modern archaeology. In Europe itself, men were trying to make some sense of the remnants of past societies they uncovered in the river valley and bogs, and in long-abandoned shell mounds. Geologists uncovered the remains of beasts no longer known to man, and the tools of men long dead.

The problems which had once been so simple, answered by reference to the Bible or to religious authority, suddenly became terribly complex. Everywhere there were men, and in many ways they were very much the same; but at the same time they were frighteningly different. The Hindu sacrificed to his gods and his morality called for his widow to throw herself on his funeral pyre. The African married many wives, and considered himself immoral if he did not. The Polynesian was seemingly incapable of feeling guilt about his unrestrained enjoyment of sex, but was convulsed with fear when approached by a man of high status. People wore clothes or none at all. They ate food unpalatable to other men and observed customs unthinkable to others.

What, asked the scientists and scholars of the early nineteenth century, made men so different? In the asking of this question, a new science was born—not yet anthropology as we know it today, but rather *ethnology*, the study of the races and cultures of mankind. Ethnology was a departure from the traditional scholarly endeavors of the time, which were circumscribed by an educational system that stressed the classical works of Greek and Roman authors and the Christian Bible. The peoples who fascinated the ethnologist were those who wrote no books, constructed no elaborate social or technical systems, and who until then had been considered scarcely worthy of the attention of men who were the intellectual descendants of Plato and Aristotle, Sophocles, Tacitus, Ovid, and Saint Thomas.

Few of these new scholars became what we now call *ethnographers*—that is, men who describe foreign cultures from direct observation. Rather, they depended on the writings of missionaries, imperial servants, and explorers. Their data and their methods were often, in the light of today's science, questionable; their almost universal assumption of European superiority was untenable; but their goal was the goal of today: to understand the immense and seemingly chaotic variation in human behavior.

BIOLOGICAL EXPLANATIONS
OF CULTURAL VARIATION

1

RACIST SPECULATIONS

Any scientist attempting to bring intellectual order out of observed chaos must first start by classifying and ordering the data with which he will work. Often quite arbitrarily, he must select differentiating criteria and then group the phenomena which share these characteristics under single categories. He will then most likely attempt to correlate one set of categories with another; if such a correlation appears valid, he will postulate some kind of a causal or dependent relationship between them. He will, in short, construct a hypothesis to see if the relationships it postulates do in fact exist.

The Nineteenth Century

To even the most unscientific observer,

one correlation was obvious: men came in many shapes, sizes, and colors. Different physical characteristics did not occur randomly around the world, but instead appeared in distinct areas of the globe where all the people tended to look more like each other (and their parents) than they did the people of other regions. This phenomenon came to be called "race." No definition of *race* has ever been totally acceptable, nor has any classification of races ever been considered finally authoritative, yet race as an organizing principle of thought tended to dominate the thinking of ethnologists and social philosophers over much of the nineteenth century. Correlated with race was the fact that styles of life differed from place to place and tended to appear in generally similar forms in specific regions. What then could be more obvious than the hypothesis that the variation in human behavior was a consequence of different "racial" heritages?

> More detailed consideration of the definition and nature of **race** is given in Part Three of *Human Variation: An Introduction to Physical Anthropology*, revised edition (Glencoe Press, 1972) by James F. Downs and Hermann K. Bleibtreu.

This explanation appeared at a time when Europeans were more conscious than ever of biological inheritance. Through the eighteenth and into the nineteenth century, great strides had been made in developing superior strains of livestock by selective breeding. Also, for centuries Europeans had thought in terms of superior and inferior peoples within their own societies. Royal or noble blood was felt to carry with it special traits of character that would manifest themselves under any conditions. Fictional romances through the nineteenth century commonly stressed the theme of the unrecognized son of nobility who, despite poor surroundings, managed to reveal his heritage by courageous or chivalrous actions which no baseborn person could ever be expected to display. The occurrence of any superior person in politics, art, and literature simply had to be explained in terms of superior inheritance or "blood." "Blood will tell" was a common and generally accepted aphorism of the time.

> See Clyde Kluckhohn's *Mirror for Man* (Fawcett World, 1970).

The late anthropologist Clyde Kluckhohn cited the instance of a nineteenth-century biographer who theorized that Abraham Lincoln's mother must have had an affair with Chief Justice John Marshall (who was also from Kentucky, although one may doubt that he knew the Lincolns), because such a superior man as Abraham could not possibly have sprung from the loins of a man like Tom Lincoln. There is no shred of evidence for such speculation, but it was seriously

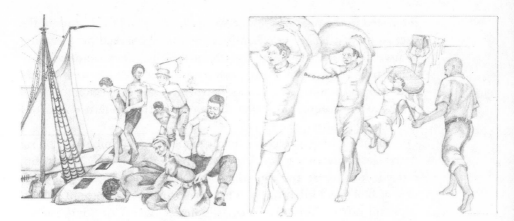

Figure 4. Slavery in America was supported by theories of racial differences. However, it had been a part of African and middle
eastern cultures—albeit in different and more humane forms
—for thousands of years.

offered and as seriously considered because the intellectual framework of the time called for biological explanations.

Science and Racism

In ethnology the biological explanation was also accepted. Differences
in custom, technology, and complexity of social organization were all
attributed to biological inheritance. This was a particularly comforting theory for members of European societies that were kidnap-
ping into slavery thousands of Africans, and usurping the lands of
other "lesser" peoples. To admit that the black slave or the Asian
colonial subject or American Indian was a biological or cultural
equal would have been difficult in the nineteenth century. On the
other hand, to assume that the African or Indian or Polynesian was
inherently inferior and incapable of cultural advance save under the
protection of the White Race gave a perfect rationale for slavery,
imperialism, and the expropriation of lands in the New World.
Had it been less useful, the idea might not have developed such a
tenacious hold on the minds of Europeans and white Americans.
In fact, it provided a "scientific" justification for the erection of
elaborate social, political, and economic structures weighted heavily
in favor of the "superior" race. And, even after the theory was disproven by science, these structures were not easily dismantled.

Once developed, the idea of a correlation between cultural
behavior and racial inheritance maintained a life of its own. Scientists

interested in the relationships between the races and the history of the races—the first to be called anthropologists—embarked on a century of investigating various physical characteristics. They examined skin color, nose shape, hair form, skull length and breadth, arm length, and an endless number of ratios between various measurements—all aimed at unraveling what they assumed was the modern product of the mixing of once pure races.

Ethnologists assumed without question that cannibalism, plural marriage, a tendency toward aggressiveness or taciturnity, along with a talent for singing and a predilection toward the dance, were products of biological inheritance. They spoke and wrote without embarrassment of the "primitive races," "inferior races," or "dark races." Thus confusing custom and biology, they would postulate biological affinity between tribal peoples thousands of miles apart and separated by oceans, on the basis of some custom they had in common. In the same manner, they would postulate the historic identity of two distant peoples because of the appearance of similar physical characteristics in both populations.

The edifice of scientific racism did not crumble until nearly a century of ethnographic reporting, historical research, anthropological investigations, and archaeology combined to prove that the supposed correlation between race and group behavior did not in fact exist at all. In the modern world such a statement cannot be made and left unsupported. Throughout the world, lines of interest and antagonism are still drawn along lines of color. It is therefore worthwhile to explore the foundations on which this denial of the racist hypothesis is based, to look at the testimony of several fields of science.

THE HYPOTHESIS DISPROVED

Various physical anthropologists have divided mankind into from three to over two hundred racial classifications. Such disagreement among men who have devoted their lives to the study of race should suggest to the most obtuse that "common sense" observations about racial differences rest on exceedingly treacherous ground. The greatest problem is of course the almost infinite variation in human appearance. A "typical" Afro-American is as rare as a white Bantu or a black Swede.

Within each racial group, of whatever classification system, only the most general statements of similarity can be made. Furthermore, many of the criteria used to establish one set of classifications often prove to have no correlation with other sets of criteria. This can be seen in comparing observable physical characteristics—eye form, nose form, skin color, hair color and form—with blood types. In theory, people of similar appearance should have generally similar blood types. This is not so, however; blood-type distributions cut right across groupings made on the basis of appearance. To put it another way, people of quite different appearance often have the same blood type.

The Human Species

There is no question that populations have developed generally different appearances that correlate with regions: that is, geographical races. There are many hundreds of such localized populations, but only three major groupings seem to be acceptable—and these with great reservation—to most modern scientists. The people of Europe, North Africa, the Middle East, and India are generally classified as *Caucasoids*. In general they are lighter-skinned than most other men, although some Caucasoid peoples are very dark-skinned indeed. Wavy hair of many shades, relative hairiness of the body, and ruggedness of skeleton are other features found with high frequency in Caucasoid populations. The people of Asia and the native American Indians are classified as *Mongoloids* although in such a vast area there are, to be sure, many variations. The general characteristics are light brown skin with a yellowish or reddish tinge, straight black hair, little body hair, and a high frequency of a special feature of the upper eyelid, the epicanthic fold. *Negroid* peoples originate in Africa south of the Sahara, and range enormously in stature and physique. Their skins are usually darker than those of the other two groups, and their hair more tightly curled. Dark populations in the Pacific islands who share only a few characteristics with Africans have been called *Oceanic Negroids*. A number of populations, including native Australians, Polynesians, and Bushmen, do not seem to fit even into these broad classifications.

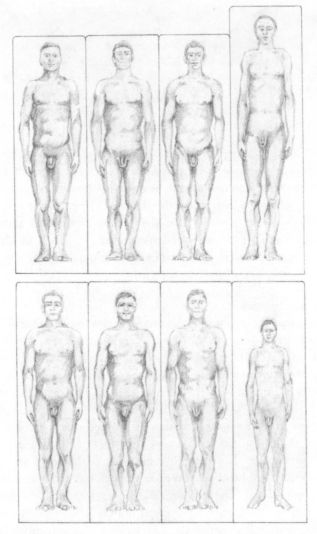

Figure 5.   Although one member of Group A is tall (raising the *average* height of Group A) and one person in Group B is short (giving that group a lower average), most individuals in both groups are the same height. This is generally true, when comparing populations.

Perhaps less than five percent of the genetic inheritance of any individual produces these "racial" differences, whereas the other ninety-five percent produces the similar organs, structures, and processes that are essential to human life. In short, the similarities among groups of men far outweigh the observable differences.

Moreover, it has been proven over and over that men are all of the same species. Any fertile male human from anywhere in the world can mate with any fertile female and produce a live and fertile child. Only members of the same species can create fertile offspring. This, of course, is the refutation of the "common sense" remark, "Horses and cows don't interbreed, so why should blacks and whites?" One answer is that men are not horses and cows, and should not be expected to act like them. But more important is the fact that while horses and cows can't successfully interbreed, black horses and white horses can, with no detriment to their species.

It has been shown many times that measurements of such factors as brain size and body stature vary *on the average* from group to group. But *average* means that there are extremes within the populations measured, so that a great deal of overlap exists among groups. The average difference in such measurements among the three major racial groupings is small indeed—almost always smaller than the variation between two individuals of the same racial category. This means, simply, that if there is a difference of N cubic centimeters in size between the average Caucasoid brain and the average Negroid brain, there is almost certainly a difference of N $\times$ 5 between the largest and smallest Negroid brains. Moreover, it means that while Caucasoids or Negroids may include a few individuals on the highest or lowest end of the scale where no scores of the other group occur, most people of *both* groups score within the same range.

Of course, all of this comparison is nearly useless because we have as yet to prove that variations in brain size, within normal ranges, have anything to do with intellectual or cultural potential. We know that, compared to other animals, all men, from dwarfs to giants, have truly enormous brains; beyond that we can say no more. What is true about cultural and intellectual potential can also be said about other measurable characteristics. It is true that some groups of people tend to have longer legs, or lungs better developed for life at high altitudes. However, these variations appear to occur quite independently of racial classifications. They result not from the unique genetic potential of a given race, but from unusual environmental conditions; given the same conditions, all human individuals and populations respond to the same biological principles.

"Primitive Traits"

Various physical features displayed by one population or another have, from time to time, been called "primitive." A precise definition

Figure 6. Indians living in the extremely high Andes of Peru have been found to display unique physical adaptations to their high altitude life. However, these features are not found in other Indian populations, so we cannot speak of them as racial "traits."

of "primitive" characteristics seems generally lacking in modern anthropological literature. Sometimes the word is used to mean an appearance reminiscent of some fossil ancestor, other times to suggest relationships to some modern ape. In fact, such usages usually carry with them a special bias. Thus, Chinese refer to Japanese as monkeys, white men speak of the ape-like characteristics of Africans, Orientals refer to the animal-like hairiness of Europeans, and so on. Where the term and idea have been used in physical anthropology, it is generally a case of an outmoded scholar of the past writing without modern scientific insights about evolution.

Outward-jutting jaws (prognathism) and heavy browridges, for example, have frequently been called "primitive" traits. If we think carefully, we can see a distinct bias in such usage. It is true that fossil man and many apes did have heavy browridges and tended to be more prognathic than modern man. It is equally true that some populations in the modern world display a greater incidence of these traits than do others. However, it is significant that other equally animal-like or ape-like characteristics are never mentioned as "primitive," perhaps because an objective examination of these features would reveal that no race has a monopoly on "primitive" physical characteristics.

When compared in terms of prognathism, hairiness, browridge development, the shape of the heel and buttocks, the average Negroid individual looks much *less* "primitive" than the average Caucasoid. That is, the features which occur most frequently in black populations—sparse body hair with tightly coiled hair on the head, full development of the buttocks, a large heel and lips—all are far removed from characteristics of apes, animals, etc. A hairy body with lank or curly hair, smaller buttocks, smaller heels, narrow lips—these are Caucasoid characteristics which are shared by apes, other animals and (to the degree we can tell) fossil men. The important point, however, is that none of these characteristics is more "primitive" than others; they all result from the lengthy and intricate workings of natural selection and genetics.

Few, if any, characteristics attributed to one race never occur in another. White-skinned people (albinos) are born among Negroids and Mongoloids. Frizzy hair appears in Caucasoid populations, as well as thick lips and broad noses, while the opposite characteristics often distinguish one "Negroid" group from another. In short, while we cannot deny that physical differences do occur in men and that such differences *between individuals* do influence individual abilities, we have not one shred of reliable evidence that such differences have any impact on the behavior or potential of the group.

The Evidence of Culture History
Another way of testing the relative creativity and cultural potential of the different physical varieties of man is to examine the record of human achievement to see if any particular racial stock has a monopoly on creativity.

From the dimmest early beginnings of man's technical progress we have so little evidence—and are so uncertain that what we do have represents the earliest occurrence of, let us say, tool making or the use of fire—that it is really pointless to speculate. Moreover, in all probability, the physical types of the Middle and Lower Paleolithic periods (see Chapter Fourteen) have so little specific relation to the modern races that nothing would be gained by an examination of the evidence. However, by the end of the Paleolithic period, we are fairly certain, the general outlines of modern human variation had stabilized; so it is perhaps fruitful to examine the subsequent achievements of man very briefly to see if there is any evidence to suggest that one racial type has been more creative than others. This idea has been cherished by Europeans for more than a century, as they have pointed to their rapidly developing technology and their successful imperial expansions into the regions occupied by other racial types. However, if we move from the present to the past, the evidence becomes increasingly disturbing.

A thousand years ago, as we mentioned earlier, Europe was a tangle of feudal states. The bulk of the population lived in abject subjugation as serfs. Intellectual achievements were limited, the province of the church. The population, from king to serf, believed in omens and amulets, visitations and witches. Justice was sought in the combat of antagonists, and the stronger swordsmen decided the issue of guilt or innocence. Technical achievements were limited.

Compare this, the world of the ancestors of the modern European, with the brilliant civilization of the Arab who was preserving the learning of ancient Greece in his universities in Cairo and Baghdad and Alexandria. Arab poets created, and Arab travelers gave birth to geography and ethnography. Arabs dominated the trade routes and the seas, administered justice according to the Koran in courts of law, and built masterpieces of architecture. At Timbuktu, an Islamic university staffed largely by Africans taught science before Oxford or the Sorbonne existed. And in the "darkest" reaches of tribal Africa, "savage" kings and chiefs heard cases at law, using rules of evidence and advocates for the principals centuries before such practices appeared in Europe.

While tenth-century Paris wallowed in its own filth and provided protection against the assaults of rapacious feudal knights, a half world away in China, Chang An, the capital of the T'ang dynasty was a miracle of civilization. Strong law protected the persons of all. Art and music flourished. Much of the foundation of later European technical achievement was being developed by Chinese concerned with the movement of the heavens, the peculiarities of magnetism, and the explosive properties of chemical mixtures. Without belaboring the point, we can say that a thousand years ago Europe, the home of the ancestors of modern Frenchman and Englishmen and Germans, was a cultural backwater that compared unfavorably with the cultures of China and the Arab world, and in many instances had yet to develop ideas and practices which were already age-old in tribal Africa.

In the days of the Romans (a branch of the white race often despised today by northern and western Europeans), Englishmen and

Frenchmen were considered savages incapable of attaining civilized status. Britain was a frontier post where civilized Romans held their noses at the odor of the natives and chuckled at their child-like customs. Franks and Germans were felt to be fanatically brave, given to debauchery and drunkenness, quite without civilized morals.

Before that, the Greeks had similarly looked at the Romans, and the civilized Minoans of Crete at the Greeks. Egyptian civilization was developed by Mediterranean peoples and when after a thousand years the culture fell into disarray, it was revitalized by the Nubians, a black African people. As Egyptian culture began to retreat from the Nile and was increasingly replaced by Greek culture, cities arose in black Africa to carry on Egyptian traditions until these in turn disappeared.

If we look at the process of technological invention, we find that agriculture was probably developed earliest by Semites in the Middle East, or by Asians in what is now called Thailand; it appeared independently in Mexico and Peru among Mongoloid peoples, and probably again in West Africa among blacks. Iron-smelting is a Middle Eastern invention, although it may have had a separate origin in Africa. Domesticated animals appear among Asian reindeer herders, Semitic farmers of the Middle East, and tribesmen of Africa and South Asia. Writing systems have been invented by Chinese, Phoenicians, ancient Greeks, Egyptians, American Indians, and Africans.

Professor William Solheim of the University of Hawaii has reported that archaeological investigations in the Mekong River valley of Thailand reveal evidence that cultivation of plants began much earlier than had previously been reported.

It would be tedious to cite more examples of the creativity of the various racial groups of mankind. These few suggest that cultural development is not exclusive to any one group, nor is cultural backwardness. The potential for technical and social development is the heritage of all men. Differences in the rate of development must be explained in some other way.

Ethnographic Evidence

A look at an ethnographic map of the modern world teaches us a similar lesson. Today, as in times past, cultural differences do not correlate significantly with mankind's racial divisions.

Figure 7. Many peasant farmers of the Middle East use methods invented millennia ago, and diffused to the rest of the world.

For instance, the simplest form of social organization and cultural development is based on hunting animals and gathering wild plant food. Before they were faced with competition from agricultural or industrial systems, some hunting and gathering peoples attained relatively complex levels of social and cultural organization. (The tribes of California and the Northwest Coast of America are recent examples.) Today and for some time past, however, the hunters and gatherers have been forced to live in marginal areas unwanted by farmers: the deserts, the frigid extremes of North and South America, and the dense jungles of Asia, Africa and the Amazon basin.

Such societies often display similarities of social organization. They frequently travel in small bands of related people, their movements in large part dictated by the availability of food. Seldom do they have leaders with permanent political authority. Hunters and gatherers often use flimsy, temporary housing, wear scanty clothing, and possess little in the way of technological equipment. Their religious systems usually lack elaborate ceremony.

Readers interested in learning more about the general traits of hunting and gathering societies should consult *Primitive Social Organization: An Evolutionary Perspective* (Random House, 1962), by Elman Service, and *Man the Hunter* (Aldine, 1968), edited by Richard B. Lee and Irven DeVore.

Hunters and gatherers have existed on all continents, composed of people from all major racial groups. The Middle East, Europe, and most of Africa and Asia have for so long been occupied by farming peoples that little trace of the hunters and gatherers remains. There are hunters and gatherers in the jungles of India with racial connections to Eurasian Caucasoids, however, and the Laplanders of northernmost Europe live on a tribal level of organization, traveling in small bands with herds of half-wild reindeer. Negroid hunters and gatherers include the Pygmies of central Africa, and a few very small groups in East Africa. (The Bushmen and Hottentots of southern Africa form a separate non-Negroid population, but the Hottentots are pastoralists while their relatives the Bushmen exist by hunting and gathering.) The tribal Samang of the Malayan jungles are considered Mongoloids, but the Indians of Alaska, Canada, and the western half of the United States are the great contribution of the Mongoloid stock to the list of hunters and gatherers.

Thus, every racial stock has representatives living at the least complex level of cultural development. Similar surveys of tribal farmers, peasants, and increasingly organized social systems would yield much the same conclusion. Until this century, Europeans might have taken comfort in the fact that only in western Europe and its cultural extensions in America had the modern urban-industrial state developed. However, the correlation between western European racial types and industrialism has ceased to exist, especially since World War I. Industrialization has spread to eastern and southern

Figure 8. Although they are Europeans, the Lapps live in bands, following the reindeer. Simple social organization is not limited to
non-European peoples.

Europe, and any differences in efficiency and productivity can easily
be explained by the shorter developmental time the new industrial
nations have had, compared to the nations that industrialized first.
Of course, the rapid development of Japan as an urban-industrial
power—surpassing Germany, France, and England, as well as all of

the eastern and southern European powers save the U.S.S.R.—quite clearly and forever destroys the myth of any racial monopoly on any style or level of cultural development.

Psychological Testing

Perhaps no problem has so totally intrigued the psychologist, particularly the American psychologist, as that of explaining the presumed differences in "intelligence" between whites and Negroes. Since the early 1900's, tests have been devised in the attempt to settle the question. A recent work reviewing the problem cites no fewer than two

The book that reviews American intelligence testing is Audrey M. Shuey's *The Testing of Negro Intelligence,* second edition (Social Science Press, 1966). Anthropological discussions of the mental processes of "primitive" peoples can be found in *The Mind of Primitive Man* (Free Press, 1965), by Franz Boas and *Primitive Man as Philosopher* (Dover, 1927), by Paul Radin. See also *Race and Intelligence,* C. L. Brace, G. R. Gamble, J. T. Bond, eds., Anthropological Studies No. 8 (American Anthropological Association, 1971).

hundred tests given between 1916 and 1960. All of these tests were designed to measure intelligence in some way or another, although the concept of intelligence itself is so difficult that no satisfactory definition exists. On the basis of these tests, blacks tested as a group scored from seven to thirteen percent lower than whites tested as a group. Surely, the reader must ask, does this not prove that the racial heritage of the black American passes on to him a lower intelligence than does that of the white person? However, when the tests and their context are examined in detail, the clearcut results seem to fade and disintegrate into endless unanswered, and perhaps unanswerable, questions.

The first stumbling block of such testing programs is that we simply don't know how to define intelligence. For some, it is a vague concept that deals with some inherent capacity for thought, based in genetics. For others, intelligence is simply performance against a standard—grades received in school for example, or ability to get along in society. Unfortunately, the only way to ascertain the degree

Figure 9. "Intelligence testing" in modern America almost always takes place in a school setting, and test questions and answers are generally based on cultural assumptions of the white middle class.

of intelligence, however one defines it, is to give tests. Almost invariably, such tests reflect the basically middle-class values of modern America, with emphasis on collected knowledge, technical devices, and education. The ability to read the test is assumed; so is the subject's familiarity with a pencil and paper, and his desire to follow the instructions and to score well. And of course, the individuals being tested are assumed to be comparable units. Seldom—perhaps never—have these assumptions been acknowledged by testers, no matter how meticulous they have been in the selection of subjects.

What, for instance, is the correct completion of the following sentence?

I sleep on the _____.

    a. table   c. bed
    b. floor   d. ice box

For the vast majority of Americans, black and white, *c.* would seem to be correct. But what of the many thousands of children of American Indian and Asian descent who do, in fact, sleep on the floor?

Or let us ask what is the correct response to another problem.

Milk is _____.

    a. white   c. blue
    b. brown   d. green

During the Depression of the 1930's, millions of American children whose families could not afford whole milk never saw milk save in the form of "blue-john," that is, skimmed milk, which has a distinctly blue color. Such obvious difficulties can be adjusted for by a sensitive investigator, but they do illustrate the basic problem of testing for "intelligence": that performances on tests may be influenced far more by the personal experience of the subject than by his inherited abilities.

This point was perhaps most forcefully illustrated in World War I, when all men inducted into the armed services were given two tests. In every instance the group scores showed whites scoring higher than men classed as Negroes. However, as analysis continued, several other results became clear. In general, blacks from northern states did better than whites from southern states. Moreover, American-born Negroes generally did better than immigrant and first generation Italians. Could migration from Georgia to New York alter a human characteristic rooted in genetics? Doubtful. The obvious key variable was the experience of the subjects—differences in education, attitudes, and aspirations—that is, social factors, many of them exceedingly subtle.

The results of the World War I armed forces tests were discussed by A. L. Kroeber in *Anthropology: Race, Language, Culture, Psychology, Prehistory* (Harcourt Brace Jovanovich).

The same reasoning that has gone into testing American blacks has been applied until quite recently to other peoples. For a generation or more, anthropologists and others discussed "the mind of primitive man" as if the psychological processes of tribal peoples were basically different from those of "civilized" man. It is odd, but nonetheless true, that such discussions were carried on in books and scientific journals and meetings by men who had lived in the field among tribesmen with whom they had often developed deep friendships and for whom they held deep respect. Gradually, it became clear that the mind of "primitive" man, or black or yellow man, is no different from that of "civilized" man, or white or brown man. All men have a similar mental makeup and, while differences in intelligence or at least performance exist between *individuals,* none exist between the groups we have called races.

Figure 10. The spread of industrialism in Japan should forever still claims that the ability to develop such an economic system is limited to Caucasians.

American Prejudice

We must ask, then, why there is such a difference in tested performance between American blacks and American whites. In its simplest and least palatable form, the answer appears to be that this difference reflects the social system of the United States—which, both in obvious and in very subtle ways, has divided the two races, always with the explicit or implicit assumption that the white was superior in inherited ability to the black. While investigators have tried very hard and with all sincerity to find black subjects who are not affected by the racial structure of the United States, their efforts are as futile as those to seek out Americans whose thinking is not in some way influenced by the structure of the English language. No factor yet considered—education, housing, or income—will erase the identification of a dark-skinned citizen as a "Negro," and that identification has far reaching and destructive social consequences.

Perhaps no better illustration of this can be found than in quoting from the autobiography of the late Malcolm X, an articulate

Readers interested in learning more about the black experience in the United States should consult *The Autobiography of Malcolm X* (Grove Press, 1964; paperback, 1966). The quotation below is from page 36 of the paperback edition.

and controversial black leader. In his youth in Michigan, the young Malcolm was a top student and class president—the kind of boy who can expect a brilliant future in America, except that he was black. One day, a favorite teacher asked Malcolm what he wanted to do in life, and Malcolm answered that he would like to be a lawyer.

> Mr. Ostrowski looked surprised. . . . He kind of half-smiled and said, "Malcolm, one of life's first needs is for us to be realistic. Don't misunderstand me, now. We all here like you, you know that. But you've got to be realistic about being a nigger. A lawyer—that's no realistic goal for a nigger. . . ."

To one degree or another, all Americans of African ancestry have had to be "realistic about being a nigger." The differential results of the intelligence tests indicate that instead of scoring Negroes and whites on inherited mental ability, perhaps the tests score America on its harmful racial structure.

Individual Achievements
The modern racist, less and less able to seek support from science, may argue: If the darker races aren't less intelligent or less creative, why haven't they done more? How have they contributed to the development of America? Where are their great men? The truth is that the black contribution to America has been largely overlooked or ignored. Where the contribution itself cannot be overlooked, the black man has often been painted white—that is, his racial background ignored. One such man was James Beckwourth, a famous western explorer; although his role could not be ignored in California history, for years textbooks simply failed to mention his race. Similarly, historians of the struggle for independence seldom point out that some five thousand free blacks served in the ranks of the Revolutionary Army. Aside from descendants of people from Great Britain, Afro-Americans constituted the largest ethnic group to take part in the Revolution. Nor have the mythmakers who write of the romantic west pointed out that some five thousand of the cowboys, not to mention a few of the pioneer ranchers, a law officer or two, and a number

Figure 11.   The Paiute Indians of the Great Basin are linguistically related to the Aztecs. But the Aztecs built great cities, established a vast empire in Mexico, and developed a complex,
diverse society, whereas the Paiutes developed an extremely
simple culture that left little room for the expression of
individuality.

of equally romantic outlaws were black. In later times, a black surgeon who had developed a new operating technique and was illustrating it in a scientific paper was asked by a major university to wear
rubber gloves that hid his dark skin. In recent years, as the ranks of
government, commerce, commercial sports, and the arts have opened
for people of African ancestry the question, "Where are their great
men?" has an increasingly hollow sound.

> The CBS–TV film documentary "The Black Soldier," nar-
> rated by Bill Cosby, described the participation of black
> Americans in the military history of the United States.

What we have said about American blacks applies to all other
racial groups. No amount of ingenuity has been able to devise a
culture-free test for intelligence. All field experience and all history

over and over again point to the fact that, individual differences aside, there is a psychological unity among all men, and thus any attempt to explain cultural differences in terms of race is in error. There have recently been criticisms that anthropology has discouraged research to seek out racial differences. However, the critics, often sincere and reputable scientists themselves, by their own utterances reveal that they are unfamiliar with the overwhelming evidence that no significant racial differences exist and the equally compelling evidence that the differences in behavior which we do see are rooted not in biology but in culture. Certainly no modern physicist would take seriously an attempt to prove the existence of ether, nor would a modern geographer or astronomer lend his support to a project devoted to proving the earth is flat. In short, the racial hypothesis has been tested by every known means and in each instance disproven. Until new methods are developed and new hypotheses offered, the argument must rest there.

Until the nineteenth century, scholars postulated the existence of a substance known as **ether**, which was believed to be the medium through which light and sound passed. Research has long since disproved the hypothesis, but for a long time it was one of the basic assumptions on which all theories of physics were built.

GALTON'S THEORY OF GENIUS

Race was not the only outgrowth of the biological orientation of the nineteenth century that was used as an explanation of man's cultural differences. Some scholars and scientists saw quite clearly that historical shifts in cultural creativity seemed to have little or nothing to do with skin color or geography. They examined the record of history and archaeology, which—as we saw earlier in the chapter—seems to skip through time almost at random from Mesopotamia to Egypt, to China, to Africa, then back to Greece and Rome, eastward again to China and India, and finally, in our time, to Europe. They realized that an explanation of cultural change that rested on the continuing possession of special creative abilities by a single racial stock would not support the facts. Trapped, still, in the biological framework of thought, they sought another explanation that emphasized biology.

In its most developed form, the theory was offered by Sir Francis Galton, a man who also studied meteorology, founded eugenics, and devised a system of fingerprint identification. Galton suggested that genius (that is, outstanding intellect) is produced at differential rates. The rate of production of genius determines a society's level of cultural development. With scientific precision Galton explored this idea, which was among the first to recognize the importance of the laws of statistical probability, but his hypothesis has two major weaknesses. The first problem is to define and identify genius, and the second is to make the theory fit what we have subsequently learned about heredity through the study of genetics.

Professor William Shockley of the Stanford University School of Engineering has become a vocal advocate of the idea that blacks inherit inferior intelligence. He was recently refused permission to teach a course on the subject, on the grounds that he was insufficiently trained in the field of genetics. Professor Arthur R. Jensen, an educational psychologist, has also advocated the idea that the I.Q. of whites and blacks is a genetically inherited factor. Neither of these men takes into consideration any possible cultural and social factors influencing school and test performance; they rely instead on a purely biological explanation. (See Jensen's "How Much Can We Boost I.Q. and Scholastic Achievement?" in the *Harvard Educational Review* 39, no. 1 (Winter 1969), and Shockley's "Models, Mathematics, and the Moral Obligation to Diagnose the Origin of Negro I.Q. Deficits," in the *Review of Educational Research* (October 1971), pp. 369–377.)

For a critique of the Shockley–Jensen approach see the *Phi Delta Kappan* of March 1971 and the special supplement to the *Phi Delta Kappan* of January 1972.

Unlike the racists, Galton was not convinced that only western Europeans possessed superior intellect. He was quite willing to accept the consequences of his own research, which suggested that at certain times other peoples had produced the greatest numbers of geniuses. His mathematics proved to him that Athens in the fifth century B.C. and sixteenth-century England had produced the most geniuses, which must have been comforting to a nineteenth-century Englishman with a classical education.

These findings, however, give us the first clue to the key weakness of the entire argument. Galton admired the fifth-century Athenians for precisely the same activities upon which he prided himself: philosophy, science, architecture, art, and government. Outstanding and appreciated works in these fields were defined as the work of genius. Less familiar with, and less appreciative of, the philosophies or poetry or sculpture of Japan, China, India or Africa, he did not see as many evidences of genius in these places. In short, by using his own time and values as a standard, Galton made his results a foregone conclusion. How is one to judge whether Phideas, the Athenian sculptor, was a greater genius than the unknown Indian of the Amazon jungle who discovered a method for removing poison from manioc root and converting the root into food? Was Genghis Khan—under whose aegis, it was said, a virgin with a bag full of gold could ride unharmed from the Black Sea to Korea—less a genius than Plato?

Using very much the same methods and standards but more willing to admit his ethnocentric bias, A. L. Kroeber reexamined Galton's hypothesis in his monumental work *The Configurations of Culture Growth*. His own conclusions suggested not that geniuses

Ethnocentrism refers to the practice of judging other cultures by the standards of one's own culture. *Configurations of Culture Growth* was published in the University of California Press in 1944.

make culture, but that culture, in fact, gives genius the opportunity for expression. The clusters of genius recognized by Galton were not the product of heredity, but instead, the consequences of environment. Kroeber's evidence filled nearly nine hundred pages, but his conclusions were brief and clear:

> ... Most of the potential geniuses born are never realized, so far as history or human values are concerned. The supply of genius physiologically or psychologically speaking ought to remain essentially constant in any race within any period which is not unduly long. However, inasmuch as even peoples possessing higher civilization have produced cultural products of value only intermittently during a relatively small

fraction of their time span, it follows that more individuals born with the endowment of genius have been inhibited by the cultural situations into which they were born than have developed by other cultural situations.

Perhaps an example would make this clearer. In the Great Basin of the United States, a number of Indian peoples, at the time they first became known to Europeans, had developed a life style dependent on the intensive and very sophisticated exploitation of plants and animals, which they hunted and collected. The Basin environment was not productive enough to support large groups of people or to allow for much experimentation. Their religious, artistic, and social life was simple. What opportunity would a potential genius have in such a situation? For women, almost the only opportunity for personal expression was in the weaving of baskets, and for men, in hunting. An imaginative Washo, Shoshone, or Paiute might compose new songs to be sung in semisacred contexts, or create original elaborations on folk tales, or become a persuasive speaker, but his accomplishments could hardly become known beyond his tribe or his own generation.

Many writers, particularly historians, have tended to see the flow of human events moving from one great human personality to another. In each chapter of history they saw a great man who, as a leader, inventor, or inspirer shaped the direction of history for other men. Kroeber's conclusions, on the other hand, suggest that the great men of history are as much the products of culture as shapers of it. Napoleon, of course, was important to European history and culture; but it is unlikely that he and only he existed at that time to play the role he played. Rather than Napoleon making history, history appears to make our Napoleons and Caesars and Robert Fultons. The expression of outstanding individual potential is often masked by society and culture itself. This is particularly true in smaller, simpler societies which simply cannot accommodate genius in any but a few contexts. In larger, more complex social systems, there are obviously more alternatives open to the outstanding personality and thus a greater chance that his impact will be felt. However, even in enormously complex modern societies, our economic system and cultural mores often mask individual potential. How many black men have been denied full expression of their potential because of the cultural pattern of discrimination in the United States? How many geniuses have worked out their lives in humdrum jobs because the economic condition of their families did not permit them to go to college or experiment with different careers? How many brilliant Russians have been denied self-expression because they did not subscribe to the party line? How many Bengali geniuses have died in the strife of the early 1970's, and how many more uprooted refugees will find nothing in life save a struggle for survival? Perhaps the genius *will* live a bit more happily than his less outstanding neighbor, but mere survival is hardly a full expression of potential.

When I was last in India, the nation was faced with the irony of an Indian scientist winning the Nobel Prize—a scientist who did his work not in India, but in the United States. India had provided no employment for a man of his training and brilliance, and so he had left his homeland and gone to the United States. Had it not been for the international economic, social, political, and technical system that allowed a bright young man from India to obtain advanced education and then go to a foreign nation to work, his life would probably have been that of another local Indian schoolteacher, or perhaps a successful businessman or government official. Certainly, at her stage of economic and scientific development, India simply could not have afforded to reward his acquired skills. Similar stories have probably existed from the beginning of human history.

THE BIOLOGICAL FOUNDATIONS
OF CULTURE

2

A TAUTOLOGY

We have seen that race is not related in any causal way to the development of culture or to the intellectual or cultural potentials of a group or an individual. It is tempting to carry this conclusion further and suggest that biology and culture are totally separate spheres which have no relation, one to the other. This, of course, is not true. We will see as we read on that culture has enormous effects on our biological selves. From psychosomatic illness to the evolutionary development of our species, all aspects of human life are subject to the predominant fact that human beings are cultural beings. The other side of the coin is equally important. We are cultural beings because we have evolved in a certain way,

biologically. Chapter One showed that with respect to men's abilities to live as cultural beings, the minor differences we call racial are not important. However, it is the basic physical structure of our species that provides the foundation on which culture is built.

It is uncomfortable for a person brought up in the western tradition of thought to consider a tautology. We prefer to think in straight lines of causality. Nonetheless, much of nature is tautological—circular—and nothing less so than man. Culture has formed the biological entity that is the human species as culture is formed by the particular morphology—anatomical, neurological, and physiological—that is mankind.

A **tautology** is a bit of circular reasoning, as when a condition is explained in terms of itself. The interrelationship between man's culture and his biology is discussed from a different perspective in chapters one and three of Downs and Bleibtreu, *Human Variation: An Introduction to Physical Anthropology*, revised edition (Glencoe Press, 1972).

Ask yourself (for a moment of fantasy) what human culture would be like if our species had evolved with the female's mammaries on her back? How would this affect the relationship of mother and child? What would be the psychological consequence to the developing youngster, and how would our standards of beauty, eroticism, and gestures of affection be changed? Or what if man, equipped with the same brain and intellectual capacity, were quadrupedal and had only a thin, prehensile nose. These *are* implausible fantasies, but if you take a moment to jot down your ideas of how your comfortable and familiar world would be different if these things had happened, perhaps you will see how important our present physique is to our capacity for culture. Let us look briefly, then, at the biological traits of *Homo sapiens* that serve as a basis for human culture and society.

HANDS AND FEET

First, man is bipedal. That is, he spends most of his time on two feet. He moves automatically on two limbs and uncomfortably on four. So completely specialized for bipedal locomotion have we become over the multimillennia of evolution that we have developed two sets of limbs with entirely different functions. This is also true of birds and bats, whose forelimbs have become wings; however, rather than organs of flying, our front limbs have become organs of holding, reaching, clinging, striking, hugging, and feeling.

At the end of our forelimbs we have a most remarkable device, the hand. Like all other mammals, men have forepaws with five digits. Our hands, however, have developed into enormously versatile instruments because one of the digits, the thumb, has become elongated and is jointed in a way which permits total opposition with any of the other fingers. Thus we can handle the most delicate of objects carefully, and yet also grasp heavy objects firmly. More importantly, we can do this while walking, standing, or running because we do not need our forelimbs for locomotion.

We assume that this ability stems from the way of life of a remote ancestor of man, apes, and monkeys who took up a life in the trees of some ancient jungle. To live successfully in trees, a differentiation of the limbs—one set for grasping and clinging and swinging, and one set for standing and jumping and pushing off—is, if not essential, certainly very useful. This ancestor's way of swinging from hold to hold with his arms is called *brachiation*. Although it does differentiate the functions of front and hind limbs, brachiation does not free the forelimbs from the demands of locomotion. We can see the results in most of our relatives among the apes and monkeys. While many of them have the ability to run or walk on their hind legs (it is much more difficult to walk on two feet than to run), they remain essentially quadrupeds on the ground.

It is interesting to speculate about how the process of evolution could have caused such an animal as man to descend from the common ancestor of ourselves and the apes. Some authorities argue that among these brachiating forebears there were some better suited to survival because they could pick up food with their forelimbs instead of remaining at the scene of a kill to fight off the buzzards and hyenas. Standing and moving on two feet gave these creatures the additional advantage of a broader horizon, since it placed their eye-level above that of most quadrupeds, even those much larger. This added visual

Figure 12.   Our bipedal posture and highly-developed arms and hands play an important role in the symbolism of interpersonal relations.

height must have been a great advantage for ancient man in searching out game and alerting him to danger.

Before we go on, think for a moment about how much of our behavior is related to our bipedalism—not simply the physical and technical surroundings which are designed for two-legged beings, but our less material culture as well. We kneel and bow to superiors, or stand at attention, to show respect. The proper times to sit and stand are rather rigidly determined by the mores of whatever culture we are brought up in. Whether one stands up straight or walks with stooped shoulders is taken to be a sign of character with symbolic value in most social systems. And how frequently our arms and hands play important social roles—in saluting, handshaking, hugging, caressing, gesturing, offering benediction, calling down curses, and asking for spiritual healing—who ever heard of the laying on of feet?—and endless and intricate systems of signs and symbols for which we must have free hands and arms.

HEAD AND BRAIN

Man has a big head, not only figuratively but literally. Compared to our bodies, our heads are large—for a human infant nearly a quarter of his length. Yet our faces are small, compared to other animals, with most of the head given over to the purpose of housing a truly massive brain. Not only is our brain larger than that of most other animals many times our size, but it is larger still in relative terms. That is, our brain takes up a much larger part of our total weight or mass. The whale, for instance, does have a brain larger than man's by a few hundred cubic centimeters; but the body of even the smallest whale is several tons, as compared to man's 100–200 pounds. The porpoise is the only animal in which the brain-to-body weight ratio is similar to man's—and, perhaps significantly, it is the only other mammal for which a linguistic ability has even been claimed. Everyone associated with porpoises in scientific or entertainment activities is forced to admit the high degree of intellect of the species as compared to any other nonhuman animals.

Although we do not know precisely how the brain works, we do know that ours is far more complex in structure than that of other animals. It is this complexity which evidently gives us the great powers of memory, the capacity for abstract thought, and the ability to symbolize which are so important to human beings. Whether intelligence alone determines the crucial human ability to use language is a question we will discuss in the next chapter.

Another important function of the head is as the site of our eyes, which face directly forward, unseparated by a nose or snout. The eyes are thus allowed to operate together, which permits us to judge great and small distances alike and to see things in three dimensions. Stereoscopic vision, as this faculty is called, is also probably a legacy from the arboreal past of our ancestors; the ability to judge distance is important to animals that need to move swiftly through the trees. We also have color vision, which gives our eyes an even greater capacity to distinguish and identify objects. Coupled with the facile hand, our vision gives us an enormously wide range of technical potentials. When these skills are linked to a brain able to ponder abstract notions, memorize a great deal, and learn through language as well as example, we have the biological basis of all human technology.

MATING AND CHILD-REARING

Culture, however, is not simply tools, buildings, costumes, vehicles, and weapons. Rather, it is a general configuration of the world which each of us carries in his head—a map, if you prefer, which provides— sometimes in general, sometimes in great detail—a guide for our behavior and an explanation for the phenomena of nature and of man himself. Each culture provides a somewhat different map, but the process of producing that map, of teaching culture to an infant and raising the infant to the level of acceptable adulthood, is very much the same for all men. That process too has its roots in our biology.

One of the great contrasts between men and other animals lies in the realm of sexuality. Most animals become sexual creatures during rather limited periods, when the female is in a state of *estrus,* or heat. For those few days she is sexually excited, not by any external

The intricacies of human sexual behavior have recently been explored by W. H. Masters and V. E. Johnson in *Human Sexual Response* and *Human Sexual Inadequacy* (Little, Brown, 1966 and 1970).

circumstances but from the working of her hormonal system. Only at such times can she be approached by adult males and conceive offspring. The precise rules of mating in various species differ, but the estrous cycle exits among virtually all mammals.

The human female, on the other hand, is not subject to specific periods of sexual receptivity. Her life cannot be divided into separate periods of female sexual or female maternal behavior. Instead she can be sexually stimulated at any time and by a wide variety of external circumstances—a male's handsomeness and persuasiveness, soft music, a good meal, looking at pictures, reading books, feeling textiles, or any one of an infinite variety of experiences. The human male is much the same. Human beings, then, can engage in sexual intercourse at any time, whether or not the female is able to conceive. This circumstance sets the stage for the development of long-term, if not permanent, unions between men and women, based on sexual attraction rather than sporadic glandular drives.

The role of sex as a unifying element in human relations has perhaps been stressed too much in recent years. On the other hand, we cannot ignore the fact that human beings do not breed frantically and promiscuously during a specific period, but selectively over most of their lives. The more or less permanent union of male and female humans sets the stage for the birth and enculturation of the human infant within a social framework.

> **Enculturation** is the process by which culture is acquired by children and becomes a part of their thought and behavior. This term is frequently confused with **acculturation,** which refers to one culture's adopting traits from another.

The birth of the infant, in turn, encourages the longevity of such unions. A young monkey is born with well-developed bones and muscles; almost from the instant of birth he is capable of fending for himself by hanging on to his mother's fur and seeking out her mammaries. Seldom will his mother share food with him, and when he is weaned he must gather his own. A similar pattern—relatively mature infants which quickly become capable of self-support—is common to most herbivorous animals. Carnivores like wolves, foxes, coyotes, and cats, on the other hand, bear young that are not as well developed and must be tended for relatively long periods. Man, although he appears to be most closely related to the herbivorous apes, displays the carnivorous pattern in that his young also require a great deal of care. The human infant is, in a sense, born prematurely; that is, it achieves its full development after birth. Or perhaps we

Figure 13.   The infant monkey clings to its mother, while the human
mother must hold her baby.

should say that the infant is simply immature as compared to the
infants of the apes and monkeys.

The human baby is totally helpless without the nurture and protection of adults of the species. In fact, an infant fox or lion is able
to fend for itself after a year or two at the most, but it takes many
years before a man's child can preserve and sustain his own life. Just
exactly when a human being can be considered capable of an independent existence is hard to define. The middle teen years seem to
be an important turning point in most cultures. Prior to the achievement of sexual maturity and the acquisition of at least a minimal
number of technical and social skills, the growing child, no matter
how precocious, is in the final analysis dependent on adults. (Industrial societies in the eighteenth and nineteenth centuries did exploit
the productive energies of very young children in factories and mills,
so that some youngsters were "self-supporting." But the long term
effects of child labor were so pernicious as to threaten the capabilities
of the adult who had been a six-year-old mill hand; the practice failed
to take hold as a culture pattern.)

The length of his childhood means that the human has many
years in which he can observe, imitate, and be taught the business of

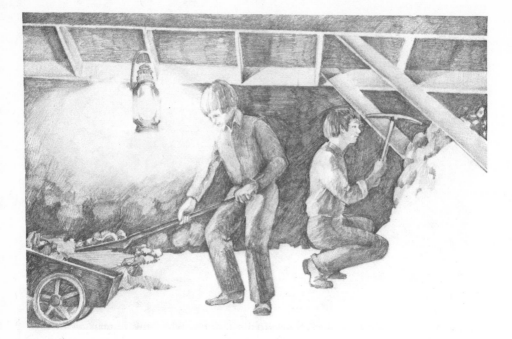

Figure 14.   While many cultures employ young children to perform some
necessary tasks in the society, only the industrial nations for
a time developed a system that exploited children to the degree that the future welfare of the society was threatened.

being a human being. Because in fact, an infant, no matter how ador-
able, is not a human being. Consider for a moment how you would
respond to a one-year-old who was six feet tall and weighed two
hundred pounds. Such a creature, with his unreasoning egocentrism,
his vast rages at personal discomfort, his lack of ability to communicate with others, and his physical clumsiness, would be a very dangerous beast indeed. It is not his parents' species alone that makes of
an infant a human being; rather, it is training and experience in the
human family that shapes each generation of infant barbarians into
genuine human beings, able to take up their assigned roles in whatever cultural context they inhabit.

The development of man's hands and feet and brain, and his
pattern of reproduction and maturation—these are biological foundations on which the edifice of human culture is erected. If any of
these factors did not exist in our species, or if they were different from
what they are, either we would not be cultural beings or our cultures
would be vastly different, perhaps unrecognizable.

SYMBOLS AND LANGUAGE

3

THE HUMAN MIND

We saw in the last chapter that biological evolution created a distinct type of animal with a special morphology upon which much of our behavior is based. Moreover we can see in the sexual nature of man, the almost total helplessness of the infant, and the long maturation process the physical foundations for human society. But had man evolved as only a clever, bipedal animal with a long maturation process and a special pattern of sexual response, we would not be dealing with human beings as we know them. The long period in which the human infant must depend on human adults, and during which it can learn, must have a curriculum—that is, something to learn. What the human adult teaches

the human child is dependent on another evolutionary development: that of the human mind. Precisely what do we mean when we speak of the *mind?* For our purposes, I think, it is enough to say that the human being is possessed of a unique and large brain, and that brain thinks in a way that appears to be quite different from other animals' thought patterns. That particular pattern of thinking, then, is the mind.

An increased amount of research with whales and certain dolphins has led us to be a bit more cautious about man's absolutely unique monopoly on thought. Porpoises and whales may indeed think and talk; but if they do, their style, molded by their particular morphology, is so different that we can

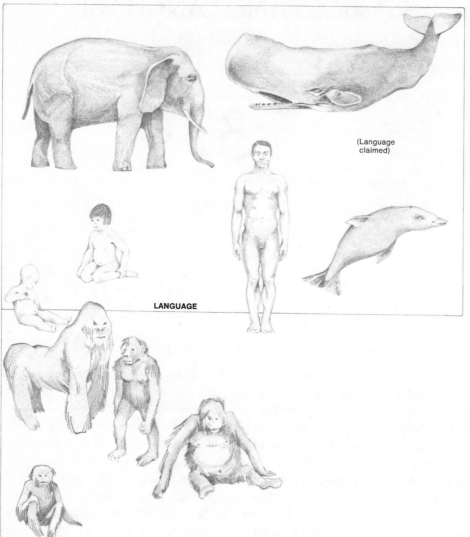

RELATIVE BRAIN SIZE

(Language claimed)

LANGUAGE

Figure 15. Only man (and perhaps porpoises and whales) has the ability to communicate using a spoken language. The elephant does not display linguistic abilities, although its brain is as large as man's in absolute terms. But the ratio of the elephant's brain size to his body weight is much larger than that ratio in man. (That is, the elephant's brain size is *proportionately* smaller than man's.) It is interesting to note that human children appear to achieve linguistic ability at the time when their brains are growing fastest.

still think of man as being quite a special creature. Our problem is to define precisely what is so special about human thought.

The answer to this is clear. Man thinks symbolically. We have all the capacity to learn and remember that other creatures do. But in addition, man has the ability to assign meaning, quite arbitrarily, to the phenomena of his life. To man, *mother* is not merely a person who has given birth to an infant. *Mother* is an idea. All mammals have biological mothers, females which bore them and nurtured them. Only man uses a permanent designation to signify a person ("Mother") who stirs up certain emotions, has certain obligations, and expects certain behaviors in return. In short, the word *mother* and the emotions and responsibilities which that word evokes are not rooted in the biological nature of the relationship between a female and her offspring, but in the symbolic meanings which human beings operating in a social context attach to that biological fact.

Later in the book we will discuss symbolism again, but for now we must simply understand that much of our behavior is guided by our ability to say X means Y and further by the fact that groups of human beings agree that X means Y. The family does for instance have an absolute biological function of conceiving, bearing, and nurturing the young. But the family continues after that function has been performed and serves, as we will see, as the basis for much human interaction quite apart from those basic functions . . . in short, the family not only *does* something, it *means* something. And so does virtually everything else in our lives. We are enmeshed in a network of symbols to the degree that we can sometimes look at ourselves objectively and laugh at our foolishness. But at the same time, we cannot conceive of a human world in which symbols do not play an important role.

LANGUAGE STRUCTURE

The most important of these symbolic systems is language, that peculiar attribute of man shared apparently by no other terrestrial creatures, although possibly used in vastly different form by some sea mammals. For our purposes, *language* can be defined as a system of sounds to which meanings have been assigned by a group of human beings. These sounds, and the way they are arranged in relation to each other, are symbols of ideas and emotions we wish to convey to other people who agree with us about the meanings of the

Figure 16. At some time in the history of civilization, each of these women has represented the ideal of beauty and sexual attractiveness for western culture.

sounds and arrangements. Different groups, of course, employ different sounds to say similar things, as in these examples:

koko kara ikimasao (Japanese)
get away from here (English)
heraus (German)
ts'ou kai (Chinese)
hele mā kahi'ē (Hawaiian)
allez vous en (French)

Each of these combinations of Roman alphabetic letters stands for a set of sounds; the spellings are roughly phonetic. Arranged in a certain way, each set of sounds means something to a specific group of people, those who speak a certain language. To people who do not speak that language, the arrangement of sounds is entirely meaningless. If the arrangement were altered, the meaning would disappear or change or become difficult to work out. If, for instance, we say "*Kara koko ikimasao,*" we have said literally, "Empty here go"— which doesn't mean much in either English or Japanese. Saying "Away from here get," makes sense in English, but the sentence sounds funny. If we change the *g* sound to an *s* sound, we get "Set away from here," which has a meaning of sorts but one which seems a bit ambiguous. If we say "tet" (changing the *s* to a *t* sound), we suddenly have an entire sentence which doesn't mean anything. It is important to remember that no one of the utterances represented above has any intrinsic relationship to the thought being conveyed. *Koko* and *here* are equally arbitrary and conventional ways of expressing the same idea. No language is easier, or more natural, or more rational than any other.

It is equally important to understand language as a system of units of sound. These are called *phonemes,* and are defined as the smallest meaningful units of sound. We have seen an example of phonemic analysis in the last paragraph. Changing the sound of *g* to the sound of *s* changed the meaning of the entire English utterance, yet neither *s* nor *g* has any meaning by itself. Similarly, adding the sound represented by the letter *s* to the end of the word changes the meaning of *cow* from singular to plural; the sound *ai* changes the meaning of *her* from a feminine pronoun to a bodily growth, and so on. Whether a phoneme *is* a phoneme depends on the context in which it occurs. Thus, we change meaning if we substitute *g* and *s* before *et,* but we find that we simply have no meaning at all if we substitute *t* or *d* or *i.* You can try for yourself to find what sounds in English are phonemes when uttered before the *et* sound.

The minimal meaningful units of sound, phonemes, are combined into minimal units of meaning called *morphemes* (or words, as
we usually think of them). The discoverable rules of altering morphemes in order to alter meaning constitute what we call grammar
or syntax. Unfortunately, all too many language teachers try to derive
the language from the formal rules rather than accept the fact that
the real rules are discoverable only by directly studying the way a
language is spoken by people. Quite often some of the most rigid
formal rules of language as taught by language teachers have nothing
at all to do with the language, but with the social symbolism we have
attached to language beyond its simple meaning. *Ain't*, for instance,

> **Phonemes** are the smallest units of meaningful sound. Al-
> though a phoneme heard out of context conveys no meaning,
> it does so in combination with other phonemes. A unit of
> sounds that has a meaning is a word or **morpheme.** Some
> morphemes convey meaning only if affixed or suffixed to
> other morphemes. They are called "bound," in contrast to
> "free" morphemes.

is a word abhorred by English teachers (and most mothers) as "bad
English." Of course, it is no such thing. It is simply a word unaccept-
able in certain social contexts. Few if any speakers of English would
fail to understand the sentence, "I ain't going," although most of
them would immediately make judgments about the social origins,
manners, and education of the speaker quite apart from any meaning
conveyed by the sentence directly.

ORIGINS OF LANGUAGE

The origins of language have long been a matter of debate and speculation. At one time speculation had run so wild, without any basis in
research (it is very difficult to even think how one might do research
on the origins of language), that a leading professional journal of
anthropology simply refused to publish any more arguments on the
subject.

One point of view is that language is a gradually evolving phenomenon and that at one time man must have had simple languages,
capable of expressing only a limited range of thoughts. We still see

this idea whenever a so-called lost tribe is discovered. Now of course the tribe in question, whether in the interior of the Melanesian islands or the Philippine mountains or the Amazon Basin, is not and never has been lost. This expression is evidence of a sense of ethnocentrism in the scholarly or "civilized" world, which holds that nothing really exists until it has been cataloged and recorded by us. Nonetheless, we frequently hear of tribes from remote and unexplored areas who have simple languages, composed of grunts and whistles and such like, which can express only a limited range of thoughts. This is simply nonsense. No such claim has ever stood up under rigorous linguistic investigation. Admittedly, a tribe in the interior of the island of New Britain does not have words or even ideas to express the complexities of nuclear fission, the United Nations, labor–management relationships or the Holy Trinity—primarily because none of these phenomena is a part of the life of that tribe. On the other hand, we average English-speakers do not have on the tip of our tongues the

Figure 17. For most people in the United States today, one word, *arrowhead*, suffices to describe a variety of rather different tools. For those who used arrowheads, a separate word might have been necessary for each type. Similar situations exist for many other categories of objects.

words and ideas to cover the complexities of witchcraft, the comparative tensile strength of wood with which to make bows, the medicinal values of hundreds of plants, or the categories of ghosts and spirits which make up the life of our hypothetical tribe. If either of us, the tribesman or the English speaker, needed to develop language to discuss these matters, we have at our command the mechanism provided in our languages to do this.

In some languages it is a matter of borrowing words. English and Japanese do this frequently—take a foreign word, give it our own phonetic treatment (that is, change sounds to be more comfortable on our tongues), and incorporate it as our own. An example in Japanese is *besubaru*, which is the way the Japanese have "naturalized" *baseball*—and with it *homurunnu, sturiku,* and much of the rest of the language of the game. On the other hand, some languages quite stubbornly resist foreign words and instead make new combinations of existing words to describe new objects or ideas. Chinese and German are like that. Thus, the Chinese, confronted with a locomotive, rejected the English word and instead said *hou ch'e,* which combines *hou* (meaning fire) and *ch'e* (meaning cart).

The Washo Indians of Nevada, in their aboriginal life, did not have lawyers, land claims, or money, but I have heard Washo speakers discuss the complexities of their tribe's suit against the government for the loss of their lands—in Washo. I have heard the Hawaiians speaking in Hawaiian (a language which is supposed to be disappearing) about the problems of an Office of Economic Opportunity program. In both cases the language expanded and developed in such a way as to include new ideas and new activities. Thus it is with all languages.

So perhaps in a sense the evolutionists are right. We can assume that in man's earliest phases his life was relatively simple compared to our own. His social units were small, the territory he could know about restricted to that which he could reach by walking, his technical life limited by his need to hunt and collect food. His language was probably simple. But it is highly unlikely that man himself was incapable of more elaboration linguistically than he was culturally. In fact, his potential to deal with new ideas and objects and phenomena linguistically was probably in large part what enabled him to invent new things, develop new ideas, and organize and deal with new phenomena.

A viewpoint with which, in one degree or another, most scientists today would agree, is that the ability to use language is a specific characteristic of the human species, like the opposable thumb. It appeared at the time the human species can be said to have become a separate episode in evolution. There are some who speculate that perhaps several pre-human species of linguistically-inclined apes may have evolved, and that because our own ancestors were the most adaptable to language they displaced the other species.

The question of exactly how human beings speak and learn languages is far from decided. One approach would hold that we have the intrinsic ability to speak any language, and that as we grow up we imitate and test ourselves against the language we hear around us—gradually and unconsciously learning the rules of proper pronunciation, grammar, and how to construct new sentences analogous to ones we have heard before. A relatively new school of thought, headed by linguist Noam Chomksy of M.I.T., argues that there are basic mental structures of sentences which we inherit and learn to use, and that these structures underlie all languages. This idea has been roundly cheered and as roundly declaimed. It rests on a great deal of speculation and very little research. Its resolution is not our purpose. Enough for us to know that man does speak, and that when he speaks he is activating that peculiar human ability to make one thing (a sound or arrangement of sounds) stand for something else in quite an arbitrary fashion.

We know that we have no special physical equipment for speech. Lungs, esophagus, larynx, palate, nose, tongue, and lips all combine to make the sounds which to us are language. Other land animals have all these pieces of equipment but do not use them linguistically. The whales and dolphins, who may well have a language analogous to our own, use quite a different arrangement of organs. Certainly we have seen human beings lacking sight, hearing, or often other organs used in speech, who have become linguistic through the use of touch, or finger signs, or by swallowing air and using it to make sounds. Thus, language is in the mind, not in the muscles.

LANGUAGE AND CULTURE

There are those who have argued that culture is simply the behavioral expression of language, or, to put it another way, that language structures reality. This was the suggestion made by Benjamin Lee Whorf and Edward Sapir in the 1930's. Their argument was that people tend to act toward things in terms of the words they use about

Figure 18.   Language affects our perception of reality and may, indeed, affect reality itself. What other examples can you think of?

them. Whorf, who was at one time an engineer for an insurance company, noted that disastrous fires were often caused by smoking in the vicinity of empty gasoline drums. In reality, an empty gasoline drum is apt to be full of fumes—that is, gasoline vapor, which is the

> The main outlines of the **Sapir-Whorf hypothesis** can be found in the book *Selected Writings of Edward Sapir in Language, Culture and Personality*, edited by David Mandelbaum (University of California Press, 1949) and *Language, Thought, and Reality: Selected Writings*, edited by John Carroll (Technology Press of the Massachusetts Institute of Technology, 1956 and reissued 1966).

form in which gasoline is most flammable. By speaking of them as empty, Whorf argued, we were saying they were safe when objectively they were most dangerous; people working around empty drums treated them as safe because they *called* them empty.

This is a very simple example. Whorf and Sapir developed their hypothesis using examples from many cultures. In the subsequent years, further investigation and thought suggests that the language–behavior relationship isn't quite as simple as that. The way we speak about things does indeed have a great deal to do with the way we look at and act toward things and phenomena and people. But, at the same time, language cannot totally rearrange reality; often we discover that a cultural system can incorporate words and ideas and subtly change them to fit some preexisting mental or cultural set. Like many other issues in the study of man we find that each side of a coin affects the other. It fits our western mode of thinking to argue that language structures (causes) reality, or that on the other hand reality structures (causes) at least some specific forms of language. In truth, however, it is probably more reasonable to assume that language and culture are constantly acting on each other—that is, causing each other—and the resulting behavior of individual human beings springs from an interaction between language and culture.

As an example we can look at Hoover Dam (which once was named Boulder Dam for political reasons and then renamed for political reasons). This huge structure was financed by government funds and constructed by an elaborate organization that included both government officials and private contractors. It is operated by the federal government and sells most of its electric power to publicly owned systems or private systems regulated by the government. And yet few Americans would want to call it a socialistic enterprise; it is called a triumph of capitalism. The Dnieper Dam in the Soviet Union was constructed for the same purposes, financed by government money with its construction supervised by the government, and it is government-operated. It is called a triumph of socialism, although many of the advising engineers were from capitalist countries. Clearly certain basic cultural attitudes are involved in the language used to describe these two great dams. Because we use words suitable to our cultural system, we are more comfortable with the dam than we would be if we objectively tried to describe the reality. But it is doubtful that simply calling the Dnieper Dam something else would make it anything different.

This section ranges rather far afield primarily to illustrate how important the ability to use language and symbols is to the formation of human culture. Think for a moment of some time in the distant past when, perhaps, man was only one of a number of species with humanoid characteristics—but the only one which had developed the ability to speak. Imagine, for instance, that a drought lay on the savannas of Africa where man's earliest ancestors might have evolved. And imagine that among the humans this statement was possible: "The water holes are all dry. I have never been there, but my father once told me that when he was a little boy he went across the mountains and on the other side there was a river. Let us go across the mountains and find the river."

Now virtually any animal could remember having been to a river. Animals are capable of learning and they do have memories. What is unique about the hypothetical incident is that the speaker himself had never seen the river—but his heritage provided him with a means of sharing the experience which his father had had in his own boyhood, and a means of transmitting that experience to others. The obvious advantage which symbolizing and language could give to such a population is great indeed. This, then, is another element in the foundations of culture: the ability to use symbols and to make symbols into language. Without this ability, much of what we do as humans, we simply could not do.

SOCIETY'S FOUNDATION: THE INCEST TABOO

4

THE PURSUIT OF A CULTURAL UNIVERSAL

Anthropology has always been faced with a paradox. At first glance, man is bewilderingly variable. His physical appearance ranges from tall, ruddy-complexioned, blue-eyed people, who appear with relatively high frequency in Scandinavia, to the tiny, almost black, kinky-haired Africans whom we call Pygmies. The means man uses to communicate language are almost as variable. Perhaps we can never know how many different and mutually unintelligible languages have been spoken on earth. Today we have record of over two thousand. Culturally, man is no less—perhaps even more—varied. It is difficult to think of a custom or practice, no matter how outrageously exotic, which somewhere, at some time, some people have not done.

Here again, the range is from one polar extreme to the other. In South India, for instance, a modest woman wears nothing above the waist. In North India, the Muslim (and much of the Hindu) population insists that a woman appear in public totally covered from head to foot—and, above all, try to prevent her face from being seen by any man save her husband. Each part of India is convinced that its standards are right, natural, and moral—and that the other region's practice is benighted, immoral, and unnatural.

Much the same illustration can be made with any human activity. The Frenchman relishes snails properly cooked, while the average American is slightly revolted at the idea. The

Frenchman, on the other hand, is disdainful and slightly sick at his stomach when he learns that Australian aborigines eat caterpillar grubs, or that the Paiute Indian relishes locusts or grasshoppers. An American insists that his steak be rare to the point of rawness, while the Chinese gourmet is revolted by the slightest pinkness in his meat. The women of one culture must appear before their gods bare-headed, but those of another are required to cover their heads. To marry two wives in America is a felony, but in Africa, not to is to neglect one's social responsibilities. Fat women are adored by many people, while girls thin to boyishness are considered the epitome of beauty by others.

> Scholars argue constantly over definitions of **culture** and **society**, but the essential distinction between the two words is generally accepted: a society is a system of roles and relations and institutions based on a common set of assumptions called culture. The boundaries of a society and a culture are not always the same; several societies may share a culture. On the other hand, a single society may include many cultures.

And yet with all this variety, the basic similarities in all men are clearly, although not so explicitly, apparent. It is a general rule that each culture tends to judge all others by its own standards and to consider other people somewhat less than truly human; this is called *ethnocentrism*. But no one who is able to associate with people of a different culture for any extended period can deny the fact (although he may try very hard to deny it) that these people are, despite all their differences, very much like his own people. This paradox has led anthropologists at different times to emphasize different things. In part, anthropologists have sought out and attempted to catalog the differences between men. At other times they have attempted to define the similarities. These are not mutually exclusive activities; to do one implies the other.

One expression of the search for human similarities was the pursuit of cultural universals—customs, social practices, ideas that are common to all men. Depending of course on how much one wishes to generalize, the list can be long or short. The more one emphasizes the differences among customs, practices, and ideas, the shorter the list. The more one averages out the differences and establishes categories of customs, practices, and ideas, the longer the list. Thus we can say that all human societies have a unit we call the family—but when we look at the wide range of familial relationships, we know that we generalize to a great extent in saying this. Similarly, all men have a religion; but the variation within the category of behavior we call religious is so great that it is difficult to justify the inclusion of two extreme sets of "religious" practices under a single heading.

One fact has been established. In all known human societies and cultures there has been a prohibition of sexual intercourse between people related to each other in a way we would describe as father–daughter, mother–son, brother–sister. Sexual relations between these people are called *incest,* and are tabooed and illegal everywhere in the world. This is not to say that incest is not committed. It does occur, again in virtually every known society. In fact, it is doubtful that a prohibition would exist against behavior that never occurred.

In a handful of cultures, permission to commit incest has been

Figure 19.   This is a sketch of a royal Hawaiian couple, taken from an old drawing. American missionaries were shocked to learn that the king's wife was often his sister. The incest taboo applied only to commoners—not to the royal family.

extended to a few people. In traditional Hawaii, ancient Korea—and for a time the Incan empire, ancient Egypt, and perhaps Persia—children of the royal family, even brothers and sisters, were required to marry each other. These exceptions do not disprove the statement that the taboo is universal. Because we allow a physician traveling on a medical emergency to exceed the speed limit does not mean that we have no speed limit.

In each of these cases, the problem of retaining the wealth and power of the royal line within the royal line was solved by permitting the children of the king and queen to marry one another. In Hawaii, the rationalization of this was that the personages of royal blood were so infused with the power of life, *mana,* that they were dangerous for common people to touch. (See Chapter Sixteen.) Thus, only a person equally infused with *mana* was a possible marriage partner of a royal person.

Other occasions for exceptions to the general incest taboo have been discovered among peoples threatened with extinction, who found themselves with no young people able to marry and bear children save a brother and sister. The answer was to dissolve their sibling relationship formally, pretending that they were not related and thus were eligible to marry. But overall, the rule against incest is a human universal. We should remember that we are speaking at this time of sexual relationships between these four relatives, what we call the nuclear family. As we will see, the variations of extension of incest taboos to cover other relatives are very great indeed.

EXPLANATIONS FOR THE TABOO

The reason this cultural universal is so important is that it *is* universal and therefore, we assume, an expression of basic human nature. At the same time, we know it is not biological. That is, people refrain from incest not because they instinctively reject the idea but because they have been taught to refrain. This being the case, we must ask, why do men thus refrain?

Every culture has an explanation of why they refrain, and an idea of what sort of punishment will be meted out by the gods, or nature, or fate, as well as by men, in the case of a violation. And at the same time, many and perhaps all cultures view themselves as having been created by incestuous unions. We have to go no further than our own Genesis to find a somewhat disguised tale of incest. Eve was created from the rib and flesh of Adam—an enormously close relationship, one should imagine, almost like that of father and daughter—and yet they were the mother and father of the race.

"Common Knowledge" Explanations

If we ask the average European or American why incest behavior is avoided, his first response is generally on a moral level. Such behavior is simply abhorrent to him. But if pressed, he will very likely suggest that the taboo is a way that man has devised to limit the birth of subnormal individuals. Close mating, he will tell us, usually produces children with congenital defects of the body or the mind. By implication, he will suggest that our ancient ancestors recognized this and began to avoid incestuous unions. By further implication, he will say that other peoples, despite the particular explanation they give, are unconsciously following the same taboo for the same reason. He will attempt to tell you why man first began to avoid incest and why he continues to avoid it—that is, the origin and the continuity of the practice will be explained in one statement.

We often do this sort of thing in popular thought and sometimes, unfortunately, in science. To explain how anything began—social practice, religious beliefs, or style of dress—does not explain why we continue to do it. To say that men shake hands because in the past this was a gesture indicating they were unarmed does not explain why people today continue to shake hands. Thus, the "common sense" explanation of the incest taboo does not explain how it began and why we continue to observe it. It may be relevant to the second problem, but not at all to the first.

Let us consider the fact that even today, scattered throughout the world, there are people who do not connect the sex act with the birth of a child—yet are obsessively concerned with the observance of the incest taboo. Are we to suppose that some ancient man or men worked out this relationship from simple observation? The act of coitus and the birth of a child are separated by nine months, and it is not surprising that the relationship between the two events is not apparent.

But what about the other element? Do incestuous matings produce inferior offspring? "Common knowledge" tells us yes—and in America we extend this belief to apply at least to first cousins. But the empiric support for this belief is not as easy to marshal as we would think. In some closely inbred populations—even those which observe incest taboos, but where generations have produced a situation where any two people are exceedingly closely related—we find no absolute support for the idea. On Pitcairn island we find many people marrying who are genetically as closely related as brother and sister (although they are not actually children of the same parents), and

> The story of **Pitcairn** through six generations is told by Henry L. Shapiro in *The Pitcairn Islanders* (Simon & Shuster, 1968).

yet the overall physical type is robust and sturdy—often spoken of as handsome and seldom, if ever, subnormal in intelligence. Other closely inbred groups produce an abnormally high frequency of certain congenital traits or inherited diseases.

This, of course, illustrates the primary fact that what comes out of inbreeding as a product is the direct result of what goes into it. That is, if the inbred pair—be they cousins, brother and sister, or what-have-you—carry the same unfortunate genetic traits, the chances of the traits' appearing in an offspring are doubled. However, if they both carry superior traits, these too have a doubled chance of appearing. One could argue that inbreeding would serve to express all the bad traits, which would otherwise be hidden because they are recessive, and thus eliminate them. This is what men do by breeding

> Some genetic traits are called **recessive** because they are not expressed in the offspring unless they are inherited from both parents. Thus, an individual may carry and pass on to his offspring a detrimental or beneficial recessive trait, without himself showing its presence. **Inbreeding** on a controlled basis can virtually remove the possibility that recessive traits will be passed on undetected, since individuals with very similar genetic structures are mated with each other systematically.

livestock, and perhaps what natural selection might do if men themselves regularly inbred. Some studies suggest that abnormalities occur no more frequently in the offspring of incestuous matings of humans than in the general population. In any event, the "common knowledge" explanation, so satisfactory to Americans because it is so scientific and practical (Americans like even their morality to be practical), cannot be unequivocally supported by science. However, men still abhor incest, and the incest taboo exists, and we must at least try to seek some explanation for this. Several attempts have been made—all of them partially successful, none of them absolutely so. Let us look at two major lines of argument.

Seligman's Argument

Anthropologist Brenda Seligman has argued that man avoids sexual relationship within the nuclear family in order to preserve the family. The injection of sexual competition and jealousy into this intimate and crucial social unit would weaken, perhaps even destroy, the family—which is essential to the continuity of the species and of society. The taboo might be seen as a cultural device created to solve the problem of the constancy of human sexuality.

See Brenda Seligman, "The Problem of Incest and Exogamy: A Restatement," *American Anthropologist* 52 (1951), pp. 305–316.

The competition among the young for the sexual favors of the parents or of each other cannot really occur in a species where sexuality is periodic. Generally speaking, the female is not sexually stimulated while she is a mother. Only after weaning her cubs, or calves, or what-have-you, will she again be ready to accept male advances. At the same time, her offspring mature and are cast on their own so rapidly that they are not really sexual creatures until after they have been freed from the mother—at which time sexual relations may well take place between parents and offspring, or among siblings. Such relations are not really relevant to the argument, however, because the female is no longer acting as a mother but simply as a female; nor is the sister really a sister, etc.

In human beings, the long period during which offspring must remain with the family means that sexually maturing adolescents will be in contact with each other and with their sexually mature parents who are, because they are human, able to be both parental beings and sexual beings at the same time. However, if they were to attempt this, so goes the argument—with the same person acting as both father and lover, mother and mistress, etc.,—the problems of separating out their obligations and responsibilities would be too great. Could a son and a father who were competing for the sexual favors of a mother and sister actually treat each other as father and son?

Seligman's argument has much to say for it, but it is not entirely conclusive. Man's instincts are real but so is his capacity to sublimate, repress, and redirect his instincts. For instance, we are all very much aware that children are apt to become jealous of a new baby and deeply resent his competition for the attentions and affections of the parents. We call this *sibling rivalry,* and, in our culture, rigorously repress it. Violent actions and hostile attitudes toward the new little brother are punished. Each child is told by word and example that he must live with and love his new baby brother or sister, and that to fail will bring about rejection more severe than that which he fears. For most of the population, this instinctive or natural jealousy is repressed and the adult grows up "loving" his siblings. Those individuals who are unable to follow the dictates of society are the neurotics who seek counsel for the problem of unresolved childhood jealousies.

In some cultures this is even more stringently observed than in ours. Among the Kota of India, brothers are permitted to share wives, and any expression of jealousy is met with the most formidable disapproval of the entire society. However, Kota men are noted for the amount of bickering and quarreling they do over other things— work rotation in the fields, money, filling ceremonial responsibilities,

Figure 20. Sibling rivalry is probably a universal phenomenon. But in some cultures, it is expressed, in others, repressed.

etc. In short, it would appear that they submerge their resentments about sex and express them in more acceptable contexts.

On the other hand, in some African cultures no one is expected to love his brother. Rather, normal sibling rivalry is allowed to express itself, and is even institutionalized in the sense that, if they are royal children, adult brothers are expected to compete for their father's inheritance, even to the point of murder. Some would argue that this is simply a matter of politics, since fratricide for political reasons has occurred in other societies; but in those cases, it has not been condoned, supported by mythology, and accepted as moral behavior.

The point of all this is to suggest that perhaps, were incest in some way beneficial or crucial to the survival of the species or the society in which he lives, man's adaptable mind would work out ways of resolving the problems which Seligman suggests are unavoidable. This is not to say that this idea is wrong simply because it cannot be supported completely by the evidence we have on hand today about human behavior. It simply remains unproven.

Tylor and White's Theory

In 1888, Sir Edward Tylor, an English ethnologist, suggested that the reason man began to observe the incest taboo is related to the family's articulation with other families. In this century, Leslie White has supported the argument. Quite correctly, they point out that the primary means of esablishing relationships between two separate social units—villages, lineages, families, or what-have-you—is by means of marriage. This produces a bond of kinship between two otherwise separate social units, which is strengthened as the married pair produces a child which is related to both sides of the marriage. White suggests that a family which insisted on marrying within itself would deliberately be cutting off these extended relationships and the benefits which accrue from them. In times of want or emergency, such a family would have no relatives on whom to call for help. In short, the basic need of human beings in a social environment would be ignored.

If such incestuous families existed in the past, White argues, they simply died out, leaving only those who avoided incest to survive —or they abandoned incestuous practices in the interests of survival. In Tylor's words, they "married out or died out." The logic here seems perfectly sound. We must remember, however, what we said earlier—that this seems to require an understanding of the relationship

Leslie White outlines the main ideas of the concept of "marrying out or dying out" in *The Science of Culture* (Farrar, Straus & Giroux, 1969).

between sexual intercourse and the birth of children. If the taboo was not conscious, why should the descendants of the surviving families (that is, all living men) have such an abhorrence of a practice which had never existed in their lines of descent? Again we have an explanation which no one would say is wrong, but of which no one can be totally certain, either.

THE TABOO AND THE LEARNING PROCESS

Both Seligman's and White's explanations are perhaps partial answers to the question of the incest taboo. They do suggest certain *functions* of the taboo: no matter what the origin of the custom or the actual motivations of the people, the avoidance of incest does produce these two results which are, it would seem, beneficial—in the sense that they allow human beings to continue to live and work in a satisfactory social context. We will use the word *function* frequently in this book, and the definition given above will, although it is very broad, be the one we have in mind. However, nothing in these explanations in fact demonstrates that human beings must avoid incest as a regular feature of human life. A truly adequate explanation would say, in effect, that people act in a certain manner concerning incest; if they acted in any other way, they could not go on living as they do. Either they would die out, or society would cease to function, which for human beings is the same thing. Such an explanation has been formulated by the sociological theorist, Talcott Parsons. We will touch only the broadest outlines of the theory before proceeding to consider other aspects of culture.

The Task of Learning
Parsons has included in his explanation essentially two dimensions, the psychological and the sociological. He suggests that the incest taboo, in a sense, serves as a point of articulation between the psychological development of the individual, and the development of the individual as a social being.

A basic assumption of the argument is that man is a social animal. Without other human beings he could not survive as an infant, develop through childhood, or function as an adult. Human life is set in a network of relationships with other human beings as individuals or as members of groups, each with some specific function in the total system. What the human infant must learn in order to become an adult are the skills and attitudes necessary to continue these relationships. He must be able to contribute to the subsistence of himself and his group, whether by catching jackrabbits in the Great Basin or selling stocks and bonds in New York City. He must be able to form a union with a member of the opposite sex, and produce the next generation, and protect and train that generation until it can assume its adult responsibility.

Taken in toto, the human being has a horrendous number of things to learn. He must learn to manipulate his body. He must internalize the system of perceptions of his cultural heritage so that the way he views his environment agrees at least in large part with the perceptions of those with whom he must live. He must learn a language in all its delicate nuances, and the entire system of complex and subtle symbols which map out the behaviors expected of him— and at every stage it is hard work. It requires enormous effort and is fraught with great frustrations.

Look, the next time you have the opportunity, at a four-year-old, trapped by his or her linguistic limitations, trying to convey an idea for which he lacks vocabulary. The exasperation and anger lead one to ask why the child persists. Think of your own clumsy attempt to learn technical skills, or the enormous fears created by your first tentative explorations into the world of dating and courtship. The annoying business of "acting your age," or the difficulty of "behaving like a young lady" are other examples of the constant frustrating pressures of learning. And yet it is the frustration of learning, as psychologists have discovered and as Parsons points out, that causes us to go on striving.

It is perhaps an oversimplification, but not too great a one, to say that we develop and learn through alternations of gratification and frustration. That is, our being unable to do something which we want to do or which is expected of us is frustrating. Often, we are in· a sense punished for not performing well—punished by withdrawal of comfort or attention or by failure to respond to our desires. In order to relieve this frustration, we increase our efforts to learn or perform until we can accomplish what we wish to, or until those around us reward us with attention, praise, food, wealth, prestige, or comfort. The nexus of this alternation of gratification and frustration for the first years of our lives is the family. Until each of us is fully adult and able to fend for himself, the family can impose frustrations or award gratifications in every sphere of our lives.

Sex as Reward for Learning

If the family can provide all the gratifications a young person requires in exchange for proper performance, what reason would anyone have for ever wishing to leave the family? Why not simply continue the cycle of striving to meet the demands of the family—to walk when expected, to speak when expected, to improve one's manners and abilities—and receive at each accomplishment level a new set of rewards: cuddling, nursing, attention, praise, protection, security, clothing, companionship, food, shelter, etc.? Something, Parsons' theory suggests, must be withheld. If the adult is eventually to free himself from childhood and become an independent entity, there must be some frustrating influence so high and so complete that he cannot hope to achieve gratification within the circle of the family.

Figure 21. This diagram represents one theory explaining the origin of the incest taboo. Who was the author of that theory?

Obviously food, shelter, protection, and education in the social skills cannot be withheld from the child, because without these the child would die. A child may be sent to bed without dinner occasionally but in the final analysis it must be fed.

How then, can the child-person be taught that someday he must leave the shelter of the family and make his own way in whatever cultural context he lives? The answer offered in Parsons' argument is simple: sex. From the very beginning, the system into which a child is born, and within which he will be able to find all the other gratifications of his early life, will deny him sexual gratification or even the prospect of sexual gratification. We all are familiar with the little boy who decides in his fourth or fifth year that he will "marry mommy when he grows up." As innocently charming as such assertions may be, they are always gently turned aside. "Little boys can't marry their mommies," the child is told. Daddy's sexual monopoly of mommy is made explicit through time, and the sexual interests of the young are either suppressed, as in our culture, or clearly diverted outside the family in other cultures.

It is interesting to note in passing that Sigmund Freud explored the **psychological roots of the incest taboo** in his book *Totem and Taboo,* edited by James Strachey (Norton, 1952). He expressed his insights in a story about how young men once killed and ate their fathers in order to usurp domination over the women. Guilt-ridden, these patricides then decided to punish themselves by forever renouncing the sexual rights they had won, and by paying homage to the dead fathers. (Although this story may reveal something important about the rivalry between fathers and sons in our civilization, it obviously has no value as historical research.)

Freud's thinking was stimulated by the fact that many of his male patients revealed unresolved conflicts between themselves and their fathers. Freud believed these conflicts were the result of sexual jealousies of little boys toward their fathers. He labelled the phenomenon the Oedipus Complex, after an ancient Greek tale about a young man (Oedipus) who killed his father and married his mother.

We have come to accept the fact that even infants display a certain amount of sexuality which continues to develop through childhood. The incest taboo is the device which shapes and channels the vague and generalized sexuality of the child into the specific sexuality of the man or woman. The message of the incest taboo is quite clear: You must look forward to a time when you will seek a partner outside the family; the one area we cannot gratify is the sexual area. Unlike hunger or thirst, the sexual impulses can be suppressed and diverted and their gratification postponed. Full participation in the heterosexual world is, in effect, the implicit carrot held out to encourage the child and the adolescent to learn the skills of his culture which would make him, or her, a suitable sexual partner.

If we examine our own lives, we can, I think, see how much of what we are taught is in the final analysis learned because we must eventually seek a marriage partner. To walk and talk as infants, to adjust ourselves to the demands of society, the manners and mores of our people, the social graces and knowledge and skills which will make it possible to support ourselves and eventually a marriage partner and children of our own—all of these things are basic to our ability to attract members of the opposite sex and to become a fully functioning adult. Even in our own society, where marriage is not essential to individual survival, it is still the normative state for most adult people.

It can be argued that human beings must learn certain skills in order to survive, regardless of how they achieve sexual gratification. Indeed, this is true—but we should remember that it is difficult indeed to tell a six-year-old that the burdens of growing up are all-important if he is to survive in later years. For children there are no later years. How much more difficult this job would be, perhaps impossible, if the child were being lectured by a member of his family who was also a partner in his sexual games and would some day be a partner in a complete sexual relationship. What would drive the young adult to want to break the bond of the family, strengthened by the attachments which would develop from a continuing sexual relationship?

This is at best a very brief summary of a complex and sophisticated argument. It does, however, set the stage for a further examination of the social network within which man must develop and survive. The biological nature of man produces an organism which is continually amenable to sexual stimulation, a situation which helps preserve the stability and continuity of the family, which in turn is needed to preserve and school the immature human infant and child. The incest taboo, then, is a counterforce which, when the infant is no longer an infant and ready to take its place in the adult world, presses him out of the family into relationships with people other than immediate relatives who are equipped with the knowledge, skills, and attitudes necessary for his survival and social continuity. The requirement that each human being marry outside of the social boundary—different in its extent in each society, but similar in its core—means that in each society each human being has relationships of two kinds. The first of these are relations we commonly call "blood" or consanguineal relationships. All other relationships are nonconsanguineal—by marriage (affinal), common interests, residence, or experiences. The number and kinds of these relationships are the basis of society, and living within a social context is essential to the survival of the human being and the continuity of human culture.

SOCIETY AND
SOCIAL BEHAVIOR

Part Two

INTRODUCTION TO PART TWO: SOCIETY

Man is a social animal; he lives with other men, and, more important, he could not live without other men. Ours is certainly not the only species that lives in a social context, but as we will see, our social environment and behavior are markedly different from those of other animals—even our closest relatives. In a culture like that of the United States, which emphasizes the worth and importance of the individual, it is sometimes a bitter pill to swallow when we are faced with our absolute dependence on others. It is paradoxical that in order for a culture to glorify and emphasize the role of the individual it must express itself in the most complicated social context. To allow the individual to function as an individual we have of necessity built the most elaborate complex of governmental, economic, and social institutions. Though simpler societies may deeply respect the rights of the individual, their members cannot afford the luxury of acting as if they could in fact get along without other men.

Our dependence on others is with us from birth. The human infant has not the slightest chance of survival without adults to care for it—not for a few days or a few months, but for years and years. We all know the worst of all punishments we can inflict on a fellow human being is to withdraw from him, to "put him in Coventry." In prisons, solitary confinement is the final lodging of the incorrigible. To

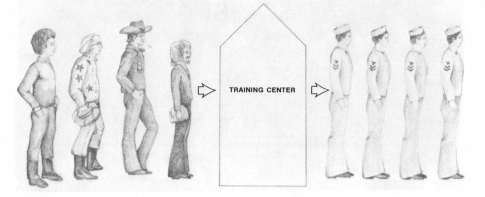

Figure 22.   The army draws recruits from many backgrounds and cultures. But it can usually produce fairly conforming and uniform soldiers within a very short time by isolating them from any value system other than that of the military.

cut someone off from human contact is to isolate him from himself, to create a situation in which he eventually questions the very bases of his own existence and is willing to accept those of anyone who will provide him with a human context within which to live once more. The success of this kind of treatment has become tragically familiar during the past two decades and is often (if used by other people) called brainwashing. The military forces of all nations know the value of isolation for the training of recruits. In our own armed services the first weeks of recruit training are carried out in isolation from any but other recruits and their instructors. All but a few trainees respond by accepting the goals and expectations of the military, no matter what their civilian attitudes were, simply because there are no other goals and attitudes to be shared with other men.

Our need of other men is not simply for food and companionship, although both of those are important. Even more important, perhaps, is the need one man has to share a set of values and expected behavior with other men. This sharing enables us to predict what will happen in specific social situations. How difficult would life be if we did not know from day to day how our teacher or friends or the people we deal with in stores would act? Will the salesgirl smile and accept my money or will she attack me and accuse me of threatening her life? Will the professor deliver his lecture today in English or Chinese? Will my friend be sympathetic to my problem or will he slap my face for bothering him? How could we live at all if each human encounter in our lives was marked by this kind of problem?

We learn to expect certain kinds of behavior in social situations through the medium of society itself. Society is the agent of the transmission of culture. In each society there are traditional patterns of social interaction, and we learn these as we grow into adulthood. Moreover, we learn a great deal more: a common explanation of the nature of the world, a common standard of beauty and justice, regular patterns of work and play and generally accepted points of view. This is not to say that human beings in any culture are all the same. They are not, of course. However, for men to live together they must be able to interact and communicate. The individual whose behavior is too unpredictable for his fellows is a deviant, in some cultures adjudged insane and in others killed outright or driven from the association of his kind.

Society is in a sense a machine designed by men to meet the demands of their environments on one hand and their psyches on the

Figure 23.   A person may play many roles in his daily life, and know what behavior is appropriate for each role. Here, possible differences between "boss" and "husband" roles are illustrated.

other. But human society is one other thing. It is learned. As we explore further, from time to time discussions will make social roles and structures seem rather mechanical and unavoidable. But we must remember that men learn their society just as they learn technical skills. They can learn imperfectly or unlearn and learn yet a new system. In this they are very unlike animals.

Animals have social relations, and certain animals within herds or hordes or bands or flocks assume various roles. Let us look briefly at social relations and behavior within a band of dog-faced baboons. The band can first be divided into males and females. But in infancy and adolescence, the sex differences are not important. Infants cling to their mothers and nurse until they are able to fend for themselves, at which time they join the adolescents who play together and collect their own food. In the playing and collecting, the young baboons develop their bodies and reflexes, and prepare for adult roles. Upon achieving sexual maturity, adolescent behavior tapers off and the young become socially adult.

For the female, adulthood means responding to periodic episodes of sexual excitement during which she presents herself to every adult male in the band. When she conceives, she joins other pregnant females and those with infants still in their care. As a member of this subgroup she is protected by the males of the band, who generally assume positions on the edges of the horde while it grazes or moves. If danger threatens, the males move to place themselves between the females and the young and the sources of danger. Among adults, both male and female, there is a clear-cut hierarchy of dominant relationships.

Dominance is indicated by which of the two individuals will back down in a confrontation, usually over food. The individual who holds his ground is dominant over the one who doesn't. In every band there is a large old male before whom all others back down, though he may be regularly challenged by others near his size and age. The older group of high-status males may sometimes com-- bine to bluff down a presumptuous younger male. And the older males generally make it their business to break up fights or suppress noisy play among adolescents. All males are dominant over females, although within the female ranks there is also a dominance hierarchy.

When one watches the movements of such a band, it is easy to describe the events in terms of human social interactions; in many ways they do seem to be the same. There is one major difference, however. Once a baboon has passed through a certain stage, he takes his position without exception in the next. No older baboon behaves like an adolescent, no male like a female, no female like a male; nor does any adolescent act like an infant. The old, dominant male is always the old, dominant male until he gives way before a challenger.

In a human society, we find that this is not always the case. What appears to be a response to genetically inherited patterns, plus some learning, among the baboons is almost entirely a matter of learning among humans. People act inappropriately. Some human males dress and behave like females to the limits of their physiology, and the reverse is sometimes true of women. Children strive to be adults, and many adults fail to act their age. Prestigious leaders may from time to time act like fools and fools sometimes are exceedingly wise.

In short, human social activities are a matter of learning, a product of the capacity human beings have for culture. This is why they can be altered, developed, readjusted to fit circumstances in a way that the social relations of animals cannot. In short, social roles are determined not by physiology but by culture. Thus, a human female does not have to act like a female simply because she is born with certain morphological or hormonal features; female behavior, or any other appropriate behavior, is a product of a cultural tradition. Human social roles are defined as specific ways of acting in specific situations, not as particular biological relationships. (This is especially important to remember since we often describe social roles in kinship terms: father, brother, mother's brother, etc. We should remember that human kinship is not biological but rather, sociological.)

Societies are often spoken of as having structures or organizations; this is another way of saying that they are composed of a number of specific roles, and there is general agreement about how a person occupying a role will act in any given situation, or in relationship to other persons occupying other roles. *Brother, sister, employee, employer, member of the congregation, veteran, member of the lodge*—all are specific social roles. With the exception of brother and sister, any person may in fact play all the roles mentioned. He will carry out certain acts in keeping with his role, depending on the situation in which he finds himself and the people with whom he deals. He will act like a brother in the presence of his sister or when her name is mentioned in other company, but when he is in the

Figure 24. Each culture clearly prescribes appropriate behavior for the roles of "customer" and "sales clerk." Describe the two roles in your culture. (Can you think of more than one model for the sales clerk role? Which do you prefer?)

presence of his employer or his employees he will act differently. He will not act like the man who pays the wages in the presence of his employer, but will in turn act that way in the presence of his own employees. In certain contexts, whether or not he is a veteran will be irrelevant, in others important, and so on.

The sum total of these positions and roles determines a person's *status*. High status, then, is acquired by occupying a configuration of high-status roles, and low status, by a number of low-status roles. Some roles do not, in and of themselves, contribute to status determination: Either a bum or a banker can be a brother; a member of the Junior League and a streetwalker can both be sisters. However, the way one lives up to the society's expectations of such roles may have a great deal to do with how one's fellows look at him.

Society can be viewed as a device that creates the environment within which the human being lives. To assure the survival of human beings, society must be flexible enough to adjust and readjust to changes and differences in the environment and in technology. In order that a society may be able to adjust to meet new demands, there must be general principles of social organization which can be applied to new specific adjustments. That is to say, relationships between roles—which in the final analysis are relationships between people—must be able to reorganize within a specific framework, or, perhaps it is best to say, spoken about in a certain idiom. For most of human history and for the vast majority of human beings even today, the basic idiom of social organization has been that of kinship. We will examine the principles used in the study of the operation of kinship relationships.

KINSHIP I: IDENTITY
AND THE FAMILY

5

WHO AM I?

Relatives or kin are those people related to you by "blood" or marriage. This second category, Americans distinguish by the term *in-laws*. The world over, most people would make similar distinctions. However, if we were to question further we would discover that people often differ on what they mean when they say "blood" relations. What one man considers a relative may in another culture be considered a complete stranger. These differences are in a very real sense differences in the way peoples in different cultural situations view themselves as individuals.

Do you, for instance, consider yourself a member of your mother's or your father's family? For most Americans the response to that question would be a somewhat bewildered rejoinder that you were a member of both sides of *your* family. To a Navajo Indian of Arizona the answer would be "my mother's family," while a Nuer from the Sudan would automatically respond "my father's family" and think you a bit odd for asking in the first place. Similarly, to ask "Would you marry your father's brother's child?" would bring a wide range of answers. The American would say, "No, that is my first cousin." A Bedouin Arab would on the other hand say that he might well marry such a relative. These differences are not, as we are so apt to think, simply perversities practiced by uncivilized savages who don't understand the "right" way to act. They represent differences in reckoning kinship between people and thus defining who you are in relation to other people. No matter what else he might be, an American is not a potential marriage partner of his uncle's children. On the other hand, a Trobriand Islander is precisely that.

Although variations in kinship systems are the rule and the details of differences from people to people almost endless, there are three major systems of reckoning descent—that is, of deciding to which family you belong. These three may be further combined into two major categories: *bilateral* systems and *unilineal* systems. Because we, along with the Hawaiians and the Eskimo, the Washo Indians and the modern Japanese and all Europeans, live in a bilateral system, let us first examine that means of reckoning descent.

BILATERAL DESCENT PATTERNS

Bilateral means two-sided, and refers to the extension of relationships equally from the mother and the father. Some anthropologists call this a "bilineal" system, but I think that term does not accurately represent the dynamics of this type of kinship. In essence, a marriage in a bilateral system creates a new unit from which relationships spread out in both directions. For a time the two sides of the system are affinal relatives only because they are simply united by one of their children being married to the child of some other group. However, when the newly married couple has a child it is related by blood to both sets of grandparents, all the parental siblings and descendants of siblings.

The key point is that in a bilateral system, relationships are seen as being equal on both sides. Thus an American cannot marry the children of either his father's siblings or his mother's siblings. He feels himself equally descended from mother's parents and father's parents.

Kin Terms and Kin Types

It is important to distinguish between a kin type and a kin term. A *kin type* is an abstraction that can be described in the same words for every culture. A *kin term* on the other hand, is a specific word in a specific language, that refers to one or more kin types, depending on the system. Thus anyone in the world can be described as having a mother's brother, but only English-speaking people can be said to have an uncle. However, in our system, *uncle* does not refer exclusively to *mother's brother*. It is also used to refer to *father's brother*, and to *mother's sister's husband* and *father's sister's husband*. Before you look closely at the American kinship chart, Figure 25, see if you can make a list of the kin types covered by the following American kin terms: *grandfather, grandmother, aunt, cousin, niece, nephew, grandson, granddaughter*. Now look. If your list corresponds with the terms and types on the chart, you have understood the difference between them.

In America we have the charted set of terms, used by an imaginary person whom we call *ego*, in the center of a kinship network. You may, if it helps think out the relationships, think of yourself as *ego*. Reckoning up from *ego*, we have *father* and *mother*, *uncles* and *aunts*. On the generation above that we have only *grandfathers* and *grandmothers*. On the same generational level as *ego* we have *cousins, brothers*, and *sisters*. On the generation below *ego* we have *sons* and *daughters* and *nieces* and *nephews*. All possible kin relationships in American society can be described with these few terms, plus the affixes *grand* and *great* and the suffix *in-law*.

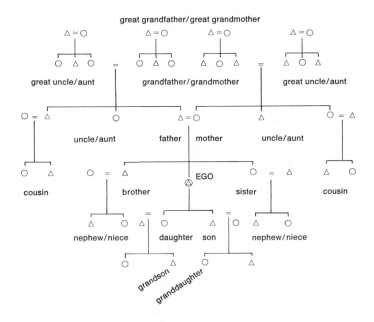

Figure 25.   American kinship terms.

The degree to which we extend these terms to include kin types within the range of our kin terms depends on how we want to use these relationships. We seldom identify with a kin term a person who is unimportant to us. It may be useful or at least pleasing to refer to a famous man as a great-uncle and include him in our list of relatives. On the other hand, a father's father's brother who died on the gallows for thievery may in fact be dropped from the genealogy and considered no relation at all for the same reason as the famous man was included.

The way persons extend relationships in a bilateral society is to raise the generational level from which two people draw a common ancestor. If, for instance, you and a new acquaintance have different grandfathers, you are not cousins. If however, you consider great-grandfathers, you might be. In theory, any two people, if total genealogies were known, could trace back to an ultimate great-grandfather and thus be cousins of some degree. For Catholics, it is important to know who one's great-great-grandfather was in order to avoid incest within the four degrees of relationship forbidden by canonical law. The core of the problem of bilateral societies is precisely this. In simpler tribal societies with small populations, it would be entirely possible to find that everyone was descended from a common great-grandfather and thus is forbidden, on grounds of incest,

Figure 26. This family crest is a visual representation of a bilateral descent system. An English nobleman has combined in one device the crests of the various families from which he was descended.

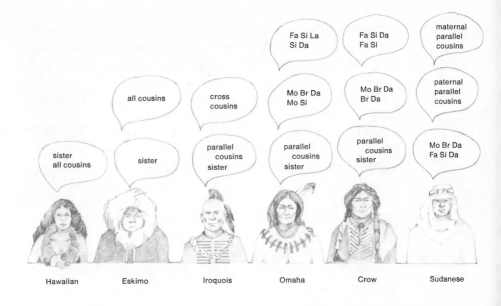

Figure 27. Almost any kinship system of the world can be identified with one or another of those illustrated, depending on how its members classify "sisters" and "cousins."

to marry. To avoid such a situation bilateral societies tend to create new unrelated people each generation by simply dropping the ultimate level of kin types from consideration. The Washo Indians of Nevada provide an example.

The Washo, an Example
The Washo lived in extreme western Nevada and eastern California, with their aboriginal range centering on Lake Tahoe in the Sierra Nevada. The Washo have been described as one of the simplest cultures to be reported in native North America. This was certainly true of their material life. They made bows and arrows and fish traps and

See James F. Downs, *Two Worlds of the Washo, an Indian Tribe of California and Nevada* (Holt, Rinehart & Winston, 1969), and Stanley A. Freed, "Changing Washo Kinship" (*University of California Anthropological Records* 4, no. 6 (1960), pp. 349–418.

during the cold part of the year, built houses. Washo women were very adept basket makers. They originally wore few clothes and they had no really permanent abodes or elaborate religious institutions. They subsisted by fishing, hunting, and gathering wild plant foods. In general the environment provided adequate food supplies but one could never count on fish or game animals or plant foods appearing every year in the proper amounts in the same places.

This meant that the Washo of necessity moved frequently and had to be prepared to take advantage of opportunities as they occurred, which is another way of saying their social structure had to be quite flexible to permit the movement of families and individuals throughout the Washo country. The Washo were bilateral, but unlike the modern American, they had some thirty-nine kin terms for consanguinal relatives and a dozen or so more for affinal relatives. Thus virtually anyone could be considered a relative of some kind and an individual Washo could move from place to place, secure in finding the hospitality which should be accorded a relative.

At the same time, it was necessary to solve the problem of having so many close relatives that no one was eligible to marry anyone. The Washo system handled it in the fashion indicated by Figure 29.

Figure 28. The Washo Indians of California and Nevada have been described as having one of the simplest cultures ever reported. Even so, tasks were specifically divided between men and women, and the Washo had to learn many skills in order for the culture to survive.

Aboriginal Washo Kinship Terms

Parent and Child Class

1. digóy?*   (father)
2. dilá?   (mother)
3. di?málu   (parent)
4. dityé·Lu   (parent)
5. diná·m   (son)
6. diŋámu?   (daughter)
7. diŋá?min   (children)

Sibling Class

8. di?á·tu   (older brother, half-brother, cousin whose parent is older than mine)
9. di?í·sa   (older sister, half-sister, cousin whose parent is older than mine)
10. dibéyu   (younger brother, half-brother, cousin whose parent is younger than mine)
11. diwitšuk   (younger sister, half-sister, cousin whose parent is younger than mine)
12. dikMílu or diMílu   (distant male relative or friend—man speaking)
13. di?ulišáwlam   (distant female relative or friend—man speaking)
14. di?ulimété liwi?   (distant male relative or friend—woman speaking)
15. disú·   (distant female relative or friend—woman speaking)

Grandparent and Grandchild Class

16. dibá·ba?   (father's father)
17. labá·ṗa?   (son's child—man speaking)
18. di?élel   (mother's father)
19. le?éleli?   (daughter's child—man speaking)
20. di?áma?   (father's mother)
21. la?á?ma?   (son's child—woman speaking)
22. digú?u   (mother's mother)
23. legú?yi?   (daughter's child—woman speaking)
24. dibɨkɨ   (father's mother's sister, mother's mother's sister)
25. lebɨkɨyi?   (sister's child's child—woman speaking)
26. disáma?   (father's father's sister, mother's father's sister)

27. lasá?ma?   (brother's child's child—woman speaking)
28. disáksak   (father's father's brother)
29. lasáksagi?   (brother's son's child—man speaking)
30. di?é·bu   (mother's father's brother)
31. le?é·ṗu?   (brother's daughter's child—man speaking)
32. ditó?o   (father's mother's brother, mother's mother's brother)
33. lató?yi?   (sister's child's child—man speaking)

Great-grandparent and Great-grandchild Class

34. dipísew   (relative of third ascending generation)
35. lepísewi   (relative of third descending generation)

Niece and Nephew Class

36. di?éwši?   (father's brother)
37. dimá?sa   (brother's child—man speaking)
38. didá?a   (mother's brother)
39. dimá·gu   (sister's child)
40. diyá·?   (father's sister)
41. dišémuk   (brother's child—woman speaking)
42. dišáša?   (mother's sister)

Parent-in-law and Child-in-law Class

43. láyuk   (parent-in-law)
44. dibu?áŋali?   (son-in-law)
45. léyeš   (daughter-in-law)
46. lámɨk   (child's spouse's parents)

Sibling-in-law Class

47. diwlá·dut   (wife's brother)
48. dime?éwši?   (husband's brother)
49. didámaw   (sister's husband)
50. dimašáša?   (brother's wife—man speaking)
51. diyáŋil   (husband's sister, brother's wife—woman speaking)

Spouse Class

52. dibumé·li?   (husband)
53. di?mé·š   (husband)
54. dimlá·ya?   (wife)

*All Washo terms are shown in the form of singular with first person possessive prefix (di)—for example, my father, my children.

Figure 29. Aboriginal Washo Kinship Terms.

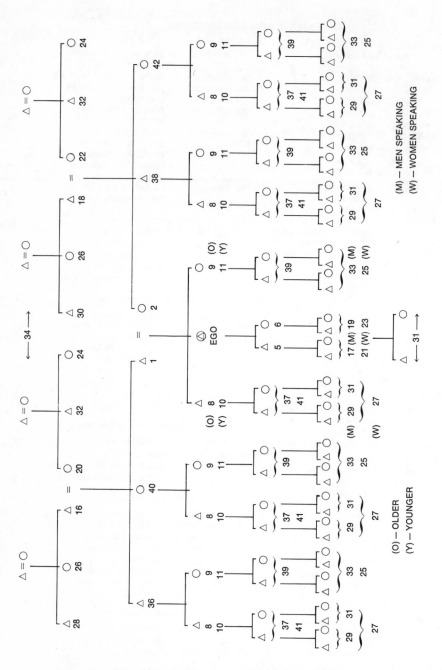

Figure 29b.   The aboriginal Washo consanguineal kinship system. Tri-
angles denote males; circles denote females; numbers refer
to the terms in Figure 29a. Source: Freed, 1960, 357.

People with a *dipisew* in common were ineligible to marry. However, if they were related by descent from the next ascending generation, they had no common ancestor *within the kinship system* and therefore were not considered to be relatives. If we put it another way, all people with a *dipisew* in common referred to each other as either "brother" or "sister" if they were of the same generation. All people of younger generations descended from people you would call *brother* and *sister* were designated by a term which literally meant sister's or brother's child. People using such terms toward each other obviously could not marry. If they shared no ancestor within three generations, however, they could marry because they used terms which did not imply close relationships. The important thing to remember is that the issue is not really biological, but rather sociological. People decided whether they were potential partners not by tracing pedigrees but by tracing genealogies—which are social documents, not records of biological descent.

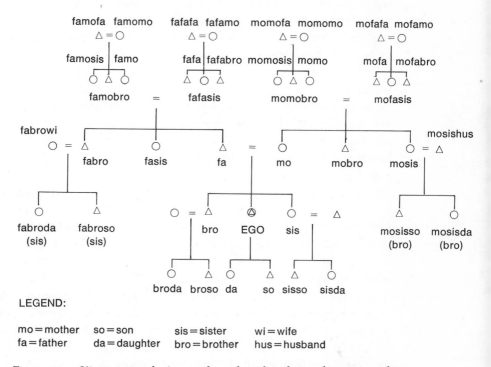

LEGEND:

mo = mother   so = son   sis = sister   wi = wife
fa = father   da = daughter bro = brother   hus = husband

Figure 30. *Kintype* is a device used to identify relationships in any kinship system. Using some terms from American kinship terminology, any relationship can be described. Contrast this with the chart of American kin*terms* on page 87.

Nuclear and Extended Families

Another way to look at a bilateral system is to think of each marriage as a stitch in a knitting pattern, with the difference being that each stitch can separate itself from one set of companions and associate with another. This unit, the two marriage partners and the children born to them (or at least to the women), is called a *nuclear family*. Such units may have any number of extraneous individuals attached to them—unmarried brothers and children, grandparents dependent on the partners in the marriage, aunts or uncles or even more distant relatives—but in the final analysis the core of the social network is the nuclear unit. We could, if it were useful even to speak of them, refer to *polygamous* nuclear families in those relatively rare situations where multiple husbands (*polyandry*) or wives (*polygyny*) share the same household with the common spouse. Far more frequent is the situation, particularly in polygynous societies, where each wife is mistress of her own household or at least her own children so that the husband plays the role of father and husband in two or more nuclear units. In polyandrous situations it is common to find all the husbands living in the same unit and sharing, in a sense, the role of father to the children born to the common wife.

In modern American society, the nuclear family is usually a separate residence unit and is more apt to make its day-to-day relationships with people other than relatives: friends, neighbors, coworkers, and the like. In some bilateral societies, the tendency is for a number of related nuclear units to cluster together into small flexible bands which cooperate in hunting, protection, fishing, and to some extent in gathering activities.

The societies we have mentioned as having bilateral descent fall into two categories: they are either hunting and gathering societies with the simplest sort of technology, or modern urban industrial societies with the most complex sort of technology. It would seem at first glance that they have nothing at all in common. However, when we examine the demands placed on the individual by the two systems we see that they in fact have a great deal in common. The Washo hunter and gatherer must be able to shift his ground easily without consulting a large family council or submitting his decision for the approval of other people. If he had to take into consideration the wants and needs and the likes and dislikes of a great collection of relatives he probably could not survive. Large family groups with fixed membership and obligations could not count on the environment in every instance producing enough to support them. Therefore,

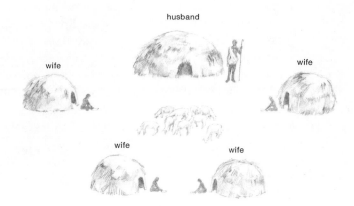

Figure 31.   In Africa, a common marital arrangement is for a man to occupy a central house (sometimes with his widowed mother), providing each wife and her children with a separate household, which he visits in turn.

the smallest viable unit, the nuclear unit, must be able to move at will to meet its own needs.

Much the same is true in industrial societies. In order to survive, a family must be able to seek out the most profitable activity—to change jobs, towns, states, even nations—in response to its own needs. Moreover, the economy is planned in such a way that it functions with this expectation in mind. Factories are built and businesses established on the premise that individual wage earners will seek out profitable work in response to their own needs. It has been discovered that one of the major problems of undeveloped nations with a tradition of large family units with fixed obligations is that it is difficult to develop an industrial work force. This is often because the needs of the extended family quite often override the desires of the nuclear family or the individual, so that even the person who wants to take a factory job finds it impossible to do so. In modern societies we tend to restrict the number of relatives and to depend on other kinds of relationships for support. In hunting and gathering societies the individual must depend on kinship for support, but he must operate in a system flexible enough to allow him to take advantage of changing opportunities. A comparison of the Washo and the American kinship charts (Figures 25 and 29) reveals the flexibility in the bilateral kind of system and reflects quite accurately the nature of the two systems.

UNILINEAL DESCENT

Unilineal systems are dramatically different from bilateral systems. Although such systems are found at least in a modified form in some hunting and gathering societies, they do not survive long in industrial societies. In general, unilineal systems are associated with agricultural societies, particularly preliterate tribal agricultural societies. In its simplest form, unilineal descent means that a person, instead of considering himself as equally descended from, and therefore a member of, two family lines, considers only one side of his family—either that of his father (*patrilineal*) or his mother (*matrilineal*).

Matrilineal Systems

Let us use the matrilineal alternative as an example. The individual's relationship to each side of his family is seen as very different. He is a member of his mother's group. He is not a member of his father's group. This is not to say that he does not recognize his kinship to his father's family, simply that he sees it as a different kind of rela-

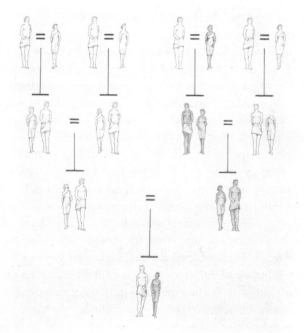

Figure 32(a). The dark figures represent people related in a single female (*matrilineal*) line of descent.

tionship. And most frequently, this difference is recognized in the kinship terminology. For instance, he cannot have uncles in the same sense that we or the English have uncles. His mother's brother is part of *his* family. On the other hand, his father's brother is not—and for that matter, neither is his father. The Navajo, for instance, will say, "I am a member of X (his mother's) clan but I am *born for* Y (his father's) clan. This recognizes that he and his father and his father's relatives have certain obligations toward each other, but they are quite different than the obligations he has toward his own family, that of his mother.

We are discussing the mother's brother because this kinsman is apt to be very important in matrilineal societies and, in fact, quite important in most unilineal societies. In a matrilineal society, he is the man of the family who will represent his mother and sisters before the world and often pass on to his sister's sons the lore and the traditions of the family. In some cases he is even responsible for their support. In the Trobriand Islands, for instance, a man—as is quite

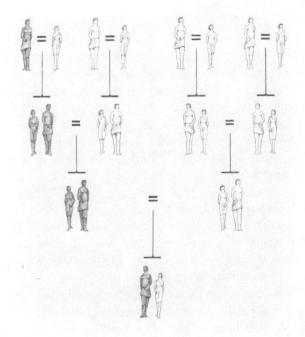

Figure 32(b).   The dark figures represent people related in a single male (*patrilineal*) line of descent.

common in matrilineal systems—moves into the village of his wife and works her farm land. At the time of harvest he takes up the season's produce of yams and delivers them to his sister. She and her husband and children will subsist on what he grew, while he will eat the food produced by his wife's brother. This is an extreme example of how important this kinsman can be, but it certainly is not a unique example.

> Almost all of our information about the Trobriand islanders comes from the work of Bronislaw **Malinowski** (see chapter seventeen), in particular his books *Argonauts of the Western Pacific* (Dutton, 1922), and *Magic, Science and Religion and Other Essays*.

The importance of the mother's brother in unilineal systems goes even beyond the possibility of his supporting sister's children. In unilineal societies, mother's brother's children are frequently unrelated to *ego*. This follows because in a matrilineal system, mother's brother is of your family but his children will belong to the family of his wife and thus not be *ego's* relatives—that is, they are eligible as marriage partners. At the same time, mother's brother is *ego's* nearest male relative and a logical person to seek out and ask for the hand of his daughter. In patrilineal systems, mother's brother's children will be of *ego's* mother's family while *ego* will be of his father's family. Since members of his family are eligible to marry members of the other, once again it is mother's brother to whom one is most likely to turn to find a mate.

Patrilineal Systems, Contrasted

Patrilineal systems of descent look in diagram very much like a mirror image of matrilineal systems. In actual operation, they are very different indeed. A descent group reckoning relationships through the male line is forever dependent on women from the outside to reproduce the line. The incest taboo prohibits marriage with one's sisters, and therefore a patriline must seek mothers for their sons from outside itself. A matriline, on the other hand, in a sense is capable of reproducing itself.

As damaging as it may be to the male ego, men just aren't as necessary in perpetuating a unilineal system as are women. The vital participation of the husband is really rather brief; once the woman has been impregnated, his presence is not really essential. The rest of the duties of men—protection, support, authority over, and training of the children—can be turned over to the brother. A descent group of men requires the presence of unrelated women for the entire period of pregnancy, and then the mother must remain to nurse and care for the child. At the same time, in order to obtain wives for their group, they must in effect trade their sisters to other such groups.

Thus, the bond between brother and sister in patrilineal societies is seldom as strong as it is in matrilineal systems. In the latter, mother's brother is *ego*'s nearest male relative who also has an interest in eligible females. In the former, mother's brother is *ego*'s contact man into a totally unrelated group. In a matrilineal system, mother's brother must be a frequent visitor in her life so that he can see to the welfare of her children and thus assure the ultimate continuity of his own line. In a patrilineal system, mother and her brother may seldom see each other since he is most concerned about the welfare of his own children and heirs.

This difference seems to produce a situation in which marriages in most matrilineal societies tend to be relatively brittle and their dissolution causes little concern. In fact, people seem little concerned about marital fidelity of either men or women in matrilineal societies. This is not to say that individuals do not become jealous and angry with the pecadillos of a partner—they often do. But in general, infidelity is not seen as a threat to the social structure in any way. In the United States a man and wife may come to hate each other over such things as failure to put the cap on the toothpaste or inability to make a good cup of coffee, but society in general remains unconcerned; in the same way, matrilineal societies generally see marital difficulties as problems for individuals to cope with on their own.

Patrilineal societies, on the other hand, tend to be far more concerned about the faithfulness of the wife. The reason is obvious. Should a wife conceive a child in an extra-marital affair, the child would belong to the lineage of the father, not that of the women's husband, and the line would be adulterated. On the other hand, some patrilineal societies permit or even expect brothers—that is, members of the same descent group—to have sexual access to each other's wives. Here again, jealousies may develop and resentments arise, but the society as a whole isn't concerned because the child of such a union is a member of the proper descent group.

A warning is in order here. One should never accept at face value an anthropological generalization such as the one just made. There are undoubtedly some matrilineal societies with very strict rules about adultery and marital fidelity. Man has an enormous capacity for variation, which is one reason anthropology is fascinating—and terribly frustrating for those who like to formulate laws without exceptions.

The matrilineal Hopi or Navajo woman may announce a divorce by simply piling her husband's possessions outside the door of the house, and he will accept it with a shrug and return to his sister's home. But patrilineal societies make divorce difficult, and in some cases virtually impossible after a child has been born. The reasons again are simple. The child, most particularly an infant, must, in order to survive, remain with the mother. In a matrilineal society, the marriage dissolution does not take that precious next generation away from the descent group. In a patrilineal system, it does.

The above paragraphs are not in any sense a complete discussion of kinship or of the differences between matrilineal and patrilineal systems. What I have attempted to do is to show how these two systems of kinship nomenclature relate to actual patterns of behavior in different societies.

Traits of Unilineal Societies

The question still remains as to what unilineal societies do that bilateral societies don't do. I think the answer again lies in the way people make a living. Among the hunters and gatherers and among the industrial peoples it is essential that each person have as many open alternatives as possible. So in both cases the focus is on the nuclear family, and kinship extends in both directions to establish the widest possible range of social contacts.

For people who make their living as farmers or herders, the number of alternatives is less important than the ability to count on having access to a single piece of farm land or grazing land from which to draw sustenance. In modern, literate societies, a person can establish his claim to a portion of land by reference to the complex system of laws that governs the ownership and inheritance of land. In tribal societies, without these elaborate legal institutions, the system of reckoning descent itself serves to verify one's rights to

Figure 33. The core of the Navajo family is the descending line of women.

a portion of the productive resources of the society. Thus, title to farm land is vested in a specific descent group and each generation verifies its right to use the land by reference to its descent from the line with established land rights.

If one reckons descent bilaterally, such verification becomes difficult. Does a son have equal rights to farm the land of his father's family and that of his mother as well? What of the daughter, and what of the rights of her children, and so on? In a unilineal system, however, the issue is quite clear. If you are a Zulu, who reckons descent patrilineally, you are eligible to farm the lands of your father's people. Your sister, in return for producing sons for her husband's descent group, will be supported by the produce of their land. In short, the use rights on the land will pass down through a single line perpetually, and the ambiguities of combined families in each generation are avoided.

Many theories have been offered concerning the origins of unilineal systems—whether the matrilineal preceded the patrilineal, etc. Today, we seldom think in these terms and simply classify existing systems without implying that one is somehow older or more primitive than the other.

It seems to be true that where the economic role of women is very important, there is also a tendency toward matrilineal systems, but this is nowise universal. It has been argued that where women do the farming we should find matrilineal systems—and yet, among the excessively patrilineal tribes of Bantu Africa, women do most of the field work while men herd cattle or go off to war. On the other hand, among the matrilineal Hopi, a man works the field of his wife's family. We can only say that in general there appears to be a relationship between unilineal descent systems and farming. The correspondence is by no means universal. Until the past few hundred years, agriculture was the economic base of virtually all human societies, at least some of which were bilateral.

This illustrates another important point about kinship systems and social structures in general: they do not change in immediate response to other aspects of culture or environment. Men, as we know, make symbols of many things. The ways they reckon descent and organize human relations are almost always treated as symbols of morality, naturalness, and propriety, and thus men are reluctant to change them even when they are not totally appropriate to the situations in which men find themselves. As a result we find an endless variation of adjustments among human societies as the traditional systems are manipulated to fit new circumstances.

Primogeniture refers to inheritance systems in which family wealth and position passes to the oldest son.
Ultimogeniture refers to systems in which inheritance devolves on the youngest son.

Bilateral systems can and do exist in agricultural societies. To do so requires that in many ways, a bilateral system act as if it were a unilineal system by making special rules about inheritance—*primogeniture*, for instance, or the opposite case, *ultimogeniture*. In Tibet and elsewhere, a family can keep from endlessly dividing the land and avoid the ambiguities of bilaterality by having all the brothers of a family marry a single woman. In the England of feudal times— and rural Ireland today—the first son inherited the land and was then entitled to marry. If his brothers and sisters wished to marry, they in effect gave up their claims to the support of the farm and found some other means of livelihood. If they wished to remain on the land, they were forced to relinquish their right to marry. In modern America, with its enormous expanses of undeveloped land, the bilateral system could continue by constantly opening up new farm lands for each generation so that new nuclear families would each have new lands from which to make a living.

Traditional China, although terminologically bilateral, was in many cases actually patrilineal, since daughters went away from the father's home to provide sons for some other family; the sons could claim only their father's wealth, and had no real claim to that of their mother's family. Somewhat the same sort of thinking developed in Japan. But keep in mind that all these examples are drawn from cultures with long traditions of land laws and record-keeping, so that the problems developing could be resolved through recourse to the law.

The children of a parent's opposite-sex sibling—that is, mother's brother's children or father's sister's children—are *ego's cross-cousins*, by kin type. In any unilineal system a cross-cousin is not a relative, or at least not a member of the same descent group as *ego*, and thus in most systems is a potential marriage partner. In many systems the best possible marriage partner one can choose is a cross-cousin. The opposite of a cross-cousin is a *parallel cousin*—that is, the child of a same-sex sibling of one of *ego*'s parents. In other words, mother's sister's children and father's brother's children are parallel cousins to *ego*. In a matrilineal system, *ego*'s matrilateral parallel cousins are close relatives, but his patrilateral parallel cousins are not. The reverse is the case in patrilineal systems. Marriage of parallel cousins is rare but not unknown. Usually it is found in patrilineal or sometimes bilateral systems, where the children of brothers marry. This, of course, serves to keep the property of a descent group together. Such marriages are considered excellent matches by the Bedouin Arabs and the Balinese.

Figure 34. According to the Bedouin of the Middle East, the marriage of the children of two brothers is an excellent match. Can you suggest a reason?

KINSHIP II: DESCENT GROUPS AND SOCIETY

6

LARGE KINSHIP GROUPS

Thus far we have spoken of descent groups or families using the latter term in its everyday sense, although unilineal systems are seldom composed only of nuclear families. Instead, larger units are considered important. We will examine some of these units.

Moieties

Many societies throughout the world are divided into *moieties,* or halves, so that each person is from birth a member of either one group or the other. Most frequently moieties have names and symbols—the Hawks and the Owls, Upstream and Downstream, the Reds and the Whites, the Land Side and the Water Side, or the like. They may even have legends about how they orig-

inated and from whom or what they descended. Frequently, as well, members of one moiety have distinct responsibilities toward members of another. In some cases moiety X must bury the dead of moiety Y and vice versa.

Not always, but most frequently, moieties are *exogamous.* That is, one cannot marry a member of one's own moiety. To determine which moiety one belongs to, it is necessary to refer to one's parentage. In a society with patrilineal moieties, one is a member of father's moiety, and if the society is matrilineal, the opposite is true. In a patrilineal moiety system one will marry a person from mother's moiety; again the reverse is true in the matrilineal system.

In some tribes, notably in Australia, the moiety is only the first of a number of important groups to which one belongs. Each moiety is divided into two, three, even four subdivisions or sections—each with a prescribed counterpart section from which mates may be drawn and each with a specific relationship, often expressed in kin terms, to all other sections. In other tribes, the moiety may be so vague that only a kind of informal rivalry between different moieties exists, expressed in choosing sides for games or races. In fact, in some groups one can even change moieties, but at that point the idea becomes so vague as to be useless in social analysis.

Clans

Clan is a very common word. We often use it in everyday English to indicate a large number of relatives without specifying their exact relationships: the "Jones clan" or the "Brown clan." We are also aware that the clan was and to a certain extent still is important among the Scots. But when we use the term in anthropology, we are somewhat more precise. A clan is a group of people who feel they are related by descent from a common ancestor, but the distinctive issue of clanship is the nature of that ultimate ancestor. When an anthropologist speaks of a *clan*, he refers to people who think they

Figure 35. Clan systems are based on the belief of the clan's descent from a common non-human ancestor. Frequently, members of a given clan wear a special insignia and share rituals that distinguish them from members of other clans.

are related because of descent from some non-human ancestor: an animal, god, spirit, natural phenomenon, or mythical person.

In a clan system, one does not in every instance have to trace his ancestry back to the mythical ancestor, but only refer to the clan of his mother or father to establish a relationship with all people who feel they are similarly descended. Of course, all people distinguish between their actual brothers and sisters and the children of other relatives, but not infrequently they will use a term like "brother" or "sister" to refer to all people of their clan of roughly the same age, "father" and "mother" to refer to clan members older than they, and so on.

See *The Navajo*, by James F. Downs (Holt, Rinehart & Winston, 1972).

In almost every instance, clans are exogamous and operate to determine who is eligible for marriage with whom. The Navajo Indians of Arizona have matrilineal clans, between fifty and sixty of them. Since there are over a hundred thousand Navajo living in an area as large as West Virginia, they cannot all be related to one another. Nonetheless, no two people bearing the same clan designation can marry. When a Navajo is traveling in a new part of the reservation he can expect a degree of hospitality from people of his clan even if he has never seen them before. Each clan has its own story to tell about how its earliest ancestors were created, appeared, or were born miraculously.

In some systems, the Navajo being one of them, clans are linked. That is, certain clans because of some incident in their mythical pasts are considered to be closely related, perhaps too closely related to permit members to marry. Thus, in a sense, entire clans view each other as kin. The Navajo, for instance, prohibit marriage between a person and any member of his father's clan, as if all members of his father's clan were somehow the same as father, and therefore their female children were like his sisters. On the other hand, members of father's father's clan are considered good marriage partners. If you draw a chart of this you can see it is almost as if clans operated bilaterally while individuals operate matrilineally.

For the Navajo, the clan serves to determine eligible marriage partners but influences very little else save in specific ceremonial contexts. The neighbors of the Navajo, the Hopi, find the idea of clanship a convenient way to organize almost their entire lives; political authority, ceremonial behavior, and almost every activity and interpersonal relationship, are determined by what clan a person belongs to. The distinguished anthropologist Fred Eggan once said that the idea of clanship is like a bag. Some people don't possess the bag at all—that is, don't think of being related to other people in this way. But those who do possess the bag put greater or lesser amounts of their lives into the bag. In some societies clans may have councils of elders, control the distribution and use of lands, serve as a basis of representation in tribal assemblies and councils, administer the law, and provide the basis for selection of men for military service. In other societies, clans may be vague entities, useful only in determining who is eligible to marry whom.

Lineages
Not infrequently, relationships based on clan identity are distinguished from relationships based on some unit or subdivision of the clan. This is very common in patrilineal systems, and widespread

Figure 36. *Lineages* and *clans* are differentiated by the nature of the ultimate ancestor. Which is a lineage, above, and which is a clan?

among pastoral peoples in Africa and central Asia. We call these subdivisions *lineages*. The lineage can be distinguished from the clan by reference to the ultimate ancestor. If the ultimate ancestor is felt to have been a real and historic human being, not different from his descendants, we are dealing not with the clan but with the lineage.

Lineages are not necessarily subdivisions of clans, although that is frequently the case. In some societies the lineage exists as the basic unit of overall social organization. Where both lineages and clans exist together, we often find that their functions are separated. For instance, clanship may determine marriage partners while lineage membership determines land rights. Lineages may be exogamous, with marriage permitted to persons of the same clan but from different lineages; on the other hand, they are not very often endogamous. Because the founder of a lineage is a real human being and because real human beings are constantly born, a lineage system has the potential of constantly dividing into even further subdivisions.

Evans-Pritchard's *The Nuer: A Description of the Modes of Livelihood and Political Institutions of a Nilotic People* (Oxford University Press, 1969) is an updating of a classic work describing this cattle-herding people of the Sudan in Africa.

The Nuer are a case in point. All Nuer see themselves as at least vaguely related because of their common language and culture. However, the population is divided into a number of clans within which relationships are seen as the result of common descent from mythical ancestors. Each clan is divided into a number of lineages, and each of these further subdivided. These subdivisions we call *segments*, and the entire system, a *segmented lineage system*. This kind of system is possible because, in theory at least, each man can become the founder of a lineage populated by his descendants. That is, a man is a member of a lineage. If he has three sons, each of them is a member of his father's lineage; but each son can also become the leader of his own lineage as he has sons and grandsons.

Stealing cattle, feuding, and hostilities between Nuer sublineages (segments) is fairly common, but if one of them is attacked by members of a lineage unrelated to theirs, they will form an alliance to fend off the outsiders. Since all Nuer are members of clans, the process of amalgamating into fighting alliances within the tribe against other portions of the tribe can go on until all the members of one clan are arrayed against all the members of another. At the same time, a threat from outside the tribe would mean that all the Nuer would ally themselves against the outsider. Although such a system sounds chaotic it actually serves to establish Nuer life. Because sublineages generally include the same number of potential fighting men, a balance is soon struck if they quarrel; to avoid a useless fight in which the outcome is not clear, the hostile parties will enter into negotiations.

Of course, Nuer sublineages are not in fact created indefinitely. By judiciously dropping generations out of the counting between the living generation and the ultimate lineage ancestor, the Nuer maintain a conventional number of six or seven lineages and sublineages.

KINSHIP AND SOCIETY

Both clan and lineage are based on kinship as a primary organizing principle of society. In such systems, virtually all other members of the tribe or nation can be placed on a kinship chart. (The devices for doing this will be discussed shortly.) While kinship as a basis for social organization is found in almost all small societies it works surprisingly well in large societies as well. The Nuer number well over one hundred thousand and with only the obligations and responsibilities of kinsmen, one to the other, manage to maintain order, organize defense and offense against enemies, and exploit their none-too-hospitable environment. They have no kings or councils of elders or political roles at all.

Such societies are called *acephalous,* "without heads." Lineage systems are not always acephalous, but the important thing to remember is that kind of political organization which we have come to think absolutely essential to all men is not necessarily so. Our television and fiction writers almost always endow "native" leaders in their stories with unlimited power of life and death over their "subjects." Nothing can be further from the truth. In most tribal societies, the forces which direct human activities are the same as those that direct your own life within your family. Seldom does family discipline come under the scrutiny of the police and the law. Mothers cannot and would not call the district attorney and ask that their children be indicted for not eating their spinach. But at the same time, mother is not without power to force her children to eat their spinach. It is the power to ridicule, to withdraw companionship or cooperation, to comment on the morality and prestige of an individual, which societies based on kinship principles can wield with good effect.

Kinship as Guide for Behavior

In terms of behavior, kinship systems provide a guide for action for the person living within the system. *Father, mother,* and *uncle* are not simply words. They are shorthand terms which define special patterns of behavior toward specific persons called "Father," "Mother," and "Uncle." One seldom speaks in the same way to, or in the presence of, one's mother as one does to, or in the presence of, one's friends or cousins. The tone of voice, even the words themselves change. You can test this yourself by simply jotting down the words and phrases you use with your contemporaries every day which you generally do not or would not use with your mother.

These differentiations in behavior are true in non-kin relations as well. Students seldom speak to professors in the same way that they speak to other students. One uses different language in court than one does on the golf course. We tend to think of this as rather random or, at the most, a matter of respect or good manners, and so it is. But at the same time, if we examine our speech, attitudes, and general bearing in the presence of people occupying different roles or statuses, we realize that our behavior changes are not random, or matters of choice. For example, we don't speak politely to a judge at one time and rudely at another. Furthermore, we find that most people we know act in very much the same way in similar situations. In short, our behavior is patterned.

Precisely what kind of behavior is expected of people in different kinship systems is one of the things which marks the differences between cultures. For instance, if an American were studiously to ignore his wife's mother, leave the house whenever she appeared, and refuse to look at her or even talk to her, he would probably initiate a domestic crisis of no small magnitude. Every gesture would suggest that he neither liked nor respected his mother-in-law. And yet all of this is exactly what would be expected of a Navajo man in the presence of his wife's mother. To speak directly to her, to look at her, or to hand her things, would be considered the signs of ill manners and disrespect. Moreover, it would be courting disaster in the form of insanity. This kind of behavior embodies what is called the *mother-in-law taboo,* and is a rather common practice throughout the world.

We know that the relationship between son-in-law and mother-in-law is often fraught with tensions and resentments. We resolve the problem somewhat in our culture by making the entire issue a matter of humor, the subject of the mother-in-law joke. But we generally live separately from our in-laws and do not cooperate in daily life with them. For people in smaller communities operating in economic systems requiring close cooperation among relatives, studied avoidance does appear to reduce the tensions and conflicts. On the other hand, there are also many potential tensions between a young woman and her husband's mother, particularly in patrilineal systems where young women are often more concerned about the character of their mothers-in-law than they are of their husbands. We seldom see a daughter-in-law–mother-in-law taboo in operation, however. Occasionally, we find a daughter-in-law–father-in-law taboo, sometimes in a kind of symmetry with a son-in-law–mother-in-law taboo. It would be nice to prove that all of these practices do resolve basic social problems and thus are entirely understandable and reasonable. But alas, we cannot. Sometimes men seem to do things for reasons totally beyond our presently limited powers of analysis.

Another common situation is to find that certain relatives have special privileges with each other in the matter of joking, particularly sexual joking. We call these joking relationships. From culture to culture the roles of people permitted to joke with each other in this manner vary greatly. In some societies, brothers and sisters can tease each other unmercifully about sex and sexual matters. In others, not the slightest suggestion of sex is allowed to enter into a brother–sister relationship. Father's sister, especially in some matrilineal systems like the Hopi, is often a person with whom a boy or young man can exchange sexual jokes and take certain sexual liberties. In some cases, the paternal aunt may indeed introduce her nephew to sexual intercourse. In other cultural systems, the marriage of a man and his sister's daughter is considered an excellent match, as it was in traditional Jewry. Among the Bathanga of Africa, a special relationship between a man and his mother's brother permits him to expropriate or even destroy property belonging to his uncle without fear of punishment.

The **Bathanga** are described by H. R. Radcliff-Brown in *Structure and Function in Primitive Society* (The Free Press, 1952).

Cousin relationships are often foci of special behavior patterns. Not infrequently, they are seen as virtually the same as sibling relationships. On the other hand, in some societies cross-cousins are expected to maintain a thinly veiled hostility towards each other, indulging in practical jokes and verbal abuse on almost every occasion. Some authorities have suggested that by allowing this sort of expression of hostility a society is preventing more serious tensions from developing into real schismatic confrontations.

In many societies, including the Kota of India and many tribes on the Great Plains of the United States, the relationship between brothers is considered an especially strong one. Thus a man called brother can require of you many kinds of assistance and cooperation, and must of course respond in kind. Not infrequently, brother relationships include the right to have sexual intercourse with one's sister-in-law. The ramifications of this practice will become clearer when we discuss marriage.

Classificatory Kinship

"What," the student is bound to ask, "happens if your mother didn't have a brother?" "Whom will you marry then?" The answer is that in societies where this is important mother *always* has a brother. But how can this be? We cannot determine how many boys and how many girls will be born to a woman. Right enough. We can't, but we must remember that kinship systems are sociological, not biological phenomena. We can see something of this in our own culture. For instance, we say that in a marriage ceremony the bride is "given away" by her father. But if her father is dead or sick or otherwise unable to take part in the ceremony a substitute is found, an older brother, uncle, or older friend of the family. This substitution is not random but rather in a decreasing order of suitability or perhaps we could say, in a descending order of "fatherliness." That is there is something, nature of the blood relation, relative age in relationship to the bride's family, something which suggests that in some way the substitute is like a father.

In a far more formalized way, this principle operates in many societies wherein kinship terms are extended to cover rather large classes of people who share in some way characteristics of relationship with *ego*. Again we can see something of this in our own society with the terms *cousin* and *uncle* and *aunt*. *Cousin* covers a number of relationships, ignoring sex, sex of parents, and whether the relationship is patrilateral or matrilateral. *Aunt* and *uncle* ignore whether the relationship is patri- or matrilateral, and in addition ignore whether it is consanguineal or affinal.

Many societies extend this principle much more widely than we do. An example might be the Siane of New Guinea, a patrilineal group with village exogamy. This means that everyone's mother is from another village. This fact provides kin terms and suitable behavior patterns toward everyone in the village of one's mother. Her brother is called something which translates as "male mother." By extension, all men of roughly his generation from that village are called "male mother." Their children are cross-cousins, and all are called by a term that indicates that relationship. Thus, terms of reference for an entire village are reduced to only a handful of words based on *ego's* relationship to *that village* through his mother. It is now easy to see how mother always has a brother. There are many men whom *ego* addresses as mother's brother and who can be called upon to fill the role of mother's brother.

The **Siane** are described in R. F. Salisbury, *From Stone to Steel: Economic Consequences of a Technological Change in New Guinea* (Melbourne University Press).

Kinship terminology of this kind is based on what is called the principle of *classificatory kinship*. At one time, anthropologists held that all kinship systems are either classificatory or descriptive, with an implication that descriptive systems were somehow a bit more advanced. Gradually we began to realize that both descriptive and classificatory terms appear in all kinship systems.

Fictive Kinship

It is not always necessary that two persons be related by either "blood" or marriage for them to use kinship terms in addressing one another. In societies where kinship is the principal means of establishing a person's role behavior and his status, kinship terms are often the idiom of all social intercourse. That is, kinship terms are systematically extended to include persons who are not actually relatives but who, for one reason or another, are expected to behave as relatives.

We call this *fictive kinship,* but should stress that there is nothing fictive about the power of kin terms to organize human relationships. Here again, we do not have to go far afield to see this principle in action. Most Americans have in their own life experiences a fictive aunt. Most frequently this term is applied to a woman of about your mother's age, often a person with whom she has a very close relationship, not infrequently one stemming from their girlhood. And quite naturally, "Aunt Mary's" husband is addressed as uncle. Somewhat less frequently, the uncle term is applied to a bachelor friend of the parents.

In some social environments, such fictive terms are used quite freely as a means of resolving the problem of what a child should call a relatively close friend of the family. "Mister" and "Missus" would imply far too formal a relationship, but first names would seem too informal for a child to use when addressing an adult. The compromise is the use of fictive kinship. In this case the term reflects a closeness of social relationship between the "aunt" or "uncle" and *ego's* parents.

We use the term "Father" to refer to priests and "Sister" to refer to nuns. Why? These terms recognize a degree of authority and potential to lead and guide the members of their parish or congregation, but most obvious is the fact that these are terms which fall within the incest taboo. Priest and nun do not marry and this is recognized by applying a close kin term. Fraternal organizations, churches, and labor unions use the terms "Brother" and "Sister" to refer to their members, suggesting the nonsexual, cooperative nature of the relationship among members. "Brothers-in-arms" has, in somewhat more floridly romantic times, been used to describe the relationship among soldiers. "Brother, can you spare a dime?" is a pathetic attempt to stir fraternal emotions in the heart and pocketbook of a total stranger.

In traditional Japan, and to some extent even today, fictive kinship played an important role in organizing human activity in non-familial or suprafamilial contexts. Selecting a promising son of a poor family, the child of a not-so-successful relative or a faithful servant, a well-to-do Japanese farmer would endow the young man with land enough to establish himself as a farmer. In return, the recipient would be obligated to treat his benefactor like a father. He would cooperate in agricultural work, contribute to the financial needs of the family, participate in ceremonial functions and use kin terms just as a real son. The home of his fictive father would be called the *honke* or "root house." His own home and those of people in similar situations would be called *bunke* or branch houses. And in succeeding generations, the relationships between the descendants of the *honke* and the descendants of the *bunke* would remain in a father and son framework.

On **fictive kinship** in Japan, see Edward Norbeck and Harumi Bofu, "Informal Fictive Kinship in Japan," *American Anthropologist* 60 (1958), pp. 102–117, and "Japanese Usages of Terms of Relationship," in *Southwestern Journal of Anthropology* 14 (1958), pp. 66–86, by the same authors.

The Japanese name for this system is *dozoku*. In industry and commerce similar relationships have been called *oyabun* (parent)–*kobun* (child) relationships. In these situations, very common in most

Figure 37.   Fictive kinship roles still play a significant part in Japanese industrial relations.

Japanese factories until recently, the foreman "adopted" his key workmen in a simple ceremony in a local teahouse. Thereafter, the group used kin terms and were expected to assist each other as brothers would help brothers, or as a parent would help a son. The foreman, "father" of his group, was in all probability a "son" in a group composed of other foremen with a supervisor "father," and in turn the supervisor was a member of another group with a "father" on a higher level. Thus the permanent work force in a company would be linked together by a series of fictive kin relations that provide financial assistance in an emergency, help with the education of children, job security, assistance in locating proper mates for children, and so on. Today the rapidly expanding Japanese economy has begun to abandon *oyabu–kobun*, but in the marginal areas of Japanese life— seasonal labor, urban criminal gangs—it is still a potent instrument of organization.

Kinship as Organizing Device

The point here is the use of kinship words and kinship thinking to extend human relationships beyond the boundaries of kinship. The practice also demonstrates how men tend, in many areas of human endeavor, to use the familiar and accepted practices and devices to do new jobs rather than create new and unfamiliar institutions. There are, however, limits to the utility of kinship as a general organizing device—limits which are most likely to appear when a society grows larger, or when it grows more complex through elaboration of technology or ideology. It is relatively easy to extend fictive kinship to nonrelatives only in a society where the differences among men are not great.

On the Great Plains of the United States, the warrior societies to which the men belonged tended to consider members as brothers, and the practice of two young men declaring their brotherhood and treating one another as brothers was widespread. Any man on the Great Plains could in fact act like a brother to any other man in his tribe. They both knew more or less the same things, lived the same way, and followed the same set of cultural directions.

See Harold Driver, *Indians of North America* (University of Chicago Press, 1969).

Figure 38. Australian aborigines have a highly complicated kinship
system. A man on "walkabout" must approach a strange
village with caution until he determines his kinship relationship with its inhabitants.

However, as technology grows, it demands specialists—people
with different knowledge, different life patterns, and different expectations. And if a culture represents the world as being full of different
kinds of people—human and subhuman races, royalty and commoners, believers and unbelievers, the clean and the unclean, upper
and lower classes, masters and slaves—the extent to which kinship
terminology can be applied is limited, too, by the boundaries of culturally conceived differences.

In some societies—the tribes of native Australia, for instance—
there is virtually no means of relating people together save in terms
of kinship. It is normal for an aboriginal man on "walkabout" to
approach a strange camp with caution and call out to the people
living there. While he waits on the outskirts someone will come out
to find out who he is. The complexities of Australian kinship systems
make it possible in most cases for any stranger to determine by what
kinship term he should be addressed while visiting a strange camp.
Thus, it is instantly determined who shall feed him and to whom he
should give the game he kills. It is known what girls he may court
and those forbidden to him, what older women he should treat with

respect, what men he can command, and whom he must obey. But should it be, as is sometimes the case, that no kinship term can be established for him, he has no choice save to run away as fast as he can. Otherwise, his erstwhile hosts would solve this little problem in human relationships by spearing him to death.

The lives of one group of **Australian aborigines** are described by C. M. W. Hart and A. Pilling, *The Tiwi of North Australia* (Holt, Rinehart & Winston, 1960), and Elman Service, *Profiles in Ethnology* (Harper & Row, 1971).

Our own society is perhaps an opposite extreme. Kinship plays a relatively restricted role in our lives, gradually growing less and less important as we grow older. Our society operates to restrict the extent and influence of kinship behavior. In government and business, the employment of relatives is frowned upon, and in many cases is outright illegal. "Nepotism" in America is a dirty word. Hiring one's relatives is felt to violate our view of equal opportunity based on ability. Not infrequently one's obligation to government, business, church, or some other non-kin institution is expected to override one's obligations as a parent or husband, son or daughter, though we accept this with some regret. A man unwilling to work overtime or travel out of town because it would take him away from his wife and children is considered lacking in ambition and certainly not destined for positions of profit and power. A young American man or woman who appears unable to strike out on his or her own, too dependent and responsive to parental demands, is considered lacking in basic character. A mother who won't relinquish her hold on a child is not playing the game as American society defines it.

We often forget, much to our collective embarrassment in this modern world, that many of the world's people see things quite differently. In many of the so-called "underdeveloped" countries where our experts despair at what they consider corruption and inefficiency, loyalty to the kin group, be it a family, lineage, or clan, is considered the highest ideal of man. To act like Americans—to refuse to hire relatives, to consider the duties of office more important than the obligation to help relatives, to abandon the parental house and authority, not to be interested in the choices and decisions one's adult children have to make—is often defined by others as the behavior of a people without basic moral standards. It is important to remember that when a South Asian politician steals from the public coffers to enrich his family he is not, in his eyes, or even in the eyes of the people from whom he steals, a criminal. Rather, he is a man living up to the highest ideals of his culture: loyalty and obligation to the continuity of his kin group.

Corporate Kinship Groups

Some kinship systems are organized in a corporate fashion—that is, the descent group is seen as a continuing entity in itself, quite independent of any individual who may be a part of the group at any given time. In our own society a corporation, while not a kinship unit, is much the same. It is an entity in and of itself with specific patterns of organization; it owns property, which belongs to it rather than to any of its members; and it possesses social identity as a kind of super individual. An industrial corporation continues to exist long after any of the original founders have died. It makes and obeys special rules for the management of corporate property, and it has an internal structure according to which individuals take up, for a time, certain functional positions. General Motors Corporation, not any individual or any group of individuals, makes and sells automobiles. All the stock can change hands, all the officers and workers be dismissed or retired and replaced, the buildings and property may be sold and new purchased. Despite all of this, the corporation continues.

The same situation exists in many societies, where the descent group is seen as a corporation, an entity with an identity greater than that of any of its members. In one society, a clan may control a portion of land which is distributed to the living members of the clan in each generation for their use, but the clan in fact retains title to the land. The corporate property may be something less material— a body of legends, a name, a special tradition or esoteric knowledge, certain skills or ritual prerogatives. Any of these things can be passed from generation to generation but not possessed or alienated by any individual. Strong corporate descent groups—governing such things as the distribution of land, the administration of justice according to customary rules—can and in many societies do carry out all the activities which we normally think of as political. The Nuer of the Sudan, you will recall, have no chiefs, councils, or rulers of any sort. Peace and order are maintained by adherence to the customary modes of behavior between families, lineages, and clans.

The burden of the preceding pages has been to show the idea of kinship as a construct of the human mind and not a biological necessity. Each of us is first introduced into the world by a group of kinsmen. As we grow into the world our range of kinsmen extends. In some societies the network of kinship relations extends to all people with whom one is liable to come into contact, and serves as a kind of map of the world of human beings, each kin term designating one's proper relationship and behavior with other people.

Kinship as we have talked of it here is a general system of organizing relationships outside the family, which is of course itself part of the system. There certainly are other principles upon which societies organize themselves and we will discuss them. But before we do we must examine in somewhat more detail the basic unit of all kinship systems, the family.

COURTSHIP AND MARRIAGE

7

THE SIGNIFICANCE OF MARRIAGE

The kinship charts in the previous chapter are combinations of triangular male marks and circular female symbols, joined by = signs. Each of these junctures indicates a formally recognized mating pair, a marriage if you prefer. The solid lines descending from these junctures and connecting other symbols for male and female individuals represent "blood" relationships. As we suggested when discussing biology and its relation to human culture and society, the union of males and females is crucial to the survival of the human species, and of course human culture. It is obviously important that we understand something of how our kind has arranged for boys and girls to get together into these pairs. The process

is not, as the street-corner philosopher would have it, a matter of chemistry; instead, complex systems of relationships and symbols guide man in his search for a mate.

The female baboon, when seized by oestrus, begins by breeding with the young and barely mature, and the weak and unaggressive. Toward the middle of the "heat" period, when she is most likely to be fertile, she copulates with the stronger, more dominant males; and as the urges of her nature taper off, she returns to the younger and weaker males until she no longer desires coitus. In other animal species, the stronger male may form a harem of all the females he can possibly service, driving off the younger, the older,

Figure 39.   A female baboon "in heat" will mate with a number of males, beginning with the younger, weaker members of the troop.

and the weaker males until he becomes injured or old and in turn is replaced.

Nowhere does man take such a casual approach to sexual intercourse, although in some societies (such as the Lepcha of Sikkim) human behavior does seem to approach promiscuity—limited always by the incest taboo. However, sexual intercourse is not marriage. Even among the Lepcha, who consider any meeting of unrelated man and woman—in a house, in the fields, or on a mountain trail—reason enough for sexual intercourse (a sort of erotic handshake, as it were), marriage is carefully considered and entered into with ritual and

See G. Gorer's *Himalayan Village: An Account of the Lepchas of Sikkim*, second edition (Basic Books, 1967).

solemnity. Marriage is not simply a sexual relationship in any society, however important sex may be. A married man or woman is always seen differently from an unmarried man or woman.

Childbearing and Adult Roles

The act of coming together to form a recognized unit or couple confers numerous other obligations and responsibilities. Foremost is the obligation or expectation that the couple will produce children. Until very recent times, reproduction hardly seemed an obligation, but was rather the assumed outcome of cohabitation. Attitudes towards childlessness reveal the social importance of reproduction, however. Many societies consider the failure of a couple to produce a child after a reasonable time as grounds for dissolution of the marriage. In parts of Africa, the husband can demand the return of money or livestock he paid over to the bride's family at the time of marriage if she fails to conceive within a reasonable period. Alternatively, he may simply ask the wife's family to supply him with another girl, a sister or cousin who might be more fertile. Because they do not want to forfeit the bride price, the request will be granted. In our own society, where having or not having children has become, through improved birth control, a matter of choice, most states recognize a partner's refusal to have children as acceptable grounds for divorce.

Having produced a child, a couple is assumed to have certain responsibilities to that child and to society. They are expected to protect and nurture the child and at the same time provide it with the training necessary to produce a responsible adult. As we shall see, these responsibilities are not always the exclusive problem of the couple, but may be widely diffused through the kinship system to include many other relatives (mother's brother, for instance, as we have seen among the Trobrianders). In addition to the responsibilities of parenthood, married people are assumed to be able to play adult roles in economic, social, and political life.

The island of Yap provides an interesting example. On this relatively large island in Micronesia, the political system is rather rigidly structured. The island is divided into districts and within each district and village there are many "offices" or political roles which must be filled by adult males. These offices are ranked in a complex hierarchy which extends over the entire island—and in the recent past extended to other islands that were part of an island empire. Political activity, council meetings, political intrigues, and caucuses are a vital part of the lives of Yapese men.

But these activities are restricted to men of mature years who are married. The age at which men are admitted to political participation is rather late; the young people are encouraged to delay adulthood for as long as possible and to "have fun," which means to spend most of their time involved in romantic involvements and seductions. The Yapese are very permissive about premarital sexual relations, and expect young men and women to experiment widely before settling down to marriage in their late twenties or early thirties.

Girls who become pregnant during this period know many ways of inducing abortion and, although abortion is overtly considered a terrible sin, regularly do so. They are abetted in this by the fact that Yapese women customarily go to a special menstrual hut during their periods and remain there until they are considered ritually pure once again. Thus, a young woman who suspects that she might be pregnant simply retires to the hut at the time her period is expected and induces an abortion without causing any suspicion.

Sex and Marriage

After ten to fifteen years of romantic adventure, the Yapese consider it time to settle down and select a mate—usually a long-term lover upon whom they have settled during the course of their experimentation. Upon assuming the status of married people, both men and women are supposed to abandon their interest in romance. Women are supposed to involve themselves in child rearing, homemaking, and gardening; the men concentrate on fishing, food collecting, and politics.

Figure 40.   Young people of Yap are urged to delay adulthood for as long as possible.

Sexual relations between man and wife are of course expected, but in the eyes of the Yapese they are perhaps the least important aspect of married life. The Yapese believe that babies are not a product of sexual intercourse, but rather the gift of the spirits to women who have proven themselves to be kind and generous and who have in general lived up to the social expectations of Yapese society. And yet no woman is expected to bear a child until she is married and has provided the children with a father.

In America we have of recent years emphasized the sexual aspects of marriage in a positive way, openly arguing that each partner should expect sexual fulfillment from the other. Not long ago, our society emphasized the sexual nature of marriage in a negative fashion, holding that women, in order to achieve the desirable status of married women and mothers, must submit reluctantly to the base instincts of men. At the same time, we stressed that sex was acceptable only within the bounds of marriage. Our linking of sex with marriage in such an exclusive way often obscures the other obligations of marriage in our society. For instance, in most states of the union two people who marry become a single economic unit through the legal device of community property. In any event, marriage alters the distribution of property through inheritance regardless of whether or not children have been born to the couple. In short, marriage means much more than two people having sexual relations, which can be accomplished without making permanent status changes. An unmarried girl is socially a virgin in our society until she marries, irrespective of how much sexual experience she might have. Sexual relations between unmarried people may imply much in terms of an emotional commitment but do not, in and of themselves, establish a marital status for either partner. In some societies, sexual relationships may imply an intention to change status and become married, and in fact society may insist on it if the relationship is discovered; but the change will be a result of a socially sanctioned and, to one degree or another, ritualized act.

MARITAL UNITS

It has been argued by some anthropologists that the married couple constitutes the universal basic unit of social organization. This is true in at least one way, because the coming together of a man and woman is necessary for the birth of a child. However, in many societies the nuclear family is submerged in larger kin units to the degree that it

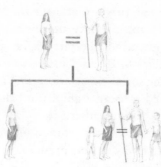

Figure 41.   A nuclear family is composed of husband, wife, and children. If they all remain in the household, an extended family is formed when the children marry. If the children establish new homes, the nuclear pattern continues.

has virtually no viability of its own; the married couple is often merely part of an *extended* or *joint* family, which may in some cases share a single roof under the authority of a single person.

Such a system existed in traditional China among the upper classes, and as an ideal among all Chinese. Under the domination of the eldest male, sons and younger brothers brought their wives into the household, often having only a sleeping room which they could consider their own. The daughter-in-law worked very much as part of a team under the direction of the mother-in-law, the sons under the direction of their father. For the Chinese the ideal family was one in which five generations lived under a single roof. In this context, the children of any specific couple were viewed as being extensions of the family and both their welfare and discipline was the responsibility of all the family members rather than only their father and mother. We can see other examples of this kind of thing as we examine various forms of marriage.

Monogamy
Our own system expects that no one will be formally married to more than one person at the same time. In addition, we at least give lip service to the idea that a couple should remain together throughout life. An increasingly permissive attitude toward divorce has made it possible to practice what sometimes has been called serial monogamy: entering into several monogamous marriages, one after another.

The idea of monogamous marriages is not at all unique to Western culture. Probably most married people, whatever society they live in, are married to only one partner. That is, if we could count individual marriages in the world, I am sure we would find that most of them are monogamous. However, the idea of lifelong fidelity is more nearly unique to Western culture. So is the idea that monogamy is the *only* acceptable form of marriage. Even in societies where most marriages are monogamous we are apt to find that other marriage forms are quite acceptable, even preferred. And in societies where monogamy is the social and legal norm, we nevertheless find a number of institutions permitting or at least accepting forms of what we might call quasi-marriages.

In Renaissance Europe, women of the upper class often reserved the right to share their husband's home with a lover who was officially part of the household. Similarly, the practice of keeping a mistress is not uncommon in European and American cultures (though it should be emphasized that a lover or a mistress is not a husband or wife). In China the institution of concubinage, that is, accepting into the household women other than the official wife, was once widely recognized. The offspring of such unions were legitimate but not necessarily heirs to their father's status. The ambiguous role of the concubine was accepted socially although it might have been bitterly

Figure 42. In traditional Japan, a man could have only one official wife. But he was allowed to take other women into his home as concubines. Until recently, concubinage was also common in China.

resented by the official wife. In other societies, partners in monogamous marriages have possessed the recognized right to seek sexual relations with persons other than their mates. The Kota, whom we mentioned before, are a case in point since brothers-in-law and sisters-in-law are considered legitimate sexual partners.

In each of these examples, we must remember that the form of marriages is monogamous. The point is that the status of married persons in a monogamous society does not necessarily include the expectation of sexual exclusiveness. Extra- or quasi-marital relationships do not alter the basic monogamous principle, although they may reflect expectations about who might become a second spouse should the first spouse die. For instance, in many societies a widow is expected to marry the brother of her late husband if he is available for marriage, and a widower to marry his late wife's sister if conditions permit. This potential situation is then recognized by a greater degree of permissiveness between these affinal relatives.

> The practice of a widow's marrying her husband's brother is known as the **leverite**; that of a widower's being expected to marry his wife's sister is known as the **sororate**.

If monogamy is the type of marriage into which most people enter, it is not the type approved exclusively in most societies. In other words, if we take societies rather than individual marriages as our unit of investigation, we find that most societies approve at least two forms of marriage: monogamy, and some form of plural marriage or polygamy.

Polygyny

Polygamy is the technical term for any system in which two or more spouses are permitted to one person at one time. If the system expects or permits a man to have more than one wife, we call it *polygyny*. Americans often see polygynous marriage as some kind of paradise for lecherous males who can dally with as many wives as they can afford and collect younger wives as their others grow old. This may once have been the case with occasional potentates of the Near East, India, or Africa, but in general it is an unfair and distorted view of polygynous marriage.

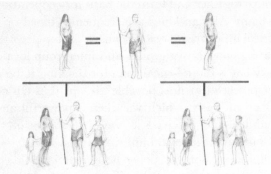

Figure 43. This diagram illustrates a form of extended or joint family based on a polygynous marriage. The two families might or might not share the same household.

We must remember that unlike mistress-keeping, a polygynous marriage places upon the husband certain specific and long-term obligations toward each wife. Certain prerogatives may be held by the first or senior wife, but the man must assume the roles of husband to several women and father to their several families of children. For many men these are onerous obligations, not infrequently entered into reluctantly, not to satisfy lust but to provide visual evidence of their prestige and success.

Some successful Americans, like Sinclair Lewis' Babbit, secretly relish the idea of living the rustic life of a hermit in a mountain cabin but instead undertake the burden of buying an expensive house and a second car; for similar reasons many an African man takes on a second wife. And just as the acquisitive American may be responding to the urging of his wife, so may the African take a second spouse to please his first wife who wishes to demonstrate her wisdom in selecting (or having selected for her) a prestigious mate.

Navajo women often urge their husbands to take second wives, too, but for different reasons. Navajo homesteads may be miles apart, and the wife's work is hard. An older woman may ask her husband to marry her younger sister or a friend so that she will have help and company. Such an arrangement also insures that the children can be cared for by someone they know if the first wife dies.

Another motivation for plural marriage is political. Affinal ties and the children stemming from them bind two otherwise separate descent groups together and form the basis for cooperation. The large harems of many African kings are frequently based on the need to extend political influence in societies where kinship plays the dominant role in creating cooperative groups and intergroup loyalties. In such a situation, what is more logical than for the king to be related to as many other powerful men as possible? It was thus ten centuries ago when the king of Tibet, which was then a powerful and aggressive state, demanded and received as wives members of the imperial family of China and the royal family of Nepal.

Yet another reason for polygynous marriages is economic. In many societies one works to help kinsmen, and employer–employee relations based on wages or barter are unknown. In such a situation one way to develop a work force devoted to special tasks, particularly tasks producing goods for sale or trade outside the society, is to marry the workers. Thus, in the middle of the nineteenth century, many polygynous marriages developed on the North American Great Plains when the Indians found that there was a market for tanned buffalo hides. Hide-tanning was the work of women, wives. It would have been too disturbing to the social system for one man to hire other men's wives. There was no real objection if men who could afford it married more than one wife, although in aboriginal times it was rare. Therefore, a well-established man, that is a good hunter with a number of trained buffalo horses, would seek out and marry strong and skillful young women, able to give presents to each and to her family, and to convince them of the wisdom of the marriage. This group of young wives could tan the hides he brought in, so that he might trade them for whiskey, cooking kettles, steel hatchets, guns and gunpowder, ribbon and glass beads and all the other attractions of industrial America. An added dimension of this arrangement was that so many strong young women attracted numbers of strong young men who were without the wherewithal to marry. They could, however, borrow hunting horses from this connubial entrepreneur and obtain more hides for his harem to process, retaining a percentage for themselves and in all probability establishing a liaison with one of the workers—whose economic rather than sexual abilities were the primary concern of the husband.

A polygynous marriage system poses a number of problems. Wives, particularly unrelated wives, are apt to compete for the attentions of the husband and strive to acquire more than a fair share of his wealth for their own children. Sometimes these problems are met by the adoption of strict rules of behavior toward the different wives. In his book describing the life of the Magyar people of Nepal, John Hitchcock records this about the household of one Maila Ba:

> In his household the eldest wife did the cooking and looked after the daughter of the absent third wife. She also cared for the animals including the buffalos. The young wife went much more often to the fields and worked there. This division was not rigid however, because the eldest wife also did field work when help was needed . . . but only the eldest wife participated with Maila Ba when he was honoring the House God. On a festival occasion such as Dasian, Maila Ba paid visits to the natal home of both wives, remaining at each for a day. . . . Also Maila Ba was discreet in his attentions to the young wife and seldom spoke to her in the presence of his eldest wife. When he did speak to her at any length, it usually was when they were working together side by side at tasks such as harvesting wheat straw.

See John Hitchcock, *Magars of Banyan Hill* (Holt, Rinehart & Winston, 1966); the quotation is from page 47.

In Africa, exact equality among wives is often insisted upon. This is assured by having the husband spend a prescribed period with each wife in her separate hut within the kraal (a fenced enclosure for human and animal occupation). Should the husband tarry longer than permitted with one of his wives, he is subject to legal action, the payment of fines, just as if he had committed adultery. In other polygynous societies, each wife is maintained in a separate homestead and visited in turn by the husband. Such was the case among the Mormons of Utah in the nineteenth century. Although they insisted that plural marriage was their religious duty, not even this could suppress the expectation of Mormon women that a married woman should have a home of her own. Some families did indeed manage to get along with several wives (usually sisters) in the same home, but most polygynous Mormon marriages were maintained by building a separate house for each wife.

Much the same situation exists for the Navajo, who are only today abandoning plural marriage under pressure of American custom. Navajo husbands often married many women, but each one

Figure 44.   Ideally, the plural marriages of the nineteenth-century Mormons of Utah should have been peaceful and free of jealousy
and tension. A few of them were. But most often, Mormon
men built a separate home for each wife.

might well live miles and miles from the others. Because of the matrilocal residence pattern, the bride commonly remained in her natal
home—bearing and raising her children, tending sheep, farming and
weaving—and was visited regularly by her husband, who rode a circuit
like a frontier judge or preacher. This was not always the case,
though; sometimes, as his first wife passed childbearing age—and
often in response to her need for help around the homestead—a man
took a younger wife. The new wife would assist her older companion,
and her children would become the focus of attention for the entire
family.

While some societies have permitted a man to marry as many
women as he could afford, others, notably those adhering to Islam,
are strictly limited to four wives. In many other societies, economic
pressures and social practices have limited the number of wives to
two. Huge harems of hundreds or even thousands of "wives" are the
product of complex and elaborate political and economic systems.

So common is polygyny that more than a few Western sociologists
and psychologists have concluded that the male human being is

Figure 45.   A Navajo married to several different women might well have
to travel many miles between their homes because Navajo
women remain with their own families after marriage. What
is such a residence system called?

naturally promiscuous, while the female is naturally monogamous.
Such conclusions are really a product of incomplete knowledge. There
is no evidence to support the idea that women are inherently any less
interested in a variety of mates than men are. In fact, there are many
societies, although admittedly they are fewer than those accepting
polygyny, which permit or require women to marry several men. This
form of marriage is called *polyandry*.

Polyandry

Polyandry is found sporadically throughout the world, but it is most
common, perhaps, in the Himalayas and on through India, among
peoples peripheral to Hindu culture. The Hindus are fiercely patrilineal and polygynous, and jealous of the favors of women; at the
same time they are convinced of the basic fickleness of women. In
Tibet, it is by no means uncommon to find a girl married to several
brothers. Generally the eldest of her husbands holds formal sway

Figure 46. *Polyandry* (represented here by a Tibetan woman and her husbands) limits births by channeling the reproductive capacity of several males into one female. It also tends to concentrate and conserve family wealth.

over the household, and the children she bears are officially his. But at the same time, as heirs of the patrilineal estate, the children are considered the descendants of all the brothers. Tibetan women with whom I have talked seem quite content with several husbands as long as, in the words of one informant, "you keep them from fighting."

In Tibet, polyandry serves a multifaceted purpose. It is often necessary for men to be away months at a time on trading journeys. By jointly marrying a girl, the men are assured that she will have the help and protection of a husband at all times. Moreover, the marriage of a group of brothers to one girl keeps the family estate concentrated in a single group of children, instead of its being divided as each son marries and sets up his own household.

Finally, and perhaps most importantly, polyandry is a birth control measure. No matter how many men a woman has coitus with, she can have children at only a limited rate. Thus, if the sexual energies of several men are directed to a single woman, the overall birthrate will be lower. A polygynous system, on the other hand, results in a single male fathering many children by different women. A maximized birthrate may have been useful over most of human history as our species has gradually expanded to cover the globe. But in certain situations where man has found himself restricted by soils or climates or social conditions, polyandry serves to limit the human pressure on the surroundings. Among the Toda, about whom we have already talked, the need to limit population is probably less a response to hostile natural conditions than to being totally surrounded by the alien culture of India, which strongly restricts and resists the expansion of this tribal people. Polyandry serves to limit births and to limit pressures to expand, thus reducing the possibility of conflict with Hindu culture.

See W. H. R. Rivers, *The Todas* (Humanities Press, 1967) for a classic description of these interesting people.

Group Marriage

The marital forms are by no means mutually exclusive. The Toda do appear to marry only in the polyandrous or monogamous forms and never in the polygynous forms. In Tibet, however, all forms of marriage appear to exist side by side, depending on the particular problems with which individuals are confronted. Thus it is common to learn of groups of sisters marrying a single man, as well as a number of men marrying a single girl. Among Tibetans and in other societies, there exist less formalized arrangements whereby it appears that in fact several brothers have married several sisters, creating a form of marriage which we have called *group marriage*.

There is much dispute in anthropological circles as to whether or not this can be considered a legitimate form of marriage. In the nineteenth century it was simply assumed that such a form existed

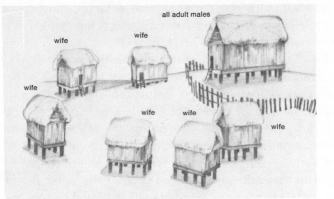

Figure 47. In New Guinea, it is not uncommon for all the adult males in a community to live in a central men's house, while their wives and children live in small separate houses. The women bring food to the central house, where it is eaten communally by all the men. Connubial visits are made secretly; some societies deny that they occur at all.

because it was a logical evolutionary transition between promiscuity and forms of plural marriage. However, ethnographers today are less certain that any society actually accepts a group of women and a group of men as being all equal partners, one to the other, with equal responsibilities throughout the group and to all of the resulting children. Nonetheless, ethnographers have reported systems of relationships which most certainly are, if not truly marriage, something different than the semi- or quasimarital situations we discussed earlier.

The most frequently cited region for these unusual arrangements is in northern Asia. In many of the hunting tribes of Siberia, a man hunting away from home is able to seek hospitality from another man and will expect, and be expected, to have sexual relations with his host's wife. A reciprocal arrangement of this kind commonly exists among several couples, so that in a sense a number of people are recognized as legitimate sexual partners.

The instances of group marriage cited appear to be devices for insuring hospitality in inhospitable environments where the method of earning a living, hunting and trapping, requires absences from home. Without hospitality survival would be difficult. The sexual union may be only incidental and symbolic of the reciprocity of hospitality.

It is doubtful though that the Siberian people involved actually view each of the potential sexual partners in the same way as they regard a wife or husband. Instead, this situation is probably analogous to those found in many parts of the world where a degree of sexual freedom is permitted to married pairs. The Eskimo are reported to share wives regularly, and it has been said they sometimes even make something of a game of it. This would suggest that this kind of sexual variety may serve to solidify small groups in their cooperation against the elements, and at the same time break the monotony of arctic life.

Before leaving the subject, we should mention the practice of sexual hospitality in which no question of marriage or permanent obligation arises. This practice is found in many parts of the world: Africa, the Arctic, among American Indians, and in Tibet and central Asia. Stated simply, it is merely offering a male guest the comfort of sexual relationships as a sign of hospitality. It is not a sign of profligacy or degeneracy in societies where it occurs, but rather a mark of good manners. Unlike the practices noted earlier, the relationship does not incur permanent obligations and is not in any sense a part of marriage.

Much the same thing appears to be more widespread than we had suspected in our own society, and perhaps for much the same reasons—a sort of an antidote to the pressures of conformity of modern life, and a defiant, perhaps pathetic attempt to establish meaningful non-kin relationships in fragmented, semianonymous, modern society.

In the nineteenth century, a group of deeply religious Americans founded and maintained what may be the most nearly genuine group marriage of which we have record. The Oneida Community was founded in 1848 by John Humphrey Noyes and a number of followers on the principle of holding all things, including spouses and children, in common. By learning and practicing a method of sexual intercourse called *coitus reservatus* the group was able to practice sexual freedom among its members without incurring too high a birth rate. As a

Coitus Reservatus, also known as the Karazza method, is a means of preventing ejaculation by means of mental and muscular control.

group, they decided which men should be allowed to father children, although all men were permitted to father at least one child. After weaning, the children were raised by the community in a way that allowed them minimal identification with their mothers and fathers. In the last quarter of the nineteenth century the experiment was abandoned in part because it incurred the wrath of neighboring communities in an area of upstate New York which was no longer remote frontier. In addition, the maintenance of a successful commercial operation on a totally communal basis was difficult. Moreover, mothers did indeed resent being separated from their children. Sexual jealousies and the like, which might have been expected to cause trouble, were apparently a rather minor element in the collapse of the experiment. If we can believe the autobiographies of some of the members of the group, communal marriage was reluctantly abandoned by both men and women.

The Nayar

Lest we overemphasize the sexual aspects of marriage, we should perhaps take a look at a unique people living on the southern coast of India in the state of Kerala, so frequently in the news because it often elects Communist officials. The Nayar are Hindus, but unlike most Hindus they are matrilineal and almost matriarchal. The continuing or corporate unit of society is a matrilineal family in which the male roles are carried out by brothers and the female by sisters, with the mother of course acting as the dowager. Obviously brothers and sisters don't marry, and yet marriage is essential for all women. On the other hand, matrilineal ties are so strong that the intrusion of an outsider as husband and father would threaten the solidarity of the family. The solution is to go through the form of marriage but not to continue its substance. Each Nayar young woman, as she approaches marriageable age, has selected for her a suitable husband of her own caste or from a higher caste, and the couple goes through the complete and elaborate Hindu marriage ritual. However, when the marriage is solemnized, the male's role is over and he leaves, perhaps never to be really a functioning part of "his" family. In time certain ritual obligations will fall on his shoulders and those of "his" children.

The Nayar are described by Kathleen E. Gough in *Matrilineal Kinship*, which she edited with David M. Schneider (University of California Press, 1961).

Paradoxically, marriage confers upon a Nayar girl—who has previously been carefully guarded—the right to engage in as many love affairs as she chooses. She may select a single lover and remain faithful to him over long periods, or she may enter into long-term relationships with several men, or she may behave in a way that our culture would call promiscuous. Her only obligation to a current lover is to allow him to remain the night in her house. His to her is to bring presents and other tokens of his love. This is resisted by his mother and sisters who do not want to see him spend too much of his substance outside the family. Children born of these affairs are primarily members of their mother's family but will be carefully designated as children of the bridegroom with whom the mother went through the wedding ceremony. Authority over and responsibility for them falls on the shoulders of the men in the family, that is, their mother's brothers.

It would be wrong to assume that Nayar men are simpering gigilos, henpecked by their female relatives and toyed with by their sweethearts. The Nayar are, in fact, a warrior caste and for centuries lived by hiring themselves out as mercenaries to the armies of rulers of India. Indeed, it is this mode of livelihood that is given as a reason for their unique system of marriage. A man is a better fighter, they contend, if he is sure that he leaves a peaceful and secure home behind him. He can feel confident because his home is composed of his mother and sisters and their children, watched over, perhaps, by another brother. If he had to leave a wife and children, with people who were in fact strangers to him, his mind would not be at peace. The point of this illustration is, however, that among the Nayar, the status of married women or men is not conferred because of sexual relationships or even parenthood; instead, it is merely a matter of ritual which formally confirms the wife in a new status.

STATUS AND ECONOMICS IN MARRIAGE

"Romance" in America

We Americans tend to think of marriage as a matter between a young man and a young woman, a result of their independent selection of mates through the process of falling in love. Most of the world would characterize this system as one in which parents are criminally unconcerned about the welfare of their children and their respective families. In fact, the late Ralph Linton has said:

All societies recognize that there are occasional violent emotional attachments between persons of the opposite sex, but our present American culture is practically the only one which has attempted to capitalize on these and make them a basis for marriage. Most groups regard them as unfortunate and point out the victims of such attachments as horrible examples. Their rarity in most societies suggests they are psychological abnormalities to which our own culture has attached extraordinary value just as other cultures have attached extreme values to other abnormalities. The hero of the modern American movie is always a romantic lover just as the hero of the old Arab epic is always an epileptic. A cynic might suspect that in any ordinary population the percentage of people with a capacity for romantic love of the Hollywood type was about as large as that of persons able to throw genuine epileptic fits. However, given a little social encouragement either one can be adequately imitated without the performer admitting even to himself that the performance is not genuine.

It is almost forty years since that paragraph was written, but the idea of romantic love has not really withered before the glaring eye of reason. Rather, the opposite is the case. In a number of nations where, in Linton's time, marriage was a matter of family deliberation with little concern for love, the idea of love has become increasingly important and disturbing. Japan—since World War II and its explosive industrialization, urbanization, and Westernization—is faced with the idea that young men and women should find each other and fall in love. The notion appears to be gaining strength in Europe as well. This suggests that reason does not always govern our behavior and that perhaps this system of finding marriage partners arises from the pattern of urban industrial life.

Ralph Linton, *The Study of Man: An Introduction* (Appleton-Century-Crofts), p. 175.

Of course, when we examine our own marriage system in detail we can see that it is not as haphazard as it might seem to a traditional European father or a pre-war Japanese mother. Study after study has shown that we indeed do tend to marry the girl next door, or at least down the street a few houses. Our system of schools geared to

Figure 48. The American "ideal" of marrying for love rather than more practical reasons is spreading to other parts of the world.

neighborhoods insures us that in general our offspring will meet and "fall in love" with a person from very much the same background as ourselves. If we restrict the number and types of people a young person may meet, it is socially a matter of indifference which one of those finally becomes our child's beloved. If, on the other hand, we do not want our child to marry a person like those living near us and attending the local school, we move away into a "better" neighborhood or at least send him or her to a "better" school.

The problem becomes complex when communities are composed of people of very different backgrounds. The practical problems of school-district administration may override the informal and unrecognized marriage pools we create. This suggests, then, an explanation for the intense resistance to school and housing integration among otherwise reasonable middle-class people. While they are perfectly content with the idea that blacks should share job opportunities and access to public facilities, they almost instinctively know what social scientists have so laboriously proven: If children grow up together they will probably "fall in love" and marry one another. That is, indeed integration will probably lead to mixed marriages. To deny this is to play the fool. The real question is: So what? If, in growing up together, black and white children do not learn the racial mythologies that haunt their elders, they will be more able to judge their peers as mates without reference to skin color. Certainly there is no biological or cultural reason why people of different races should not marry.

Another device we have used to limit the choices available to our youngsters, particularly those who leave the home town and go away to college, is the fraternity and sorority system. By emphasizing the prestige involved in belonging to one of these groups—which until recently were openly segregated racially, religiously, and economically —parents assured themselves that their child would not meet unsuitable potential mates. The traditions and customs of the system tended to insure that a fraternity boy would not long or comfortably court a nonsorority girl without losing his place in the caste system on campus. Similarly, and with even more rigidity, girls were forced to choose between dates with fraternity men or gradual, genteel ostracism from their peer group.

Figure 49. College fraternities and sororities serve as effective devices for mate selection within a particular social framework.

Some, of course, refused to conform, but over the years most "Greek" students have been content with a system created by the elders to give them the illusion of free choice without the danger that romantic emotions might bring "the wrong kind of people" into their families. Little wonder, then, that the resistance to removing racial restrictions in fraternities and sororities has often come from the old alumni rather than the students. The alumni understood what the system was all about. The children didn't.

Dowries and Bride Prices

Most societies, however, do not have to revert to such subterfuges. Marriage is generally a matter of family concern, in which the wishes of the individuals are given consideration only if all other factors are acceptable. Marriages are seen as contracts between two families, assuring one of continuity and the other that their child will be well treated and comfortable. To achieve these ends, a number of devices have been worked out, the most notable being the dowry and the bride price.

Dowry is essentially a payment made by the family of the bride to the groom's family, or to the groom himself, at the time of marriage. Generally in Europe the dowry was in fact considered to remain the possession of the bride although the husband had use of the funds or property. It is difficult to arrive at any explanation for the dowry system that correlates with the reasoning behind the bride price, which we will discuss later.

One suspects the custom might well have arisen with the thrust of new European entrepreneurial classes to better themselves in social as well as economic position. Many families of nonaristocratic background began to become wealthy in the early phases of the Industrial Revolution—but wealth alone does not ensure one a place in the social hierarchy. It might be suggested that the dowry was a means of attracting upper-class husbands without funds for lower-class girls with funds. Similar alliances in Japan between merchants and impoverished samurai formed the basis for the modern Japanese commercial families.

Dowry, of course, is not limited only to the upper and rising classes, and it is quite common among the peasantry as well. Perhaps a better answer is to be found in people's attitudes about themselves. An expression of this point can be found in a famous film, *The Quiet Man,* starring John Wayne and Maureen O'Hara, and produced by

John Huston. In the film, an Irish lady (Miss O'Hara) marries an American who is thoroughly hated by her overbearing brother. In revenge, her brother refuses to relinquish the money and furniture which constitute her dowry. The bride's angry response is to refuse to consummate her marriage, even though her groom is rich and does not want the dowry. In her eyes, to come to the marriage bed without her "portion" is tantamount to losing her own identity and individuality and becoming a chattel of her husband. Thus we might suggest that a dowry in theory served to protect a woman from mishandling and mistreatment at the hands of her husband by providing a modicum of economic freedom. In some areas where men are in short supply and all women must be married, a direct payment is made to the bridegroom. In India, the dowry for a daughter is one of the greatest financial burdens a family must bear. A man with only daughters is fated to a lifetime of debt.

The bride price is often misinterpreted as a direct purchase of a wife, and from time to time in the press we see semihumorous stories quoting the current price for a bride in certain parts of the world, particularly Africa. In fact, few societies (if any) actually practice outright purchase. Money, goods, and livestock may well change hands, but the husband does not obtain absolute rights to the person of his wife. It appears that the bride price payment made by the family of the husband is actually in exchange for the childbearing capacity of another family's daughter.

The payment of a fixed sum of cattle (as is frequent in Africa), horses (as was so common on the American Great Plains), or some other valuable, including money, also acts as insurance to the girl's parents that their daughter is entering a family with sufficient wherewithal to support her. It assures them that the girl is not marrying beneath herself. Moreover, it assures the girl of at least a relatively good position in her new family. If her husband or his family were to mistreat her so badly that public opinion or tribal law considered it grounds for separation, the girl could leave his bed and board and her family could keep the bride price. Inasmuch as the husband's family, often including remote relatives, contributes to his bridal payment, there is a collective interest in seeing that the girl is well treated. On the other hand, the price tends to insure good behavior on the wife's part. If she is shrewish and refuses to tend to her wifely duties, her husband could send her home and demand that his bride price be returned. Inasmuch as the payment is most likely to be immediately invested in a wife for a brother or a cousin, a demand for a return of her bride price would probably be a family catastrophe.

In short, the institution of the bride price creates a situation in which a number of relatives of the couple have a material stake in the survival of the marriage. We have already spoken of the relation of bride price to the childbearing capacity of the bride. The assumption by her family of the obligation to provide in her place another girl who might be more fecund, should she prove sterile, reflects once again the idea that marriages are apt to be agreements between two families rather than between two people. (The idea of male sterility is relatively rare, and not well accepted even in our own society.)

Another facet of the bride-price phenomenon, which disproves the idea that it is a matter of actual purchase, is the seemingly irrational economic behavior that is usually involved. Young men seldom shop for a modestly priced bride but rather tend to seek out the the highest priced girl they can as a means of displaying their own substance and standing in the community. (Of course, we see this kind of conspicuous consumption in other cultures as well—the purchase of large houses, elaborate wardrobes, and expensive entertainments, none of which follows the logical rules of economic behavior.)

Perhaps the most clear-cut case of this is to be found among the Hupa Indians of northern California. Among these people, a young man and his family strove mightily to accumulate as large as possible a bride price, paid in obsidian blades, woodpecker scalps, and strings of haliotis-shell "money." More than simple prestige was at stake in these transactions, because the original bride price of a woman became the lowest acceptable price for her daughters; the father could ask more for his daughters, but to ask less would be a grievous insult to his wife and her family. Thus a high investment by the husband's family would eventually be returned multiplied several times—unless the bride was unfortunate enough to bear only sons.

The Hupa are described by A. L. Kroeber in *Handbook of American Indians* (University of California Press, 1925; reprinted by California Book Company in 1953).

In many societies, the difficulty of raising the bride price is recognized by making arrangements for installment payments over many years. As an alternative, in many places the groom may live with the bride at the home of her parents until he has worked off all or part of his debt in what we call bride service, after which he can take her to his own home.

Another means of establishing the fact that the intermarrying families are entering into an equal bargain is a mutual exchange of gifts between the two groups. This is common in many of the cultures of the Pacific Islands. The goods—food, tapa cloth, and other valuable items—should ideally be equal, establishing in public the fact that both families can hold their own in social competition. Of course these systems can be combined with other broader systems of partner selection. Exchanges may take place within a certain prescribed group such as a caste or class, or within an ethnic or religious group, so that a basic equity is assured before marriage is even considered.

Choosing Partners in Other Ways

The selection of a mate is a singularly important aspect of the lives of each human being. In tribal or peasant societies it is difficult for the single person to survive without help. A man cannot both hunt

Figure 50.   In traditional Japan, an astrologer was often consulted by parents to determine whether or not a proposed marriage was suitable according to the stars.

and work a farm, nor can a woman gather plant foods and fish at the same time. In order for one person to live, two or more must cooperate in a division of labor. In most tribal societies a spinster or bachelor is an unthinkable social role. There frequently is no place for a spinster or unmarried uncle in peasant societies, and the lot of such people is far from enviable. Most certainly, the single woman cannot play a full adult role, and must be content with tending other people's children and helping to maintain the homes of other women; not infrequently, she must foreswear sexual life altogether, or risk ostracism. Similarly, in most societies, a bachelor will never be fully accepted as a man until he marries, no matter what his age.

We could perhaps continue for hundreds of pages about how an eligible young man sets out to find an eligible bride. The details vary from culture to culture and the range of variation is very great indeed. Ideally, among the Chinese and Japanese, it is a problem for the young people's family. Using the services of a go-between, and not infrequently an astrologer to ascertain if a given match is suitable, the parents of a young man look over the eligible young women and eventually enter into negotiations with another family. After the important matters have been agreed upon by the families, the principles may be given a final veto but most frequently they accept the decisions of their parents.

To young Americans such an idea is shocking; letting your parents pick your spouse seems spineless, cowardly to them. For the Japanese, such is not the case. Children are brought up to expect that their families have this responsibility, and they would be deeply disturbed if their parents did not find a mate for them. Only in recent years have young Japanese even begun to develop the social skills needed to meet, get acquainted with, and finally win a member of the opposite sex. As Japan has become industrialized and young people have gone into factories, it has become common for the company for which they work to play the role of the parent and assist in arranging marriages. For a period after World War II, the millions of young people leaving their families and coming into the cities were so helpless in this matter that they demanded the government establish a bureau to assist in the problem. In modern India the newspapers are filled with want ads for husbands and wives, placed by the families of young people seeking a socially and economically acceptable mate for their children.

Even family-arranged marriages, however, may merely formalize an already existing relationship. In rural villages the rigid separation an already existing relationship. In rural villages the rigid separation of the Japanese sexes was not so closely observed. Not infrequently a peasant boy and girl would become lovers through the institution of "night crawling." This custom, widespread in the Pacific and also found in North America among Indian tribes, is one in which a boy, after the girl's family has gone to sleep, creeps into her house and bed, remaining their until just before her family awakes. In Japan, his first visit was made with a towel wrapped around his face so that if advances were rejected he would be able to pretend that the young woman didn't know who he was and therefore would not be embarrassed when they met openly. In some societies that permit night crawling, the young couple manages to be discovered by her parents, who will insist that they be married. In others, the visits are never mentioned or admitted but the couple obliquely informs the parents of their desires. The introduction of electric lights around the world has done much to discourage night crawling. Such are the costs of progress.

Among the tribal peoples of upper Burma and also in the islands of Melanesia, young people often live separately from their families in special houses. In some cases a house for the girls is separate from that of the boys. In other societies, only one sex will have a dwelling and the opposite sex will visit them there. In yet others, both boys and girls will share a large house. In many cases the assumption is that the young people will freely experiment until they decide on a mate, but in some societies actual sexual intercourse is forbidden although the youngsters may become very intimately acquainted.

In general, we might say that while marriages are usually not considered matters of love and the families of both parties are usually an important influence—perhaps more important than the bride and groom—most societies leave room in their patterns of behavior for courtship and experimentation. In many cases, a young person ready to be married will have had romantic relationships or sexual intercourse with every person of the opposite sex with whom it might be possible to marry. In more rigid systems, some way is developed to permit at least an expression of preference or the exercise of romantic fancies.

An example of how the romantic urges of a young man are indulged in a very strict society where family considerations are paramount can be found in the poignant novel by Narayan, *The Bachelor of Arts*. In this novel, the protagonist, a young Indian man, carried on the most explosive romances with girls he had scarcely seen, primarily in his imagination. My own research assistant in northern India, a man in his seventies, had very much the same experiences in his youth, before he was literally presented with a bride whose face he did not see until after they had been married and conveyed to the connubial chamber.

However it is arranged and solemnized, a marriage establishes the basic social unit within which a child will be born and begin to find his way into the world of men. The unit may be independent, called a nuclear family, or part of some larger unit such as a joint or extended family. It may be only a sham as among the Nayar or it may be dissolved easily as among the Hopi and the Navajo. In whatever form it appears, its function remains the same; to produce a child and nurture it until it can take up the full mantle of humanity.

CASTE AND CLASS

8

CASTES

Kinship—the intricate web of relatives, clans, families, phraties and the like—plays an important role in all societies. In some so-called primitive or tribal societies, kinship provides the basis for all social organization. Societies of surprisingly large population can manage their affairs without governors, judges, policemen, or departments of social welfare, by dependence on the obligations expected of kinsmen. However, there are other dimensions of social organization yet to be considered, which transcend kinship but are in a sense logically related to it in any discussion of social organization. These are the phenomena of caste and class. One or the other or both play a singularly important role in the culture of all complex societies.

Caste is more closely related to the phenomena we have studied thus far. It is a pervasive organizational principle, though we commonly associate it with India. The United States is another large nation in which caste organization is important. In India, caste is supported by a religious philosophy which holds that the human race is divided into caste people and noncaste people, and that caste people are further subdivided into four general types.

In the United States, caste is maintained on a foundation of racism, which holds that people of different races are irreconcilably different and should not mingle and associate. The fallacies of such thinking are monumentalized in the burned-out ghettos of American cities and the abandoned

Figure 51. The question of caste in the United States can be confusing. To what caste do these people belong—a black surgeon, an educated chicano labor leader, the "dropout" children of wealthy white parents?

gas execution chambers of Germany. Race, of course, is not a social unit. It is simply a vague idea. Biologically we can talk about race, as we have seen, but socially or culturally, it is a useless term. The members of the Caucasoid race are not all members of a single social system or unit; nor is this true of the Negroid or Mongoloid races. Nevertheless, race is an idea often used to justify certain kinds of social arrangements that are prejudicial to part of the population. It was, for a time in this country, used as the basic ideational support for slavery—that is, a society divided into those who owned people and people who were owned. Today race is the justification and organizing principle of the American caste system and the division of Americans into distinct "racial" groups—such as black, white, Indian, Mexican, or Oriental.

How does one define a caste system? Is it simply categorizing people as members of a Negro or white or Chinese caste? No, because caste is a social reality aside from any ideational content used to explain it. Many peoples divide humanity into racial groups but do not have caste system. Other societies are homogeneous racially but do have caste groups. A caste system is one in which various groups are considered to be separate and their association is rigorously controlled. The first restriction is on intermarriage. A caste is considered an endogamous unit—that is, one within which members of the same unit must marry. If members of two caste groups do marry they are considered to have lost caste or to have committed a grave sin, and are subject to punishment. Inevitably caste systems are organized in hierarchies, one caste being higher than another. Frequently, many other restrictions between castes are developed, such as prohibition on members of two caste groups eating together, or being under the same roof, or touching.

Readers interested in learning more about **social stratification and economics** in the American South should see John Dollard's classic study, *Caste and Class in a Southern Town* (Doubleday, 1957). Max Weber's *The Theory of Social and Economic Organization* (translated by A. M. Henderson and Talcott Parsons, The Free Press, 1947) gives a theoretical overview.

Castes in the United States

Generally speaking, caste systems also designate specific occupations for members of each caste. These may not be observed in every case, but they do form a picture of the proper position of each caste in the minds of the people. In the United States until after World War II, there were very clear-cut ideas about suitable employment for blacks and whites. In our Army, blacks were almost always enlisted men. Only the demands of war on American manpower forced us to open commissioned ranks to nonwhites. In the Navy, blacks were permitted to hold positions only as officer's stewards. Marines were, by definition, white. Sports were equally segregated. Not permitted on major professional football and baseball teams, blacks were required to play only in all-Negro leagues. Only a few blacks found positions on college teams before World War II. There were no black radio announcers or newspaper reporters, except those who worked for "Negro" stations or papers. There were very few Negro lawyers, doctors, or dentists, and these were largely restricted to black clientele. Rigid segregation of craft unions prevented most Negroes from entering skilled trades. The low-pay, low-prestige jobs of seasonal farm workers, unskilled laborers in laundries and factories, domestic servants, janitors, and the like, were virtually reserved for nonwhites.

In America, these caste–job relationships are not as rigid today as they once were, nor are they absolute in every case. Negro business-men have become rich, and white men have been bootblacks. But the general feeling is there. Our caste system evolved in the agricultural South, where the vast majority of American blacks lived until a generation ago. In general, the more powerful positions—such as land-owners, businessman, professional man, politician, or law enforcer—were open only to whites; the lower jobs—such as fieldhand, cotton-picker, sharecropper, wet nurse, cook, or servant—were open mainly to Negroes. Even if a Negro became a landowner or a businessman, his caste position remained the same. The same was true for the white man in a "Negro" occupation, although he would have a more diffi-cult time of it, perhaps. However, if either were to violate the specific caste rules—that is, intermarry, eat with members of the opposite caste, or associate on a familiar basis—their caste position would be weakened. The Negro might be punished, even killed; the white more frequently would be ostracized, but sometimes killed. Perhaps it is easier to understand the clown-like behavior of Lester Maddox "defending" his restaurants from Negroes, and the determination of those same Negroes, when we accept the fact that they were quarrel-ing, not over the right to sell or not to sell fried chicken, but over whether or not the entire caste system of the South would continue.

As unpleasant as it is to accept, caste systems often work quite well and for very long periods under certain circumstances. Inevitably the caste system has its base in agriculture, and most likely in the kind of agriculture practiced before the 1930's in the United States or in traditional societies. This kind of agriculture requires large expendi-tures of human labor, but also needs a number of specialists to main-tain it—blacksmiths, millers, storekeepers, and the like. Nor does caste lend itself to a system of rapidly changing technology. Stability is the first essential if social units are to form in such a permanent way around technical roles.

In addition, such a system must be accepted; that is, the idea-tional basis of the system must be believed by all or most members of the system. Thus, if only the upper caste believes in its superiority and the "naturalness" or "divine inspiration" of the system, a caste system cannot develop, or certainly cannot endure for long. It is difficult to accept, but within the caste system that has developed in the United States, the bulk of the population—both black and white—accepted for some time the idea that blacks are biologically inferior to whites. The effort used to support this idea has been tremendous: segregated and underfinanced schooling, deliberate failure to recognize the accomplishments of black individuals, and regular repression of black ambition. All these tactics worked to convince the whites they were right in their feeling of superiority, and to reinforce the idea of inferiority in the minds of Negroes. In India, the ideational basis of caste is not biological theory but rather religious doctrine that holds that the human race is separated into distinct divisions. To be a Hindu of any caste is to accept this idea.

A third requirement of caste systems is that within the framework of its culture's particular definition of adequacy, each caste group must receive what it believes to be a fair share of the resources of the system. This is not to say that everyone should have the same, but that no group should receive less than what the entire system believes to be minimally enough. Given stability, agreement on the ideational basis of the system, and adequate distribution of resources—no matter how unfair the rationale or unequal the distribution—a caste system can operate for generations, and centuries. However, if any one of these factors is lacking, a caste system is subject to tremendous stress. The change in agricultural technology in the southern United States, the increasing disbelief in inherent inferiority, and the increasingly unequal distribution of resources to the blacks, both North and South, have made the American caste system a thing of the past.

Castes in India

The caste system in India is far more complex and has a much longer history than that of the United States. It is based on the religious idea that man was created in four major divisions: the *Brahmans, Kshatriya, Vaisyas,* and the *Sudra.* People not falling into one of these major divisions are considered noncaste or outcastes. The measure of caste in India is not biological as much as it is religious, and the four groups are ranked in order—the highest being more ritually pure and thus in a sense nearer to God. A belief in reincarnation provides an emotional comfort by permitting the lower-caste person to feel that if he lives his life well, in whatever position fate has dealt him, he may find rebirth in one of the higher castes; eventually, if his progress is not interrupted by base behavior and consequent rebirth at a lower station, he is able to escape the earth and its suffering forever.

> For more detail on **Indian castes**, see Dhirendra Nath Majumbar, *Caste and Communication in an Indian Village* (Asia Publishing House, 1958) ; and Adrian C. Mayer, *Caste and Kinship in Central India: A Village and Its Region* (University of California Press, 1971).

In the actual working of the Indian caste system, however, we find a great deal more complexity. People are not simply *Brahman* or *Sudra,* but rather members of one or another sub-group or *jati* which is, in turn, identified with one of the major levels. There may be in a single district many *jatis* equated with the *Brahman* caste or *varna,* each one observing slightly different customs, and each identifying with a somewhat different role in society. In theory the *Brahmans* are priests, but in fact most people belonging to Brahman *jatis* may not be priests; they may be in trade, which is thought to be the prerogative of the *Vaisya,* or in farming, the traditional occupation of the *Sudra.* But because of their birth, they remain on top of the hierarchy of the local caste system.

Not in India or in any other caste system is it inevitable that the members of a higher caste be in control of wealth and resources. In fact, very low-caste people may become quite rich or high-caste people may be poor, even dependents of the low. This does not alter their relative positions in the system, and the form of caste relations will be observed, even between a low-caste money lender or landlord and a high-caste debtor or tenant. The *jatis* of India are many, and some scholars have spent virtually their entire professional lives attempting to understand the details of *jati* organization and the interaction of *jatis.*

This interaction, called the *jajmani* system, determines the way the various caste segments of an Indian village or district relate to one another in order that the necessary work be done and the entire population survive. Thus, since farmers need rope for their work and pottery for their households, the ropemakers and the potters make these items on order and supply them to the farmers. And when the farmer attends the village temple or holds a wedding he needs the services of a priest, and these too are his as he needs them. Similarly,

Figure 52. Although not as rigid as they once were, castes in India still have a heavy influence on the country's social fabric.

because Hindu ritual often requires that a man must be shorn and shaved properly before he can perform religious rites, the farmer and the priest both need the services of the barber. And because touching the carcass of a dead cow or carrying away waste is defiling, the high-caste villager is dependent on the presence of the outcaste sweeper who hauls away the dead animals and the waste.

These interactions within our own society would most likely be supplied by the municipal government in the case of sanitation, or through regular commercial transactions. However, in the Indian village, instead of paying for each service or for each product of the artisan, the farmer awaits the harvest time and then—keeping necessary food for himself along with seed for the following year and perhaps land rent if he is a tenant—he presents to the barber, the ropemaker, the priest, and the sweeper an amount of grain agreed upon by tradition. From each farmer each specialist receives a similar amount of grain, and in the end his year's food supply is assured. In addition, traditional and customary presents of clothing, cloth, and condiments are exchanged among all the caste groups. Thus the village continues, with each segment of the society receiving at least an agreed-upon minimum. If, however, as has occurred in the recent past, the farmer discovers he can profitably sell his wheat on the open market and use the money to buy cheaper rope instead of using the product of the village ropemaker, the system is quickly threatened. Nor does traditional India survive without stress when confronted with material culture items not part of the tradition. Ball-point pens, flashlights, kerosene, and bicycles are not produced within the old system, and the desire for these things and the need for money to obtain them quickly threaten it.

We must not forget, however, that such a system, while it can be analyzed as a simple division of labor, quite rational and understandable, is not seen in this way by the participants. The Indian villager does not pay out the traditional measure of grain to the ropemaker because it seems the reasonable thing to do, but because it is the only thing to do. It is right, ordained by God, and follows the patterns of accepted morality. Nor does the southern white or black simply shrug and say the social patterns of the South were, after all, only an economic arrangement. Rather, it is "the natural order of things" that the black Mississipian should chop cotton, live in a shack, and never dream of voting. Racial intermarriage is not looked upon as the most despicable of events because it would upset a rational economic system, but because it is contrary to accepted morality.

These attitudes illustrate how social systems and culture interact, how ideas and beliefs serve to support and shape social practices. They also suggest why it is so difficult to effect changes in social systems. It is not enough, in an Indian village, simply to show a farmer a new way of growing wheat or demonstrate to a mother a new way of caring for her child. One must also understand how these new patterns of behavior might create stresses within the existing system and how the villager might find himself doing things which, although they seem reasonable acts to us, to him are immoral.

Another important feature of a caste system is that in the minds of the participants it is immutable. There is no way for a black man to cease being a black man or for a member of a lower caste in India to become a member of an upper caste. The lines of division are seen as existing throughout time and impenetrable. In fact, individuals can sometimes beat the system by disguising their backgrounds and taking on the customs and manners of another caste. Thus, a "Negro" who lacks the readily recognizable features of "blackness" can sometimes, by denying his Negro heritage, pass for white. Similarly, a low-caste Indian can, in a strange locality, sometimes successfully pretend that he is of some other caste. The amount of this kind of movement between caste groups is hard to determine. We know of its existence only because failed attempts have been brought to our attention. Such a potential is, of course, a constant fear in a caste society because it threatens the very foundation of the system. In South Africa, for instance, the government maintains agents who decide by visual examination whether a person is "white" or "colored" or "native—a task which, of course, is scientifically impossible to accomplish.

Caste is not found only in India and the United States, nor is it only an element of complex societies. In some tribes of East Africa, tools and weapons are made by specialists in blacksmithing. These men lead quite a different life than their fellow tribesmen, and are in part cut off from them. Viewed as a combination of sorcerer and devil, they are often despised and must marry among themselves. At the same time they do not take up the warrior's life and are exempt from danger in intertribal wars. In Japan, there are many hundreds of thousands of people known as *Eta*—or *Burakumin,* a somewhat more polite form. To the foreigner, the Eta are indistinguishable from other Japanese. The Japanese insist they can always identify an Eta. This was probably true in traditional Japan, where the Eta lived in special sections of town and were restricted to certain occupations; it is unlikely that Eta can be so easily identified in modern Japan.

The **burakumin** or outcastes of Japan are discussed in DeVos and Wagatsuma, *Japan's Invisible Race: Caste in Culture and Personality* (University of California Press, 1966).

Castes or caste-like groups have existed or still exist in many other societies; these examples serve only to illustrate the basic mode of social organization that castes involve. Most often such societies use the caste group as a basis for stringent social control. Within the Indian village or district, each *jati* traditionally has a council that oversees the behavior of members of their group and represents them in interaction with other groups and in governing their common regions. And in our own system the black community is always felt to have spokesmen who can exercise influence and authority over "their" people. It may be an indication of the gradual collapse of our caste system that it is increasingly difficult to find such persons.

CLASSES

Social classes are even more widespread than castes, at least in complex societies, which in fact are defined largely by their existence. In many ways, a class society is like a caste society, but it differs in certain crucial elements; in the final analysis it is a separate social phenomenon. While we can think of a poverty-stricken Brahman and a wealthy outcaste in India, or a dirt-poor white tenant farmer and a Negro millionaire, it would be incongruous to speak of an upper-class beggar or a lower-class millionaire. This shows that class is, in large part, determined by control over resources and wealth and thus, power. And because this control can shift with changes in politics, environment, and technology, so class systems are apt to be more dynamic than caste systems. In addition, a class system inevitably has within its recognized structure some means for individuals to change class—that is, to sink or rise in class affiliations. Rigid class societies will resist such changes strenuously, but they will recognize the possibility of their occurring. A caste system does not.

Some tribal societies, such as the Natchez of the North American Southeast, displayed class characteristics. The upper or ruling class held an enormous amount of power and received great deference from the lower classes, or "Stinkards," an unusual occurrence in usually egalitarian native North America. However, a complex set of marriage rules made it possible for a Natchez to lift his social status—and also almost inevitably assured that his descendants would eventually sink back into the lower classes. In Africa, class societies seem not infrequently to be the product of conquests of one people by another. In many ways they resemble caste systems, save that intermarriage occurs and often confers upper-class status on the offspring. Similarly, in the Near East, the children of slaves, if fathered by a free man, were no longer slaves.

The Traditional Classes of Japan

Traditional Japan is an example of a class society—one in which every effort was made to stabilize the relative positions of the various levels in the structure. This structure was formalized in the seventeenth century by the Tokugawa Shogunate, which attempted to quiet the warring and disturbed islands of Japan by establishing a series of rigid laws governing the structure of society. On the top of the heap were the noblemen or *daimyo* who held, under the *shogun,* tracts of land just as did the aristocrats of feudal Europe. Serving

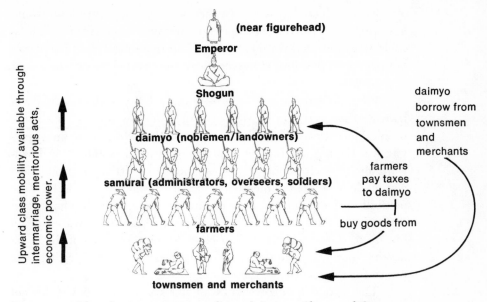

Figure 53.   The class system in traditional Japan. Class mobility was available through intermarriage, meritorious acts, and economic power.

the *daimyo* as administrators, overseers, and above all professional soldiers, were the *samurai*. Below them, paying part of their produce to the *daimyo* as taxes, were the farmers; and finally, on the contemptible bottom of the social heap were the townsmen and merchants. At the apex of the pyramid was the almost powerless, but sacred, emperor, in whose name the shogun ruled.

For more on **Japanese class structure**, see G. B. Sansom, *Japan: A Short Cultural History* (Appleton-Century-Crofts, 1962); and Ezra Vogel, *Japan's New Middle Class: The Salary Man and His Family in a Tokyo Suburb* (University of California Press, 1967).

These positions were reinforced by a network of sumptuary laws governing such things as the kind of clothing permitted to each class, whether they could bear arms and what type, the nature and size of their houses, the kind of transportation they could use, and a host of other details of life. (Similar sumptuary laws were an integral part of European feudal system.) In theory these sumptuary laws would have prevented interclass competition, because members of each class could not aspire to own goods other than those prescribed for people of their social position. However, there were two chinks in the armor of these laws.

First, the Japanese did not deny the validity or the possibility of marriage between classes. Although such unions might be considered unsuitable, they were not absolutely forbidden. Nor, in the final analysis, was the ancient Japanese pattern of upward mobility—or downward mobility, for that matter—abandoned. Although every effort was made to freeze the members of each class in position, at least the possibility of moving up as a reward for exceptionally meritorious acts existed. And downgrading was possible for those who did not live up to the standards of their class. Many thousands of the lower ranking *samurai* voluntarily gave up their warriors' privileges in return for the security of the farmer's status.

The second major weakness of this system was that it did not take into consideration the movement of money. The economic system was founded on agricultural production, primarily rice. Thus, the farmer made a payment in rice to the *daimyo,* and he in turn paid his taxes to the state, maintained himself, and made payments to his *samurai* retainers—all with rice. In theory, then, each of these classes had their basic food supply in hand; but requirements other than food had to be purchased with cash, although the only commodity readily available to all the people of the three upper classes was rice. Very soon, as the life of the *daimyo* became more and more luxurious and secure, and the obligations of the *samurai* became more those of administrators than of warriors, their own desires led both classes to mortgage future rice crops to the despised merchants—and then, of course, they used the money to buy things from the merchants.

The natural outcome was that the lowest of all classes, the merchant and townsmen, became the richest of people. Condemned to wear the plainest of clothing, they lined them with silks. The interiors of their simple houses were elegant and luxurious. But the rich man who is a member of a powerless group is constantly threatened with seizure of his wealth. To prevent this, the merchants exercised economic power by suggesting that their children marry the children of *samurai* who were deeply in debt to them. As humiliating as it may have been, many *samurai* families had no other choice but to make marriage alliances with merchants, thus bringing the grandchildren of merchants into the upper classes and linking through kinship ties all of the merchant's relatives with all of their own.

This illustration suggests the dynamic quality of class system when contrasted to caste system. A caste system would have been able to continue because intercaste marriages would have made the participants outcastes. And although the despised caste might well have become economically powerful, the basic divisions in the society would not have been challenged.

Class Mobility

Much the same series of changes occurred in Europe to bring about the collapse of the feudal system which, despite every legal effort, was even more permeable by class mobility than the Japanese system. Class systems may often develop an ideational element which we might say attempts to imitate caste thinking. In medieval Europe, justifications of the class structure were made in theological terms and the hierarchy of the classes given divine sanction. And with the collapse of feudalism, the new classes that formed on the basis of the industrial revolution found much justification in the new Protestant churches, which held that the evidence of God's favor was to be found in the rewards one received on this earth. Thus, the rich were rich because they were elected of God, the poor were poor because they were not, and one could only submit himself to this clear-cut evidence of divine will. Today, not infrequently, we hear arguments based in pseudoscience explaining that the poor are poor because they lack the biological or psychological qualities which would enable them to become rich. Or we hear the Social Darwinist, attempting to transfer biological theory into a social framework, suggest that successful people or nations are simply the superior products that would naturally win out in social competition.

See F. L. K. Hsu, *Under the Ancestors' Shadow: Kinship, Personality and Social Mobility in China* (Stanford University Press, 1971).

Not all class systems produce these justifications, although some do and some are almost as rigid as caste societies. The traditional Chinese system, which divided the world into imperial officials, nobles, mandarins, merchants, farmers, and lower classes, explicitly provided

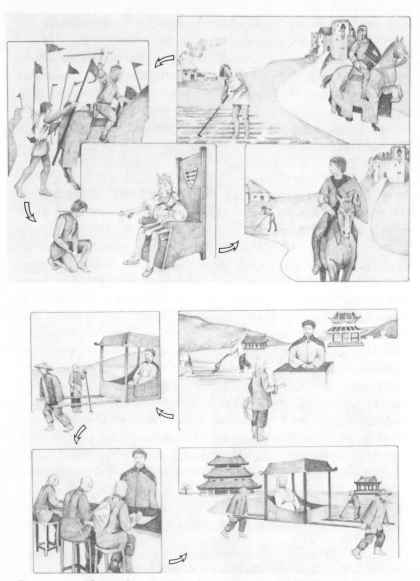

Figure 54.   The paths of upward mobility in feudal Europe and tradiditional China. In Europe, military service was a major means
of increasing one's wealth and special position. Even the
lowest commoner might be rewarded for exemplary or faithful service in battle. In China, education was the key. If a
commoner could obtain an education, he might sit for the
imperial examination and qualify for a government appointment. Even military appointments were dependent on education.

a means of upward mobility. Almost everyone was eligible to obtain an education and sit for the imperial examinations, if he could afford it. If these were passed the successful candidate was then eligible for appointment to positions in the imperial government—and access to wealth and power. Obviously, every attempt was made to see that one's sons and daughters remained in the upper class. But with each generation, according to estimates, five percent of the new officials were sons of lower-class people. On the other hand, failure to carry out the expected responsibilities of upper class—to live according to Confucian doctrine, to insist on education for the sons, etc.—was often the prelude to a family's gradual decline back into the masses from which it had arisen. Pearl Buck's memorable trilogy, of which *The Good Earth* is the first volume, describes the rise and fall of a Chinese family. In fact, this cycle of rise and fall was a common theme in much Chinese fiction.

Our own society, in addition to its caste system, is organized along class lines as well. Within each of the caste divisions there are further divisions according to control of resources and power, which is another way of saying control of money. As the caste lines blur there is an increasing tendency to see the black and white division merging through intermarriage and other social interactions. Compared to traditional Japan, and England in the recent past, there is less emphasis on class differences in America. Rather, America tends, through universal education, mass production, and mass media, to obscure the symbols of class differentiation.

Many of the symbols of class distinction of the recent past have disappeared. The private university finds itself increasingly hard put to survive and increasingly responds to pressure to admit into its halls—and thus into eligibility for the upper class—members of lower classes and minority groups. Mass-produced automobiles, which before World War II were symbols of different social levels—low, medium, and high-priced, each quite distinct in design and model names—have been replaced by broad-range production of many similar models under a few names; today, the "low-priced three," in fact, produce very high-priced automobiles. The stately mansion on a hill has increasingly given way to the expensive but essentially mass-produced house in a suburb. More and more graduates of public universities are finding their way into the upper classes through entry into the professions—medicine, law, and higher education—which were previously occupied almost exclusively by upper-class people.

Distinctive regional and class accents are becoming obscured and mingled to the extent that a writer recently describing the tones of what he called Real Society mentioned that upper-class people speak a curious combination of southern- and New England–accented English. Moreover, people of the upper classes—or the lower classes, for that matter—will seldom openly state their own class position, either modestly or hopefully suggesting they are really "middle class."

The basic themes of American culture repeat over and over again that anyone can lift himself through hard work and application, and insist that the law must be applied equally to all people. The fact that neither of these ideals is, in every case, true is probably irrelevant in an overall analysis of our own system. As long as we insist that they are, we cannot openly suppress the individual who chooses to take advantage of these expectations and seek his fortune.

Class Differences and Conflict

Class systems differ from caste systems in another way. They are seldom as well organized. In an Indian village, each caste ideally has its own internal structure for the keeping of order, relating to other caste groups, cooperating in political decisions and activities. Seldom, however, does a class system display such a definition of structure. In part, this may be because it is not necessary. Class systems are defined by actual control of wealth and power by one class to the disadvantage of the others. It is this fact which led social thinkers like Karl Marx and those influenced by him to argue that a basic process of history has been class conflict—that is, attempts on the part of the exploited classes to obtain all or part of the control, or rewards stemming from that control, held by the ruling class.

While no one can deny that peasant revolts, revolutions, labor strife, food riots, and the like have occurred throughout history, it is doubtful that the recognition of class differences alone gives rise to them. Rather, only when the system places a great disadvantage on one segment of the society does conflict occur. Perhaps one of the most disillusioning episodes of world history was the discovery by the various socialist factions in Europe and America that the presumed common interests of the international working class did not prevent workers from fighting each other in World Wars I and II. The Communists, who dreamed of a world society dominated by the working class working together in the common interest, must indeed be disturbed by the obvious development of classes in all socialist nations and the clear-cut supremacy of nationalism over socialist solidarity in the socialist world. The more philosophical of American union leaders have also had to face the fact that common interests will not weld an entire class into a single social unit to oppose real or imaginary enemies of the workers.

Class organization appears to be a natural outcome of the differentiation of life styles that becomes increasingly common as societies become more complex. And while kinship ties within classes may be very strong indeed, kinship as an overall organizing principle of a society must inevitably suffer in a class society. A member of the royal class cannot admit kinship with a commoner. How would such people relate to each other—as king and subject, or as cousins? Thus, while it may be necessary—as it was in Japan—for individuals to establish kinship ties within an upper class in order to assure their descendants of a firm place in the class, it is equally inevitable that one must either bring his relatives into the upper class along with him or cease to recognize the relationships, should they remain behind. In essence, then, a man's position in the class system can and often does override his position in a kinship system.

The ideological foundations of class systems are usually undefined. If they exist, the population may not recognize them; on the other hand, they may develop a complex superstructure of ideas and symbols that serves to accentuate and perpetuate class differences, and thus relative positions. And yet, no matter how rigid such distinctions may be, a class society cannot fail to include mechanisms whereby individuals (or groups) who control power and wealth can be incorporated into the upper class. Otherwise, the old ruling class would quickly be displaced, as was essentially the case when the knightly aristocracy of feudal Europe gave way before the increasingly powerful mercantile and entrepreneurial classes. Today in Britian, where the different classes still speak quite different versions of English, the political representatives of the working classes are upper class by virtue of having acquired political power. Having achieved admittance to the upper class, they have very quickly adopted the style in clothing, language, and other behavior that is symbolic of upper-class position in British culture.

This implies that classes are seldom, if ever, definable units save in contrast to other classes. Within any single class, there may be many schisms and divisions that contest with each other to enjoy the prerogatives of the class. But when confronted with another lower class striving for control of resources and power, the class may act in relative consort to preserve its position. Thus, in a large and complex society the definition of any class is often quite difficult; it becomes a problem of studying the configuration of behavior patterns, obligations, and privileges held by each class division. In smaller societies, a class may act as something of a social unit—but never in the same way as the Indian caste system, with its social expressions of specific *jatis* in specific regions, each *jati* having recognized leaders and mechanisms of control over its own members and a clear-cut system of interactions with other *jatis*.

In actual practice, caste and class may be very much the same—a means of organizing work and dividing duties and responsibilities within a society. The caste system, however, invariably finds clear-cut social expression in social units organized around an ideological foundation. The class system tends to be more dynamic and flexible, ideologically less coherent. Both caste and class systems have operated in traditional agrarian societies from Japan to Rome and Greece, to the Inca and Aztec of the New World. However, caste seems unsuited to the problems of industrial societies—their complexities and everchanging technological and economic base. Thus, class would appear to be the style of social organization most likely to continue in the modern world.

Soldier   Laborer   Senator

Figure 55.   Caste systems existed in Roman and other early societies, as well as more recent civilizations.

POLITICAL UNITS

9

TERRITORIALITY AND KINSHIP

One's kinship ties and caste position or class relationship in society are in the final analysis based on the status of his parents. There is, however, another singularly important dimension of social organization: that of territoriality, relations between people based on proximity. We should not think that some societies are kin-based and others territorially based, because in fact these two principles combine and complement each other in all societies.

The Washo Indians of Nevada and California, for instance, reckon almost all relationships in terms of kinship. However, their territory was roughly divided into four sections, only three of which could be occupied all

year round. In addition to his place in the kinship system, each Washo was also identified with one of these sections, and considered to be somehow more closely related to other people from that area than from the other regions. In general, a person was considered to be of the section where he was born, but if he chose to move into another section, his old identification faded and a new one developed. The Washo lived in small bands or, as they were called in western Nevada, *bunches.* Usually members of each bunch were related, but unrelated people could and frequently did attach themselves to a bunch, traveling, cooperating, and working with them. Under these circumstances it was difficult to tell where kinship ended and proximity began as organizing factors.

There were no clearly political roles in Washo life. No one had any permanent authority. The leader of a bunch was able to control his little band through the vague authority exercised by an elder kinsman, coupled with proven wisdom in making decisions about movement, hunting, fishing, etc. If his decisions proved unwise, his following soon melted away to find another leader. If, however, he was singularly strong-willed—a person able to convince others, whose decisions were more often right than wrong—his influence was apt to spread to other bunches in his area and his voice had some effect over a rather large region. To be sure, there might be kin relationships between the various bunches, but it should not be thought that the powerful leader's authority or influence extended along kinship lines. At some distance, his decisions and ideas would be unfelt, even among people closely related to him.

In general, the Washo had no notion of firm boundaries for their lands. Rather, they tended to defend specific resources. A band of Paiutes would be unopposed were they to come into Washo country to pick some plentiful plant crop, but they would be violently attacked if they attempted to fish. On the edges of the Washo country the proximity of Washo and Paiute bands often led to intermarriage and the formation of bands composed of both peoples. In short, even in this simple and kin-based society, the role of physical or geographic proximity was important.

Marriage and Residence

One of the important questions anthropologists ask about all people is where a young couple establishes residence after marriage. Like descent systems, postmarital residence can be considered in three categories. *Patrilocality* describes a situation wherein a young man brings his bride into the home of his father, or, if not into home, into the village where he was born and raised. *Matrilocality* is a matter of the groom's coming into the family or neighborhood of the bride's family. With *neolocality,* a couple is expected to establish a new home unit without special reference to the natal home of either partner.

Logically, these three residence patterns should correlate with descent systems. But human culture is not necessarily logical, nor is society such a perfect system that we always find what we expect. Neolocality can and does occur in bilateral, matrilineal, and patrilineal systems. Patrilocality may occur in matrilineal societies, or matrilocality in patrilineal societies. Or variations may be developed, such as *avunculocality* wherein a young man brings his bride to reside in or near the home of his mother's brother; this is not at all uncommon in matrilineal societies.

If, however, a strictly observed postmarital-residence rule does occur with the corresponding descent system—strict patrilocality with patrilineal descent, for instance—a situation is created wherein a residential unit (territorial) coincides precisely with a descent unit (kinship). Such is the case in the highlands of New Guinea, among the Siane. In this patrilineal and patrilocal group, each groom brings his bride to the village in which he was born and raised. His children, of course, are members of his descent group, as are the children of all the other men in the village. The patrilineal descent group and the village have the same limits. All people within the village boundaries, save the mothers brought in from the outside, are relatives and forbidden to each other under the prohibitions of incest. Occasionally a village will be composed of two descent groups, each occupying a different section but generally not intermarrying; this extends the kin-based taboos against incest to a territorial designation.

In fact, the practice of insisting that a person marry outside his immediate residential area is widespread and often referred to as *village exogamy.* In India, field researchers have constructed elaborate charts showing the complex relationships between villages in the matter of finding mates without violating this prohibition. In such a unit, where kinship has become territoriality, or perhaps territoriality has become kinship, the roles of leadership and responsibility are frequently those of real or fancied kinship, and thus there is little of what we would call real political organization. Just as a family seldom calls the police to make little Johnny finish his breakfast, so a village seldom has need of courts and judges and councils. The informal dynamics of family relationships can be brought into play to enforce proper behavior.

If a rule of residence is not strictly enforced, as among the Navajo, where as many as fifty percent of the newly married do not live with the bride's mother as called for in the cultural ideal, the bounds of kinship cannot take a firm root in the territory. The pastoral Nuer (of whom we have spoken) and the pastoral Navajo provide an interesting contrast. Among the Nuer, government and kinship are virtually the same. The hierarchy of kinship units, at once contending and cooperative, organizes a large number of people inhabiting a vast area. The Navajo, on the other hand, have never been able to organize large blocks of land along strictly kin-based lines. Because the children take the clan of their mother but matri-locality is not strictly observed, nearly fifty percent of them in some places are living with patrilineal cross-cousins, children of their fathers' sisters. This means that in each generation a given piece of land is apt to have representatives of two or more clans using it cooperatively.

See Mary Shepardson, *The Navajo Way in Government* (American Anthropological Association Memoir 90, 1964).

Among the Navajo, affinal relationships are important, along with the need for cooperation in herding and farming, and in earlier times fighting and raiding. Out of this situation we see the development of the *nataani*, a purely political role. In every area of the Navajo reservation there are men who, irrespective of clan or kinship, are considered to be leaders; to them, people bring domestic problems for solutions. Disputes between grazers are adjudicated, and public decisions guided by his counsel. Not infrequently, because he is a member of the largest clan present, he will have many relatives in the area, but his authority transcends clan lines. This authority is limited to giving advice and counsel, and is virtually unenforceable. The issue here is the nature of that authority.

The position of *nataani* is what we should call an *achieved* status, conferred by others after demonstration of wisdom and good character. On the other hand, the elder of a clan or lineage is an *ascribed* status, conferred at birth. Much has been said about the difference between achieved and ascribed status. We will not dwell on it here, save to suggest that in societies where relationships tend to be based on proximity rather than kinship, achieved statuses are more common. However, even in modern nations—based, as we shall see, primarily on territorial principles—ascription is not unknown. Kings are born, not made. Royalty is royal and commoners are common, and nothing a single commoner can do will make him king without disturbing the entire social system in a revolution.

Kin and Countrymen
Most societies combine the two principles, territory and kinship, in

order to organize themselves. For a kin-based system, we might depict the hierarchy of relationships as something like this:

Immediate blood relatives
More distant blood relatives
Classificatory relatives
Fictive relatives
Immediate affinal relatives
Distant affinal relatives
Classificatory affinal relatives
Fictive affinal relatives
—*and finally*
People of our own kind (caste, class, race)

People in the last category may or may not, depending on the view held by the society in question, be seen as real relatives. Not infrequently—because they subscribe to the same rules, speak the same language and practice the same customs—they will be included in some overall word meaning literally Humans or True Humans. Thus speak the Navajo when they call themselves *Dine*.

The hierarchy of relationships in territorial systems is perhaps a bit simpler:

People I live with (family)
People I live next to (neighbors)
People with whom I associate (friends)
People who live within our land (countrymen)

It is obvious that some of these people may be kinsmen, but the principles being considered in these classifications are entirely different than those of a kin-based classification.

Within the category "countrymen," a number of subdivisions of relationship can be accommodated. Some divisions might be based on real-kinship principles: my family, clan, or lineage. Others may be based on broad fictive-kinship principles: my caste or my class. At the same time, a degree of closeness may be felt toward all people from the individual's town, district, state, or region—particularly if these divisions correspond with common customs, language or dialect, or religious differences between the people living in different areas.

It would be difficult to say overall which of these two principles is the stronger. Patriotism, love of country, nationalism, or whatever you might call it, does indeed invoke the strong emotions which have not infrequently led men to make enormous sacrifices and commit acts of both nobility and barbarism in the name of country. On

Figure 56.   Isolation and ridicule are the means used by the Eskimos to control unruly members. This method has some features in common with the Amish practice of "shunning" members who have committed wrongdoings. Can you think of comparable methods in your own society?

the other hand, the ties of "blood" are strong, whether those ties be real or imagined; among tribal and peasant peoples whose view of nationhood is ill-developed, kinship ties are virtually unbreakable.

In tribal societies, proximity, in addition to kinship, does play an important role. A tribe may, in fact, be a number of villages, each with its own relative autonomy and identity. Such units existed among the Yokuts of California for instance, with whom seldom more than two or three villages constituted a tribe. The leader of one of the villages was recognized as having some authority in all the villages, and some vaguely defined territory surrounding the villages was considered "our" land, although it probably would not be defended simply on principle.

The Use of Force
Another way of looking at a tribe is to attempt to learn how force or coercion may be applied. A system which allows, or requires, that

each man be prepared to defend only his own life and property against all attacks might be considered one end of a continuum depicting the varying allocation of the use of force in different societies. The Eskimo appear to be an example of this. There is no machinery of control among the Eskimo save through ridicule, admonishment, and withdrawal of cooperation. Should a bully appear and threaten the lives or safety of other Eskimo, no automatic mechanism operates to stop him. If his actions become too annoying, a group of people may decide he must be killed and, as a group, do it. But no court or police force or army exists to make such a decision.

The Tiwi, of Melville and Bathhurst Islands off the coast of Australia, appear to be much the same. Each man is responsible for himself; and to his support he may be able to call his kinsmen or those indebted to him, but there is no certainty of this. Only in the case of a young man challenging the authority of the old men of the tribe is there anything like a court. The trial is relatively simple in the sense that the old men are permitted to throw spears at the youngster, making him jump and dodge, perhaps even wounding, but rarely killing him. But for this there will be no revenge, as would be the case of a man wounded or killed in a fight.

See C. W. M. Hart and A. Pilling, *The Tiwi of North Australia* (Holt, Rinehart & Winston, 1960).

Among other people, such as the Nuer, the right to use force rests with the kin group and one can call upon his relatives to help him redress a grievance against others. In some complex tribes there exist councils of elders, or even what must be considered courts, where evidence is heard and weighed and decisions made. Seldom, however, do punishments include the application of force; banishment to prevent the development of feuding, the payment of fines to the offended party, return of stolen goods—such forms of redress are far more common. Of course, the decisions of such courts—or the balance of terror which exists among the Nuer—extend only to the edge of the "tribe," which is more apt to be defined by kinship relations, languages, and custom than by a specific geographic boundary. However, whereever institutions exist which monopolize to themselves the right to use force within a certain territory, without fear of reprisal, we are dealing with a different kind of social unit: the state.

THE STATE

We will not become involved in the argument of how the state evolved from a tribal level of existence, how relationships based on common residence within a boundary replaced those of real or fancied kinship. We can only say that something like the state appears to have developed in company with another phenomenon we will discuss later: civilization.

In essence, the state is a means of organizing people who are not relatives, who perhaps do not even share the same language or culture, by establishing statuses and roles for the application of force to require observance of certain rules of behavior we would call law—as distinguished from custom. It is important to make this distinction or we find ourselves trapped in an intellectual maze where any custom is a law and any law without the sanction of custom is invalid. The weight of tradition and our idea of good manners, for instance, force us to shake hands with people under certain circumstances. A refusal to do so may mark us as boors, cause people to be angry at us, and lead to the withdrawal of cooperation and companionship, or simply to pity and ridicule. But it will not, in this country, lead to our being arrested and brought before a court. In the United States, no one can force you with muscle or weapons to shake hands. Force can be used to prevent you from speeding or entering a house where you do not belong, and to punish you if you do. On the other hand, in Japan, public rudeness may indeed attract the attention of the police.

Within this country and any other organized along state lines, the law, and thus force, will be applied not because of your family, clan, or lineage, but rather because you live in a certain place. In a state-society, force is also monopolized with respect to its use outside the boundaries of the state. Thus if one uses force against a neighbor, the state in the form of the police forces him to desist, and in the form of the courts may well punish him for violating the peace and require that he pay damages to the neighbor as well. If the neighbor was living on the other side of an international boundary—in Nogales, Sonora, for instance—it would not be the United States police and courts, but those of Mexico. But one additional element would be involved. In a sense, the single act of a citizen of the United States against a citizen of Mexico within the boundaries of Mexico would involve the entire structures of two countries. The United States citizen, no matter how guilty, would be represented, at least in theory, by an official of the United States. If a band of American citizens raided Mexico, it would be expected that our government would put a stop to it. If it did not, it would be assumed their actions were officially approved and the entire people of the United States were at war with the people of Mexico.

Such a situation did occur in the reverse when, early in this century, the Mexican revolutionary Pancho Villa attacked Columbus, New Mexico. Villa most certainly did not represent the government of Mexico. At the same time, that government was not strong enough to stop his depredations across the border. Finally and very reluctantly, it agreed to allow United States troops to enter Mexico in pursuit of Villa. The invisible line between Mexico and the United States made the difference between the raid of a revolutionary and an act of war against another country.

Thus, it is common for the institutions of a state-society to control in one way or another the maintaining of armed forces. Private armies are forbidden or at least rigidly controlled in any state. In our own Constitution, the right to keep and bear arms in order to maintain a militia had to be specifically protected; it is not a right readily given by most nations. Armies may be drawn from a single military class, or from the entire manhood of the nation as a whole. They may be manned by volunteers or conscripts. But in a state-society, they must be under the final control of the state rather than individuals, kin groups, or corporations.

During the sixteenth and seventeenth centuries, armies were often a private-enterprise activity—free companies selling themselves to the highest-bidding king. Private regiments were recruited and maintained by corporations like the British East India Company to conquer and police areas they had been licensed to exploit. However, in these instances the king had the final authority to issue a license. Many of the great wartime heroes—Drake, Hawkins, Captain Kidd, even Jean Lafitte—were men who raided the sea lanes of the sixteenth, seventeenth, and eighteenth centuries under licenses from one state or another. To attack a ship without the authority of some government was to become a pirate with all the world's hand turned against you.

Forms of States
The authorization and use of force is the final and determining mark of statehood. Unless that is present, along with a defined geographical boundary, we are not dealing with a state. Where it is present, no matter how simple and primitive the society may appear to be, we

are dealing with a state. To use and control force, however, there must be some established institution, a government. The structure of governments can be wildly varying. "Who is authorized to use force?" is another way of asking, "What form of government do these people enjoy?" A *monarchy* authorizes a king—that is a hereditary status role—to command armies and set into motion the use of force. A *republic* is in essence any form of government which does not have a hereditary king but which, by any number of different devices, selects a leader or leaders who control the machinery of force.

The complexities of investigations in this area are many. Tribes may have hereditary rulers who have at least some authority over the use of force but who cannot point to specific territorial boundaries; we might call such rulers chiefs instead of kings, though the difference would be slight. On the other hand, tribes such as the Iroquois had no hereditary chief, but rather a council of sachems representing matrilineal clans and elected by the members of the clan—thus, perhaps, a tribal republic. A state may be ruled by priests and called a *theocracy,* or by officials elected by the faithful and be called a theocratic republic. Just how we would categorize Tibet, where until recently the rulers were priests who were said to be reincarnations of previous ruling priests, it is hard to say. And at this point in our study of man, undue sophistication is not really needed.

What we must remember is that a state is a society in which the use of force within a specified geographic area is reserved for a specific governing institution. To one degree or another, relationships between men in a state are more apt to be based on the fact that they live within its boundaries than they are on kinship. Examine your own life, for instance, and ask how many decisions each day are determined by where you live. The schools you go to, the side of the street you drive on, the language you use in business and government, the mathematics of your currency and weights and measures, the materials and construction techniques of your house, the price of the goods you buy—these are but a few of the things that are determined by were you live. And if you have a relative living in another country, your kinship to him is much less important than the fact that you live in different nations. This was most clearly brought home in the two world wars, when first- and second-generation American citizens went to war willingly, even if sadly, against their cousins, even brothers who had remained behind in the Old Country.

In the last paragraph we used the word *nation.* It is necessary to draw a distinction between a nation and a state. A state is a rather clearly defined political unit, usually a large one. A nation on the other hand may be a single state or many, because the word refers not to political or social structure but rather to culture, language, and common tradition. Thus Roman and European writers spoke of the German nation for nearly two thousand years before Bismarck united the fragmented German principalities into a single state. In fact, this task was not totally finished until Hitler attempted to bring all the German-speakers of Austria, Czechoslovakia, Poland, and Alsace-Lorraine under a single flag. We often speak of the Cherokee or Sioux or Apache nations among American Indians because these peoples shared a common language, traditions, and cultures. None of them, however, had a form of social–political organization we could call statehood. On the other hand many states have existed now and in the past which cannot be called nations. Switzerland, with its four distinct languages and traditions, has been a separate state for several centuries, but never a nation. The Soviet Union is a state, but with two hundred minority populations and nearly as many languages and cultural traditions, it cannot be considered a nation. Our own pledge of allegiance to "one nation" is more of a hope than a statement of fact.

The nation-state is an idea developed fairly recently in western Europe—and like steam engines, airplanes, and a number of other Western inventions, it has spread rapidly throughout the world. A corollary to the nation-state idea is the philosophy of self-determination that is held in such high esteem today. "Self-determination" is a term which gained currency as the empires of the nineteenth and early twentieth centuries collapsed rapidly after World War II. It meant at that time that people living in India, let us say, should rule themselves, not be ruled by the British. But once that end was achieved, the term increasingly came to mean that the people of one part of India—or, more importantly, people speaking one of India's many languages or having a distinct pattern of culture—should be ruled by themselves.

The recent civil war in Ghana, during which the short-lived country of Biafra was formed, resulted partly from the idea that people of one tribal heritage should not be ruled or share a government with people of another heritage. But even as Biafra was born and died, other tribesmen, who did not share the culture of the dominant Biafran population, were beginning to speak out for their own self-determination. And so it goes. It is hard to say where culturally and linguistically based demands for self-determination will stop.

Seldom do language and cultural boundaries form such a distinct line that one can draw political boundaries without isolating some people from their fellows.

The demands for a separate Islamic government in India resulted in millions of Hindus' being isolated in Bengal (East Pakistan), and nearly fifty million Muslims remaining in India. The differences in language and culture between East and West Pakistan were in part responsible for the founding of Bangladesh in 1972. In the 1950's, the Sikh population of the Punjab, certainly not even a majority of the people in that area, successfully campaigned for a separate Indian state oriented toward their language and culture. The other half of the old Punjabi region was peopled with Hindus, and they next demanded to be separate from the new state of Punjab; thus was formed Harayana, a state whose language is officially Hindi although most of the people have been raised to speak Punjabi. The problem lies in equating cultural identity with political identity—a notion which seems to have come from the European-born philosophy of the nation-state.

Bases of Authority

Since the development of tiny city-states in Asia, the Middle East, and the eastern Mediterranean several thousand years ago, man has struggled with the problem of justifying the position of leaders. In many large and complex tribal kingdoms, the role of king has been justified by divine sanction. We believe that the rulers of the earliest city-states in the Middle East were priests, and the role of the ruler has always been related in some way to the religious system of the country.

Experiments with representative government—that is, systems based on the idea of the people being ruled by human means, subject to the will or at least responsive to the desires of the ruled—are not new. Many of the city-states of Greece were republics with democratic institutions, and so was Rome, at least in its beginnings. But it is important to remember that the idea of representative government, after over two thousand years, is still developing. The leaders of Athens ruled in the name of a very small part of the population: free men who bore arms. This was true also of Rome. The larger part of the population—bound servants, foreigners, women, and slaves—were not considered part of the body politic.

Figure 57.   Monarchs in many early kingdoms were considered to be divine—or at least, to rule by divine right.

It is true, no matter how unpalatable, that representation in government has generally been accorded only to those obligated or permitted to bear arms. Almost inevitably, systems with a small and elite body of fighting men have fallen under the control of those who bore arms. Tribal societies generally assume that all or virtually all men will be warriors in time of need. More complex societies, however, not infrequently develop military classes. Seldom in history have such classes resisted the urge to sieze the power of government through the power of their arms. Even when the military is accorded low status, as it was in traditional China, military officials play an important role in government. In Rome, the decline of the original republican model can be seen to coincide with the increased use of foreign mercenary troops instead of Roman citizens, until the soldiers literally auctioned off the imperial throne to the highest bidder.

The reverse is true in modern Europe and Japan, where the introduction of firearms made it possible to train large numbers of commoners in a relatively short time, instead of the years required to train a knight or samurai. As the exclusive right to bear arms was eroded, so was the political control of military aristocracy. Universal military service exists in virtually all western European democracies, monarchical or republican, save England. In Japan, the power of the warrior nobility was overthrown in 1868 by the supporters of the emperor, who increasingly depended on the common people and universal military service. Universal service obviously does not guarantee a democratic form of government, but military exclusiveness does seem to tend toward military control. This is one of the fears voiced in the United States about an all-volunteer army. Such fears may be groundless, but they are based on real historic evidence.

Warlordism and Feudalism

Warlordism is seldom described in formal courses in political science, and yet it has, and does, play an important role in human affairs. Defined simply, it is a situation where, within the boundaries of a nation-state, actual control of affairs in various areas is in the hands of leaders (warlords) whose claim to power is sustained by their control of armed forces. China, from the revolution of 1911 to the rise of the Chinese People's Republic, is a good example. Although various "governors" of provinces were theoretically loyal to the central government, in fact they were virtually independent because they controlled large armies. The central government remained in its position only by carefully balancing the power of these men and avoiding con-

> Although scholars have seldom included **warlordism** among formal classifications of types of governments, the workings of such a system are well described by Barbara Tuchman in *Stilwell and the American Experience in China 1911–1945* (Macmillan, 1971).

frontations with them. (One warlord, quite independent of the government in Nanking, declared war on the British Empire.) Unlike feudal systems, warlordism appears to have no ideological content at all. Power is maintained with power; whereas a feudal king might call on his barons to support him against a recalcitrant nobleman because of oaths sworn and loyalties expected and enforced by religious sanctions, the leader of a nation of warlords can only appeal to the self-interest of the warlords to keep them in line.

Feudalism is a system of government with a wide distribution, and is seen by some to be a transition between a simpler form of tribal government and the state. In Europe and Japan, it was the system devised to replace large but weak centralized governments—or in the case of Europe, no government at all, after the gradual erosion of the power of Rome. In essence, feudalism is a system based on a number of ascending levels of loyalty and obligation. In theory, all the kings of feudal Europe owed a spiritual allegiance to the pope in Rome, but the pope never had enough military or political power of his own to assure that loyalty.

The fascinating subject of feudalism on the continent and in England may be approached through Marc Bloch's *Feudal Society*, 2 vols. (University of Chicago Press, 1961); and George C. Homans' *English Villagers of the Thirteenth Century* (Harvard University Press, 1941).

Below each king were various classes of citizens, each depending for support on the class above. The king distributed land to his barons, who in return promised loyalty and military support. To collect the armed men they had promised to the king, the barons in turn distributed land to lesser nobles, and they in turn provided incomes for fighting men. At the bottom of the heap were the peasantry, who were tied to the land—but in theory, at least, were exempt from military service and supposedly immune from the terrors of war.

In practice, feudalism was more complex than this. The tangles of rights and obligations in feudal relationships—the rights to kill deer in the forest in a certain month, to graze sheep on the common land, to collect firewood, and any number of other privileges and perquisites—are almost beyond comprehension; they made the feudal period one in which litigation before the courts was a regular part of the life of at least the upper classes.

The conflict between the kings and barons was a constant tension. The king sought the right to exercise direct power in the lands held by the barons. The barons, on the other hand, held that their obligation to support the king justified their retaining control over the people within their various domains. They claimed that the king's authority should be exercised indirectly through them, except in the lands held by the king himself. The agreement between King John of England and his barons, which we call the Magna Carta, was not a declaration of freedom for the common people of England; instead, it was an agreement forced on the king, dealing with whose tyranny the people would be exposed to—the king's or that of the particular lord who held dominion over the lands on which the commoners lived.

Feudal states are fragile because the interests, ambitions, and loyalties of the component members may well transcend the geographic boundaries of the state. A man might hold land from two kings or two barons, promising each his loyalty. In thirteenth-century England, many noblemen found themselves in the uncomfortable position of being both liege men of the King of Scotland and claimants to the throne of England at the same time. It was on the rocks of such a paradox that the feudal ship of state went aground.

The Meaning of the Vote

Another tension in most political systems—and most certainly in ours—is the conflict between individuals and group interests. This tension is symbolized by the slogan, *One man, one vote*. To us, in the middle of the twentieth century, that seems unarguable logic; but throughout most of American history, and over much of the world, it didn't and doesn't make sense. Whether in the councils of large tribal societies, the courts of kings, or in parliaments or congresses, the more general pattern is to distribute representation in terms of large groups of people—the elders, warriors, and individual clans; or the nobility, merchants, and clergy; or property holders, financiers, etc.

The English Parliament retains something of this pattern; the House of Lords represents the titled nobility of the country, and the House of Commons represents nontitled people. Commons, of course, holds the predominant power at this time, but the older form remains. Similarly, in the United States, senators represent not people but sovereign states. Thus, the votes of two senators from California (population 18 million) and two senators from Hawaii (.75 million) are equal in the voting of the Senate. Each member of the House of Representatives, on the other hand, represents about the same number of voters, at least in theory.

Beyond this, however, it is necessary to examine the system of voting to determine who is actually represented. Until fifty years ago in the United States, only men were allowed to vote, women and children being dependent on them for political expression. Until the 1960's, over much of the country, blacks, Indians, and Chicanos were kept from voting by a welter of legal and illegal devices. Frequently, particularly in state and local systems, only property owners were allowed to vote.

There is always a conflict between interests and individuals. In some nations, even though voting takes place, established interests are predominant. For example, the military, in theory composed of individual voters, in fact often stands ready to intervene forcibly if the vote goes against the candidate favored by the generals. This largely explains the fact that South American republics often possess large, well-equipped armies and air forces although no real external threat exists. The tanks and planes and a large military budget are the price they demand for not seizing power directly. Thus, to understand modern politics it is necessary to understand a great deal more than what one learns in civics classes.

An article by James C. Scott, "An Essay on the Political Functions of Corruption," *Asian Studies 5* (December 1967) discusses different styles of "corruption" in various governmental systems.

No matter what the formal organization, one must examine a political system as another aspect of culture. It is necessary to understand how decisions are made and what are the cultural patterns of the people. Political structures conceived in one context are not always easily transferred to another—no matter how high-minded the attempt may be. Particularly in many Asian nations, the individual traditionally had no standing in the politics of the state. Instead the village or the family was responsible to the government. Taxes were charged to the village. The number of men required for the army, or a statement of needed repairs, was transmitted to the village headman or the head of the family. If a member of the village committed a crime, it was the village's responsibility to deal with him—to fail was to invite punishment of the entire village. Thus, for most people government was distant and removed. Little wonder, then, that Vietnamese villagers find it difficult to understand general elections, representative government, and other democratic forms. For them, life within the village has always been governed by custom. A population with this background sees government not as a protector, but as an intruder— the more so because many new nations are not able to live up to their own expectations.

Lack of trained personnel, lack of funds, and unfamiliarity with self-government after long periods of colonial control—all combine to make it difficult for new national governments to operate efficiently. Thus, laws passed in the capitol are seldom effectively enforced in the provinces. Such a situation makes a population much more concerned about how effectively the laws operate than about who passes them in some distant city. People tend in these circumstances to be less concerned with national political problems than they are with seeing that their interests are represented at a local level. Instead of devoting their time and energy to national elections, they prefer to influence personally the way laws are administered, through influence or bribery.

Such behavior shocks Americans, but we tend to forget that, in contrast to Vietnamese or Filipinos, when *we* vote for congressmen or senators or presidents we are placing men in positions of *real* power, and it therefore behooves us to be concerned about who wins these positions. We react quite violently to corruption that would sabotage our intentions as expressed in voting, but we often spend a great deal of time and energy attempting to influence the votes of legislators, congressmen, and senators, and we find it very difficult to establish rules which prevent large, rich organizations from exerting too much influence. Our situation is opposite to that of the citizens of a small, poor, or new nation. Because we know that in general a law passed in Congress will be enforced, we are concerned with what laws are passed. The citizen of India or Vietnam is as certain that laws passed in the Lok Sabha or national legislature will not be enforced, and so one must see to it that local officials are well disposed toward one's interests. It is all politics—a matter of channeling and sharing power; only the situation is different.

How Power Changes Hands

One of the problems with which man has wrestled for millennia is, How can power be transferred when one ruler dies or is superseded by another? In the past, power was said to reside in the hands of one group or another for religious or supernatural reasons. This justified the status quo in terms the population would accept—at least as long as everyone felt that the government was reasonably just in whatever terms justice was seen. However, the death of a ruler has always led to confusion and struggles to succeed him. It was to reduce the possible claimants to the throne that Africans once set out to slay their brothers, as mentioned in Chapter Four. Hawaiians, Egyptians, Koreans, and Peruvians allowed incestuous marriages to take place among the royalty. In Tibet, a council of respected priests sought a supernatural message to tell them where to find the new reincarnation to rule when the reigning Dalai Lama died.

Since the sixteenth century, the principal religious figure in Buddhist Tibet has been the **Dalai Lama**, resident in Lhassa. Each Dalai Lama is believed to be a reincarnation of *Chen-re-zi*, a manifestation of Buddha and patron of Tibet. In 1641, the Dalai Lama gained not only spiritual authority, but also temporal power over all Tibet. The present Dalai Lama, the fourteenth, fled to India when the Chinese invaded Tibet, and remains there in exile with about 100,000 of his people.

Some nations in the modern world have depended on well-established bureaucracies—functionaries of government who carry on their duties no matter who is the ruler. Others have retained a monarch who remains as head of state while politicians struggle for the reins of government; such a system can reduce the chances of revolution because it would constitute an attack not merely upon the government but on the king—a subtle but important difference.

The United States has been remarkable in this area. No government of the United States has ever been overthrown by disgruntled losers of an election. Only once was there even such a threat in the air—and although the South rejected the election of Lincoln, there was no attempt to overthrow the government; rather, the Confederate states tried to establish their own nation-state. Even though American presidents have been assassinated, the murders were not part of a revolution or seizure of power, despite hysterical claims to the contrary.

This aspect of American history has often puzzled foreigners, because our president is both chief of state and head of government. When a contender for the White House criticizes the incumbent, he is, in the eyes of many foreigners, treading close to treason. To Americans, it seems entirely reasonable. Just why Americans—otherwise not a particularly law-abiding people, certainly prone to violence—are able to effect peaceful changes of government is not clear. Certainly it cannot be credited to an overall superiority of our political system, which falls far short of perfect. For the time, we must accept it as a characteristic of American political culture—a subject for further research.

This discussion of power and politics has painted, in rather broad strokes, some of the major and recurring problems man has faced in trying to manage very large groups of people. A mere glance at today's headlines will prove how important these problems are and how far we are from an understanding which would effect their total solution.

DEFINING AND STUDYING CULTURE

Part Three

INTRODUCTION TO PART THREE: CULTURE

Part Two of this book dealt with what may be called the social foundations of culture—that is, the actual ways in which human beings organize into groups in order to get the business of living done. Man, it seems quite certain, is a social animal. The life of a single man cannot be described apart from the lives of other men or aside from the groups of men with whom he lives. This is true of any number of other creatures. Buffalo, deer, porpoises, and tuna fish—all live in groups. This means that the presence of other individuals of their kind influences not only the environment but also the behavior of individuals who are interacting with the environment and with each other. Even the complexities of the most modern nation or most elaborate civilization of the past can be matched in the animal kingdom. Allowing for a bit of anthropomorphising in the choice of words, we find classes and castes, royalty and commoners, and an elaborate division of labor in beehives and anthills. Ants even display the kind of behavior we would attribute to warring nations, and the vicious racism which has marked Mississippi and South Africa.

However, we can stretch these analogies too far. Ants and bees inherit their patterns of behavior genetically. In a beehive, a commoner is a commoner and a queen is a queen because of inherited physical characteristics. A worker ant cannot be anything but a worker ant because he is not physically equipped to be anything else. A queen bee will always be a queen bee; though she might be assassinated, she can never lose her status and fall into the lower classes. Many people would like it very much if things were as clear-cut in human societies as they are in anthills, but human beings do not inherit their class positions by virtue of genetics; a human's class position is mainly a result of historical accident, social heritage, and cultural patterns.

It is difficult to distinguish in human beings between social behavior on one hand and cultural behavior on the other. Some have said it is impossible, and others imply it is a waste of time. Yet we will find it useful to make a conceptual distinction between the social aspects of man's behavior and the other aspects, though we must remember this can only be done in the mind. We must never expect human beings to act in a totally social way or a totally cultural way—or in a totally physical way, for that matter.

What I am trying to say is that human beings are social animals, and in fact depend for their continued existence as individuals on the existence of other humans to whom they can relate certain kinds of behavior; this can be seen over and over again in human groups, irrespective of their history, language, or particular cultural tradition. This is most striking, perhaps, on the simplest level of human organization—the hunting and gathering bands which we discussed in Chapter One.

Simple descriptions of the social structure of the Bushman of the Kalahari desert, the Paiute and Washo and Shoshone of the Great Basin, the Semang and Saki of the Malayan jungle, or of the aboriginal peoples of Australia—all sound dramatically similar. The size of the groups, the division of labor, the degree of specialization, the relation of men and women, and the means of reckoning descent are very much the same for these widely separated and probably unrelated groups of people.

So, also, would purely social-structural descriptions, of Japan, the United States, and the Soviet Union sound the same. There are classes of people with different life styles and differential access to

Figure 58.   Commuter trains—whether in New York or Tokyo—share a similar atmosphere, despite differences in the racial and cultural heritages of their passengers. Similar economic systems tend to produce similar behavior patterns.

wealth and resources (much as the Soviets would deny it, and no matter how reluctant we might be to admit it ourselves). Classes of people do appear to behave in predictable ways, just because there are classes. Members of the upper class (read upper class in America and Japan, Communist party members in the Soviet Union) do try to restrict entry of newcomers, and they do use their access to wealth or resources in order to do this.

In short, I am sure that at first glance an observer from somewhere off the earth would see much that was the same about many of the societies we think of as quite different. But while man must indeed live in a social context, and because of that respond to social realities, he does not live by society alone. Nor is society in any sense a separate and independent entity. That brings us to the question of culture.

No matter how similar the social structure of the Paiute and the Australian aborigine may be, no one could mistake one for the other if he saw a Paiute bunch or an Australian horde. The same can be said of modern complex civilizations. The social structures of Japan and the United States are becoming more and more alike in many essential and central ways, and yet no one would ever be confused as to whether he was in Los Angeles or Tokyo, or whether he was in a factory operated by Toyota or General Motors. Because as much as society influences the culture of a people, so does culture influence society. Differential access to wealth and resources implies, of course, that wealth exists in a society. And wealth is not an objective or an abstract concept; it is what a society (or more properly, a culture) determines it to be.

Although the hills and streams of California were full of wealth in the form of gold, California Indians did not consider it wealth and so their access to it made no difference. To them, wealth was counted in certain kinds of shells, the scalps of a species of woodpeckers, and a number of other things. The possession of such objects was what made a difference in the life of the Yurok or Karok or Hupa. Things, including human beings, could be bought and sold with them. Death could be avenged by demanding payment in them. Neighbors could be made to feel inferior by displaying them. Wives could be obtained only by offering them.

California Indian cultures are described in considerable detail by A. L. Kroeber in his *Handbook of the Indians of California* (California Book Company, 1970; original edition published in 1925).

There are probably environmental explanations as to why these things should be precious. Haliotis shell was relatively rare, and it must have taken much time and skill to catch and scalp a woodpecker. But neither of these materials was more rare than any number of other items in the environment of Northwestern California. Nor, am I sure, did it require any more labor to drill a hole in a haliotis shell or scalp a woodpecker than it would have taken to pan golden nuggets from the streams. And had they wanted to, most certainly the Karok, Yurok, and Hupa, could have applied their technical skills to gold-panning. The simple facts were that as children they had been brought up to believe that woodpecker scalps and haliotis shell were wealth and that gold nuggets were simply another kind of pebble. In short, the cultures of northwestern California defined the environment quite differently than did other cultures.

Now some anthropologists would say, *"Cultures* don't do anything—only people do." That, I think, is simply nit-picking. *Culture,* as we will see in this section, is a word we use to describe the assumptions and knowledge shared by a group of people. In the abstract, culture is the unique potential human beings have to make these assumptions and develop and learn and teach this knowledge. It seems childish not to sum up all this in a word and go on about one's business. But it seems singularly wrong-headed to then make that word into reality and refuse to ask how and why cultural things happen.

Culture has been defined in many ways, and a great deal of effort has been devoted to attempting to isolate culture just as one might try to isolate a chemical element in a complex compound. I remember once hearing one of the world's most famous anthropologists discuss *seriously* the argument that an Indian driving a herd of domesticated horses was culture but that the trail of hoofprints left wasn't. We must accept such silliness as a part of the human mental makeup. After all, learned medieval theologians spent a great deal of time speculating about how many angels could stand on the head of a pin. And after months of deliberations, a group of rabbinical scholars once decided that if a young man fell off a roof onto a young woman walking below, and if he fell in such a way that his penis entered her vagina, there would be no sin. All of this goes to prove, along with the hoofprints, that even the most profound and logical sequence of thoughts can turn into silly illogic if allowed to progress to its "logical" conclusion without the imposition of common sense.

What we will do in this section is look at a number of ways of defining culture, or perhaps a number of different kinds of culture, if you wish. Each of these points of view has been useful and still is useful to understanding certain kinds of questions. There is a tendency among scholars to argue constantly that only "our" generation knows the truth (or conversely to argue that the elders learned the truth and no alteration can be made to it). So today many younger and not-so-young anthropologists are suggesting that certain new techniques of eliciting information have brought about revolutionary revisions in the concept of culture. Hardly. Very little of what they say is theoretically new, and many of the approaches they use would be of no use at all to a scientist exploring questions other than the ones they ask. However, we will begin with this new approach because it is new and because it is undoubtedly useful; oddly enough (and, I suspect, to the horror of some anthropologists) it is the most easily explained to introductory students and most easily put into application.

CULTURE AS A MAP

10

SYMBOLS AND CATEGORIES

As we said many pages ago, man is uniquely endowed in body and mind to do things other creatures cannot. He can make symbols of things. That is, he can arbitrarily assign meaning to things. A flag is perhaps as simple an example as we can think of. The American flag, flying from the flag staff of a warship or standing in the corner behind the speaker's stand in a public hall, is simply cloth: stripes of red and white cloth, a patch of blue cloth and a number of white "star-shaped" things (and that in itself is interesting —we call them stars, but stars don't really look like that at all). If the stripes were green and blue, the stars black, and the patch lemon yellow, we would look at it and say, "That is a funny looking flag," or "What flag is that?" But because it is colored and shaped as it is, we take our hats off in its presence, hold our hands over our hearts, salute it, pledge allegiance to it, try to prevent it from touching the ground, hoist it at certain times and lower it at others. All for a piece of cloth. And oddly enough, students who didn't agree with the national policy of having troops in Vietnam burned the flag.

Obviously, we are all not completely mad. We know that this particular arrangement of color and shape does indeed stand for something, and we know that other arrangements of shape and color stand for other things. Thus, we recognize that a peculiar

For more on symbols and symboling, see Leslie White's *The Science of Culture* (Farrar, Straus & Giroux, 1969).

combination of red and white crosses on a blue background stands for England and the British Empire, and that one arrangement of red, white, and blue stripes stands for the Netherlands, and another of identical colors for France. But there is nothing intrinsic in the shapes or arrangements or colors to relate them to what they stand for. Why red, white, and blue, and not green, pink, and yellow; why not spots instead of stripes, and little eagles instead of stars? Indeed, why not? No reason at all, as nearly as I can see—save that there is a general agreement that certain colors mean certain things, and others don't.

Figure 59.   An American flag at half mast means something to virtually every American. What? Would it have the same meaning if the flag were blue with a white cross on it, or divided into red, yellow, blue, and black quarters?

Thus white is for purity, and red for courage, and blue for faithfulness or the sky or something. Lavender just wouldn't convey to us the same set of feelings. But when we look around a bit we discover some interesting things about color. White, which we consider a symbol of purity and assign to brides, children taking confirmation, and the like, is not considered so among the Chinese; they wear white for mourning, and assign red to brides. Black is the mourning color for us, but the color of everyday dress for a Vietnamese peasant—and so on.

Or, consider the mark *A*. All Americans know what that is: it is a letter and it stands for a sound. But really, it stands for several sounds. A is the symbol we use for the sound in *cat, ate, car, aunt,* and *at*. Now, there is no reason why we couldn't have used the symbol *B* to represent those sounds, and *A* to represent the first sound in *bat, burg,* and *bean*—thus, the spellings *abt, aurg,* and *aebn*. Why not? For no reason at all, save that over a long historical development of our alphabet those two symbols came to stand for those several different sounds. We assign meaning to things quite arbitrarily. We know it is arbitrary because we find that other peoples often use the same symbols we use, but give them different meanings. Even the symbol *A* is given quite different sound values in written Cherokee, although the alphabet developed by Sequoya was inspired by letters he had seen written in English.

Sequoya was a Cherokee Indian who, although himself illiterate, was inspired by seeing European books to invent for his native language a writing system that was later adopted and used for books, newspapers, and public records.

This ability to make symbols is the basis of language, spoken and written, and in a sense at least is also the basis of culture itself. Man identifies himself not objectively but symbolically, and moves through life responding far more often to symbols than to objective reality. Some anthropologists find it difficult to come to grips with this simple proposition, despite the abundant supporting evidence to be found on every hand. They try desperately to relate each human practice to some "objective" factor in the environment or in the economic system without realizing that even the environment is not an objective reality, but rather a projection of the symbol system of one society or another; similarly, economic activity is based not on absolutes but on the symbolic values and needs of a given society.

What has man's symbolizing ability to do with the title of this chapter, "Culture as a Map"? A map is not reality, but rather a set of agreed-upon symbols that represent those aspects of the environment the makers of a map have decided are important. A heavy dark

Figure 60. A map and a sketch of a corner neighborhood in Hilo, Hawaii. Neither is an absolute representation of reality. But the map is composed only of conventional symbols. It makes no attempt to depict the visual scene.

line is not a road; it merely stands for a road, just as a yellow dot may stand for a city with a population of over 10,000 or a wiggly blue line represent a river. Take out an ordinary roadmap while you are driving (or, better yet, have your passenger do it) and see how many things in the environment are simply not indicated on the map. Fields, most buildings—all sorts of natural and man-made features are not included in a road map because they are not relevant to the purpose of the map. Furthermore, those things which are indicated are represented symbolically, not pictorially. Now look at another kind of map, a Coast and Geodetic Survey map, for instance. A number of other things are indicated—vegetation, elevation, natural features, roads, and even some structures—but still they are represented only as symbols, and even they tend to leave out other specifics which yet some other kind of map might include. In short, these maps do not give you a picture of the environment in absolute detail. What they do is provide a general guide for the person using them. So, in a way, does culture.

We are provided by a culture with a mental map to life, through the agency of people who share that culture. An infant begins almost at birth to learn about culture's map, at first from parents and siblings, then from other relatives, and gradually from other children, neighbors, schools, or churches. He learns a set of general rules about how to act and react, and what to expect from other people and from the environment. We do not receive detailed instructions on how to behave in every specific situation throughout our lives. Rather—like a person reading a roadmap—we are provided with general guidelines and must constantly use them to decide where we are in the real world and what rules apply to each specific case. Thus we learn to walk and speak and in so doing we learn a particular language, and, as often as not, a walk which will distinguish us and our kind from people brought up in other cultures. We learn how to talk to other people in different situations, and how to court a girl and to get married, how to perform coitus and to urinate and defecate, and what is beautiful and what is ugly, and when it is appropriate to wear clothes or not to wear clothes, and what clothes it is appropriate to wear. We learn the symbols which distinguish people of one status from those of another, and we learn a culturally defined version of time and space, heat and cold, full and hungry, polite and impolite—on and on, endlessly. Virtually every act we perform, awake or asleep, in right mind or insane, is directly or indirectly influenced by the cultural system within which we are born and raised.

We must reemphasize that culture does not provide a detailed script for life. We do not learn, for instance, how we should behave if we go insane—at least we don't receive specific, conscious instructions. Rather, we inherit a cultural map which guides our behavior in such a way that we tend to respond to many situations in terms of the *general* instructions of the map. Young men in America do not learn consciously that if they become homosexuals they will engage in one kind of sex act, and young Englishmen are not taught that in the same circumstances they will act in a different way. Nonetheless the general patterns of the two cultures cause this kind of differential response to develop.

COGNITIVE ANTHROPOLOGY

Each culture, with its ideas and responses and patterns for behavior, can be called a *cognitive map*. The assumption is that the cognitive map for all Americans is generally the same, although it may differ in detail or even in interpretation from one generation to another and from social group to social group. This idea, in one form or another, has been around in anthropology for a long time. We have spoken of the perceptions of a group of people in trying to describe how they saw the world in a way that was different from other peoples. We have spoken of world view, and in a way the very basis of cultural relativism is the assumption that different cultures see things differently. In recent years, the cognitive map has come to be seen as a system of classifications of objects and phenomena; some anthropologists have attempted to find out in a systematic way exactly how the people of specific cultures classify certain phenomena.

These anthropologists were motivated by several needs, not the least of which was to make anthropological research more rigorous—that is, to do research which was more like that done by biologists

Figure 61.   In traditional north India, women were in purdah (seclusion), always covering their faces in public. In the south, women regularly went nude above the waist. In fact, it was not respectable for a woman to cover her breasts.

and physicists, or even sociologists or psychologists. They sought methods of research that could not reflect the biases of the investigator, producing results that could be repeated in detail by another scientist using the same techniques. This feature, which is called *replicability*, is an important criterion of scientific research; in most sciences, it provides the only way a proposition can be proven or disproven. If a biochemist says substance S taken in certain amounts, will kill bacteria, he must be able to prove it. He and others can prove or disprove by repeating the experiment over and over. If the results are consistently the same, the proposition or hypothesis is proven. If not, then something is wrong.

Many scientists have criticized anthropological research because it is not replicable. Two different anthropologists often go to the same village or tribe or region and return to write quite disparate reports. The most famous of these contradictions occurred between studies of the village of Tepoztlán in Mexico, produced by Robert Redfield and later Oscar Lewis.

In fact, it has always seemed to me that much anthropological work is actually replicable. For instance, while there are minor variations in the collections of kinship terms done by many anthropologists working among the Navajo, there is general agreement that if one asks about Navajo kin terms he will get the same list from almost any Navajo. After several investigators have done this there seems to be little reason to go on doing it. My own field work among the Navajo seemed to produce results and information that was in agreement with information gathered by at least a dozen other anthropologists. I doubt that I would ever have received the funds to go there had I simply wanted to see if Professors Kluckhohn or Aberle and Riechard were right. I went to ask questions about areas of Navajo life other investigators had not asked about. I am sure that if anyone went into the Navajo country and conducted his work in the same manner I did, he would receive much the same information as I did.

However, it is true that anthropological research has not developed a tradition of reexamining past work to see if it was correct—quite the opposite. In the earlier years of the science—perhaps because it was felt that there was too much new work to be done—no one even thought of going back to a people to "test," as it were, someone's work. Rather, once a tribe was reported on the science would move on to study other groups. Today, anthropologists may return time and again to the same people in order to explore areas previously unexplored or test hypotheses based on previous field work—but seldom to replicate the work of others simply to see if they were right or not.

Perhaps they should—other scientists would say that indeed they should. Whatever your opinion, such is seldom the case in anthropology. The advocates of what has come to be called *ethnoscience*

A key work in this new anthropological field is *Cognitive Anthropology* (Holt, Rinehart & Winston, 1969), edited by Stephen Tyler. It includes the work of Lamb and Hansen that will be discussed later in this book.

or *cognitive anthropology* believe that at least there should be a method of research that would make a reexamination of results possible. In general, their approach is to elicit from informants statements that indicate how certain objects, or classes of objects or phenomena or practices, are classified by the people in question. One of the earliest such studies was conducted in the 1950's by Harold C. Conklin, working among the Hanunoó in the Philippines with the main aim of discovering how they classified medicinal plants. He discovered, among other things, that these tribal people identified over three hundred plants. Now that in itself, except to the hardheaded who choose to believe that other peoples are simply unintelligent, is not so remarkable. However, Conklin learned that the classifications used by the Hanunoó were not the same classifications as an American botanist would use. We tend to look at our scientific classifications with their Latin names as the "real" classifications and "native" terms as somehow in error and unreal. Many anthropologists had in the past collected lists of native names for plants and then poured over botanical texts to "identify" the plants which a native informant had already identified. Conklin, because his work was so systematic, was able to show that the Hanunoó classification system was just as systematic and as meaningful as our own. It simply used different criteria for making its categories. More important, perhaps, was the fact that every step of the reasoning which led Conklin to his conclusions could be followed by another anthropologist.

For many anthropologists, the analysis of data has often been preceded by a mixture of logical argument and intuition. The major contribution of the ethnoscientist is in using a method of analysis that can be followed and repeated, and errors discovered if they exist. The price of his rigorous methodology, according to many other anthropologists, is a sacrifice in breadth of interest. Ethnoscientists tend to collect really large amounts of information about subjects which many of us consider not really worth all that effort. On the other hand the development of scientific methodology must begin somewhere, and ethnoscientific techniques may possibly be applied to broader subject areas in the future.

All this is something of a digression but one worth taking, I think, because it illustrates that a science is not magic, that it develops differences of opinion, that it explores and probes to find ways of collecting data, and arriving at conclusions. Seldom do all scientists in any field agree with all other scientists in the field. If they did, we would probably not be dealing with a science any longer but rather a dogma.

SYSTEMS OF CLASSIFICATION

We began all this by talking of classifications. Just what do we mean? A simple illustration can be found in Tyler's book, *Cognitive Anthropology*. Drawing from yet another study, by Lamb, Tyler takes the term *livestock*. In English, we classify livestock in the following manner:

cattle	*horses*	*sheep*	*swine*
cow	mare	ewe	sow
bull	stallion	ram	boar
steer	gelding	wether	barrow
heifer	filly	lamb	gilt
calf	colt		shoat
	foal		piglet

One who has spent much time around livestock might question these classifications. I have never heard a farmer regularly speak of a "piglet" for instance, and most farmers speak of hogs or pigs, not swine. Nonetheless, we can see general themes in this classification; age and sex (or lack of it in the case of steer, gelding, wether, and barrow) are important criteria.

But we also have other ways of classifying horses—for instance, by the work they do. So the question might be: How many kinds of horses are there? Riding horses, light harness horses, draft horses; and these classifications might further break down:

Riding	*Light harness*	*Draft horses*
saddle horse	carriage horse	plow horse
cow horse	coach horse	brewery wagon horse
hunter	harness racer	etc.
show jumper	trotter	
flat racer	pacer	

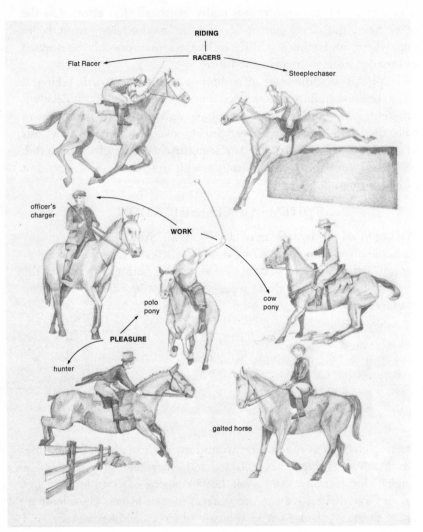

Figure 62. The term *horse* refers to a particular kind of animal—as compared to all other animals. But there are many kinds of horses. They can be—and often are—classified by a variety of criteria—breed, color, and size, to name a few. Many classification systems are situational, rather than static. For example, this illustration shows a system based on the horse's *use*. Note that each "type" of horse is associated with a human being in a different kind of costume. Thus, this classification system describes not only horses, but the behavior of human beings in certain relationships with horses.

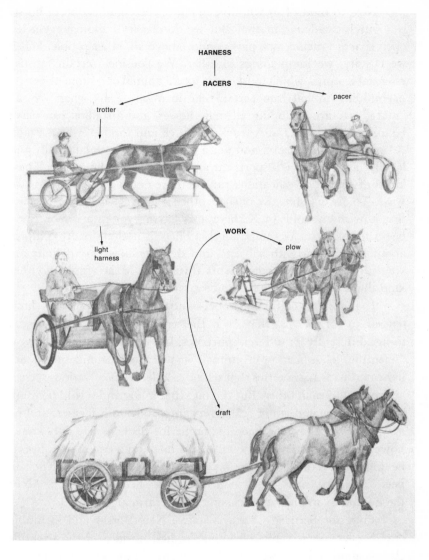

What does all this mean in everyday terms? A great deal. If we go back to the starting point and think of culture as a map that classifies people, situations, objects, and phenomena according to features that do or do not appear, and then gives general instructions about proper behavior in each case, we can see culture as the most immediate force in our lives. Let us look at some specific examples drawn from field experiences.

Now to most of us who live in cities, the classification of horses is a purely academic matter. But we do classify buildings, vehicles, open spaces (vacant lots, parks) and, above all, other people. When we classify, we lump things together. We consider certain (to us) essential features, which must occur for an animal or custom or person or building to fall into certain classification. Thus when we say "mare," we are excluding all male horses, and a stallion can never be a mare or vice versa. A truck is a truck and can never be a sedan. A taxi is definitely a taxi and not a pleasure car, both culturally and legally; a sports car is a sports car and a limousine a limousine. These kinds of simple classifications can be represented graphically in two ways. To discover how we or some other people classify things, we ask first how many kinds of X there are; having gotten a response, we begin to ask if an X_1 can be an X_2. There is nothing really complex about this. Try it with a friend and discover how very definite are your ideas about how things; work through it. Make graphs of either kind illustrated in Figure 63, and see what you come up with.

It is important to remember—and some anthropologists have tended to forget this—that even the simplest culture may classify things differently for different purposes. In Western culture we have a "scientific" classification of animals in which genus and species are indicated with Latin terms that tell us to a degree how various species are related to each other. But the fact that a hog and a wild boar are very closely related is not really very important to a farmer, and he may not even know the scientific name for his hogs. He does know, however, the difference between a lard hog and a bacon hog, just as he understands the differences between draft horses and riding horses, beef and dairy cattle, wool- and meat-type sheep, and so on. All of these fall into an important classification: farm animals.

Professor Bernard Cohen, a native New Yorker and incurable city dweller, once commented that he had no idea of the scientific classification of the trees around his suburban house. He was interested only in whether the tree in question dropped leaves which required raking in the fall. In his life, there were only droppers and nondroppers. I suspect his classification of trees is far more significant to most modern Americans than the classifications of the botanist or the lumberman. Check it out at the nearest nursery, and see how quickly the nurseryman mentions the fact that a certain tree is "dirty" or not, and how little work maintaining one kind of tree is compared with another.

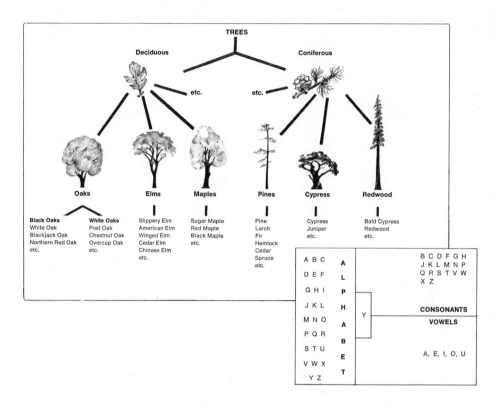

Figure 63. Two methods of classification.

Not too long ago, I was in Seoul, Korea, walking in the early morning from my hotel to make an appointment. I saw a window advertising COFFEE SHOP, and was struck by my need to have a second cup before really getting started with the day. Now "coffee shop" is an American classification of food-dispensing places. It is related to "hot dog stand," "cafeteria," and "restaurant" as a place where prepared food is served and eaten. One has a fairly good idea of what one will be served, what quality of the service to expect, and the appropriate price range. In addition, you have a good idea of how you should dress and act, and what size tip you should leave in relation to your bill.

In the Korean coffee shop I was not presented with a menu, but was given a small cup of hot water (which I later learned was barley water). While I sat uncomfortably before the steaming cup I was jolted (I can think of no other word) by being presented with an absolutely raw egg in a shot glass (as our culture would classify it).

Before my consternation reached panic proportions, a small cup, half full of coffee, was served. Anthropologists, if they are to survive long, soon learn to hide panic and watch carefully. I saw the other customers down the egg in a gulp (some even seemed to *chew*), then sip the coffee, and finally drink the barley water. I noticed too, that while waiting they seemed to hold the hot water cup as a kind of hand warmer in the bitter Korean winter.

Now what I have just described as an experience that hundreds, perhaps thousands, of Americans have had in Korea. It makes an interesting story to tell at cocktail parties. But for an anthropologist— or rather for anthropology—it provides in addition a small foundation on which to stand as one tries to learn more about coffee shops in Korea, and thus about Korea. Obviously the classification "coffee shop" includes different things in Korea than it does in the United States. Coffee, one soon discovers, is considered not a food beverage but an entertainment beverage, like soda pop or a highball or wine or beer. And Korean coffee shops seldom serve much more than coffee and raw eggs in the morning. Moreover, they function not as places for dispensing food but as places of entertainment. In the evening one notices very quickly that the waitresses in a Korean coffee shop are not the starched and efficient ladies of an American coffee shop: there are too many of them, and they spend a lot of time sitting with male customers, joking, flirting, and allowing certain very limited intimacies. In short, there is a complete behavioral style indicated to a Korean by the classification, "coffee shop"—a style completely different from what the term indicates to an American.

Or let us take another example, even more important. Arensberg and Kimball report in their study of rural Ireland that a male, no matter how old or what his experience, is considered a boy by the villagers of Ireland until he has inherited the family farm or become

See Conrad Arensberg and Solon Kimball, *Family and Community in Ireland* (Harvard University Press, 1968).

the proprietor of a farm by some other means. Now, one doesn't consider the opinions of boy in the same light as he listens to the advice of a man, and so it is in rural Ireland. There, to be a man means not merely to have certain physical characteristics, or to be of a certain age, or to have had certain experiences; one must also own a farm.

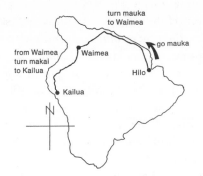

Figure 64. This map of the island of Hawaii illustrates the Hawaiian system of giving directions—in terms of topography, rather than cardinal points.

Until then he is classified as a boy and treated as such. And one finds that much of Irish rural culture centers around "boyish" things— soccer and football, horse racing, casual drinking, and an occasional friendly fight at the pub.

The fact that different peoples see things differently is not in and of itself a new discovery. Anthropologists have recognized this fact almost since the beginning of the science. They have spoken of cultural perceptions and the "world view" of various cultures and have stressed as part of the doctrine of cultural relativism that each culture has its own logic, meaningful within its own context and perhaps not so meaningful outside of it.

For instance, almost any tourist to Hawaii soon learns that in Hawaii the cardinal compass directions are seldom used in giving directions. Rather, people speak of traveling *mauka* or *makai*—"My house is on the *mauka* side of the road." What tourists do not learn is that these directions are part of a total Hawaiian system of locating things, a way of classifying directions, if you will. *Mauka,* which literally means "toward the center of the island," and *makai,* which means "toward the sea," are two vital reference points to any island dweller. In fact, since all islands are in a sense circular, north, south, east, and west aren't really very meaningful. High islands are seldom transversed; travelers usually move around the edge of an island instead. Thus, on the island of Hawaii, the little town of Kailua *is* west of the city of Hilo, but to get there one travels first north, then west, and then south—or first south, then west, and then north. Is one traveling west?

Far more meaningful is a statement as to the spot one is headed for. Thus, to get from Hilo to Kailua one travels first *Hamakua* (up the Hamakua coast), then turns *mauka* and travels toward Waimea; and then from Waimea, *makai* toward Kailua. In the city of Hilo, directions are not given in cardinal points but in references such as: "The accident occurred as the Puna-bound car was turning *mauka* onto X street." I once read in a police report: "The body was in the *makai Hamakua* corner of the room." Through careful questioning and recording, an anthropologist can establish the critical factors which combine to provide Hawaiians with a system of directions and locations. It is interesting that Icelanders, confronted with much the same kind of topography, solved their problems in much the same way. To make the comparison, however, comparable data must be collected; this is what modern ethnoscientists are able to do.

According to cognitive theory, modern anthropology ought to be able to describe a culture completely from the viewpoint of that culture, in terms intelligible to an outsider, by simply presenting all its classification systems—kinsmen, natural phenomena, men, animals, weather, etc., etc., etc. And it is exactly those three etceteras which cause the trouble. No one has seriously tried to do such an exhaustive job and no one as yet has even suggested it is practically possible.

Nonetheless, the cognitive approach—that is, viewing culture as a map which guides our actions, and also the ethnoscientific methodology that enables an anthropologist to demonstrate precisely how he came to his conclusions about the way a culture classifies a particular phenomenon—this approach is a useful and important step forward in man's investigation of himself. Prior to the introduction of these methods, anthropologists often gathered and presented voluminous details about one people or another, and stated their conclusions about how this people looked at the world, but were often unable to demonstrate precisely how they came to their conclusions. For many of us, were the truth to be known, it was a matter of not quite knowing ourselves; of responding to "feel," or a sense of the people or place, or long practice by trial and error to know what was expected of people in a given situation. This special feeling is not something that can be abandoned even by the most systematic field worker, particularly when he attempts to describe the larger dimensions of a culture, but it can be supported and buttressed by modern field methods, such as ethnoscience.

CULTURE AS A PATTERN

11

THE CONCEPT OF PATTERN

A pattern is not the thing itself. One buys a dress pattern, which provides a model for cutting and stitching the dress. A mold provides us with the pattern of the eventual casting, and so on. In this sense, then, to examine culture as a pattern is to search for the ideals of behavior and attitude that are held by a people—the ways things ought to be done, not necessarily the ways they are done.

This distinction has caused endless debate in anthropology which seems needless to me. Every culture appears to have standards of behavior, a view of how a real person ought to act. Not infrequently, a person will describe behavior in terms of such standards when, in fact, he and most of the people in his society do not actually behave the way they say people ought to behave. That is important. But it is also important that people are often aware that their behavior or attitudes do not always jibe with culturally accepted patterns—and they generally have a culturally acceptable reason to justify this variation.

An example is postmarital residence among the Navajo. The Navajo pattern—that is, the ideal for a young married couple—is to take up residence near the home of the bride's mother; in short, they are matrilocal. However, a number of field workers have pointed out that this is not invariably the case.

In many parts of the reservation, almost half the married couples live somewhere other than with the bride's mother. Therefore, some people have argued that earlier investigators were in error—that the Navajo are *not* matrilocal. However, if one pushes on in his investigations and questions people as to why they are living where they are living, he discovers that in every instance a Navajo has a good reason for not living with the bride's mother—but nonetheless admits that living with the bride's mother is the "right" or "best" way to arrange one's life. Furthermore, a Navajo informant seldom speaks of living with the groom's father (that is, patrilocally); rather, he says he is living with the groom's *mother*.

What does all this have to do with pattern? First, we find that Navajo regularly respond to the question, "Where do you live when you get married?" by saying, "With the bride's mother." And even when they do not, in fact, live with the bride's mother, they emphasize the female relative with whom they do live rather than the male relative. All of this confirms a theme in Navajo culture that emphasizes the female side of society. One is a member of one's mother's clan. One lives with the bride's mother. A man's children belong to the clan of his wife. The birth of a girl baby is celebrated more than the birth of a boy baby. In religion, the dominant figure is that of the Changing Woman—and so on. Thus, the pattern or recurring theme of Navajo life is an emphasis on the female. There are many acceptable reasons why an individual cannot live up to the ideal pattern, but this in no way challenges the fact that the Navajo do respond in a certain way to most of life's problems.

These might be called *specific* patterns, but some anthropologists have suggested that each culture has an *overall* pattern that gives coherence to the universe and to the relationships between people. Ruth Benedict, in her book, *Patterns of Culture*—one of the most widely read anthropology books ever written—develops this theme most completely. Comparing the culture of the Zuñi Indians with that of the Great Plains, she argues that these people had two different general patterns of gauging all behavior. The Zuñi, she argues, were

Ruth Benedict, *Patterns of Culture* (Houghton Mifflin, 1934). Mentor Books issued a paperback edition in 1946, and it has been reprinted many times since then.

Figure 65. Although each society appears to have a cultural ideal image for each sex, there are always those who violate the norm. The Hopi of the Southwest United States prize harmony and peacefulness above all else. But some individuals were still bellicose, despite the norm. The ideal Zuñi man was also calm and non-aggressive, although there were individuals who did not live up to the ideal. Among the Indians of the Great Plains, almost the opposite male image existed. But the non-aggressive male in those cultures could choose to occupy a "woman's position" without disgrace.

Apollonian; that is, they sought in all things a balance, a lack of conflict, a degree of harmony and organization. This, she argues, was explicit in their styles of interpersonal relationship, in their social organization, ritual and mythology. On the other hand, she says, the Plains Indians emphasized the exciting, the highly individualistic, the orgiastic aspects of life—a pattern she labels *Dionysian*. Some other anthropologists have criticized her by pointing out that the Zuñi did compete with each other, gossip and feud, and otherwise acted in ways counter to the Apollonian ideal she describes.

The critics' information is no doubt true, but to repeat, the pattern is not the dress. Nor is behavior the pattern. People violate patterns—act in ways which do not adhere to the standards set by the pattern. No culture can be so rigid as not to admit to human variation or not to have developed accepted ways to meet the exigencies of life. The Zuñi, for instance, did have a system for waging war when they had to. They did not, however, glorify war and the warrior. To them, war was an unpleasant necessity. To the Plains tribes, in contrast, war was the reason for a man's being born. If it did not occur, one went out and made it happen. Both people fought and had warriors and weapons, but the difference in their *attitudes* toward the war is the issue.

This is not to deny that there may have been individual Zuñi men who gloried in war—who enjoyed the danger and the risk and the approbation of their people when they acquitted themselves well in a fight. However, for them Zuñi life in general must have been something of a burden. Similarly, there most assuredly were Plains Indians who did not seek recognition in warfare, and there were men who did not respond to the rigorous, individualistic, religious system in which each man sought his own dream and guiding vision. For them, life on the plains was no great pleasure. For some, Plains culture provided an escape valve which allowed them to choose the role of a woman and abandon completely the life of the hunt and the war trail. There were some who advocated cooperation and the submission of individual desires to the goals of the group. There were, indeed, times when that was exactly what was done among the Plains tribes. The individual who hunted the buffalo before the tribe as a whole had begun the hunt would most certainly suffer severe punishment. But in general the Plains Indians saw the world in a different way than did the Zuñi.

Anthropological studies that discussed culture patterns were the basis of later work, particularly during and immediately after World War II, called *national character studies*. In a sense, these studies sought to isolate the general cultural patterns of modern nations in an attempt to provide a basis for political policy-making predictions about how each country would act under specific circumstances. They have often been criticized because in many cases the writers did not do field work in the subject country but depended on interviews with expatriots, motion pictures, literature, etc. Nonetheless, such studies often proved to be remarkably useful. Perhaps general patterns reveal themselves more clearly at a distance than they do in the intimate field-work situation. Perhaps the writers were simply very insightful, after the manner of novelists rather than systematic scientists.

In any event the bulk of our experience with the study of culture suggests that one of the vital facts of culture is that it is patterned and produces patterned behavior. That is, people within a single cultural context tend to behave in similar ways, often in situations where it is difficult to understand precisely how the pattern was communicated. It was a shock and a relief to many millions of Americans to discover how similar their sexual behavior was to that described by the respondents in the research conducted by Dr. Alfred Kinsey. Americans had tended before this pioneering work to think of their own behavior as somewhat deviant. "Am I normal?" was the question most frequently asked of Dr. Kinsey's investigators. Certainly very little overt instruction was given in American culture as to sexual behavior, and yet the statistics showed a remarkable amount of similarity—that is, patterned behavior. The Americans interviewed tended to make love in a certain way, have certain kinds of sexual experiences at certain points in their lives, and the like. In a sense, each person had thought himself a violator of a set of absolute standards, which everyone else obeyed. When he discovered that this was not so, he was surprised and relieved.

See Kinsey, Pomeroy, and Martin, *Sexual Behavior in the Human Male* (W. B. Saunders, 1948); and Kinsey, Pomeroy, Martin, and Gebhard, *Sexual Behavior in the Human Female* (W. B. Saunders, 1953).

EXAMPLES

Let us take another example. Once, when traveling in Japan, I ran out of funds and was forced to borrow one hundred and fifty dollars from a Japanese friend of mine. As soon as I returned to the United States, I sent him a check for one hundred dollars. By return mail, I received a letter acknowledging payment and a package containing an expensive string of cultured pearls, which I knew he must have bought with part of the money I had sent him. The pearls were a gift to my daughter, he said. Shortly thereafter, I was back in Japan and had dinner with the same gentleman. I gave him in an envelope (it is less than good taste to handle money openly in Japan) the remaining fifty dollars I owed him. As we said goodnight at my hotel, he presented *me* with an envelope containing twenty-five of that fifty. A gift for my youngest son, he said. In short, he would not let me repay him completely. He politely but stubbornly rejected my attempt to relieve myself of the obligation I had to him.

See Ruth Benedict, *The Chrysanthemum and the Sword: Patterns of Japanese Culture* (World Publishing, 1967).

This is simply an incident, but if we read Ruth Benedict's work, *The Chrysanthemum and the Sword*, we find that her research led

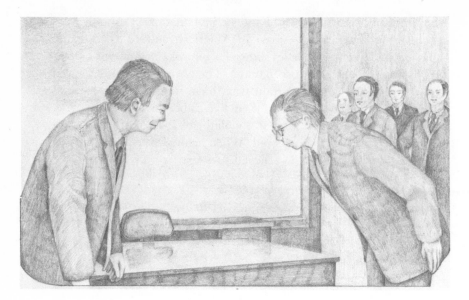

Figure 66.   Which of these Japanese businessmen is the social superior of the other? What was the basis of your answer?

her to conclude that there is a pattern in Japanese culture that encourages a person to attempt to keep others obligated to him, but to avoid obligation, if possible. Those are rather abstract terms and I am sure most Japanese do not wander around repeating that rule to themselves. Rather, in dozens of situations they simply act according to those principles. Two elderly men will alternately bow to each other time and again until one stops, thereby acknowledging that he owes a bit more respect than he received and thus is obligated in a sense to the other—and in this case it is most apt to be the older who ends up being owed by the younger, or the social superior being owed by the social inferior.

This reveals another pattern of Japanese culture, the hierarchial ranking of almost every human relationship. The basis of the hierarchy may be social position, education, age, or any number of other factors—or combination of factors—but however things are combined, no two people are ever absolutely equal in Japanese culture and this inequality must be recognized in one way or another. Contrast this to an American pattern which, rather than emphasizing natural or social differences, always tries to mask them. The publisher of a newspaper in public speeches usually boasts that he once was, and still is at heart, just a newspaper reporter. Generals, despite their medals and stars and prerogatives, like to intimate that they are simple soldiers just like the troops in the ranks. Industrialists emphasize their humble origins and the hard work in their past, and try to give the impression of being "one of the boys." The differences are just as real as they are in Japan, but this pattern of American culture requires that we publicly minimize them while, in Japan, cultural patterns require that they be maximized—invented if they do not exist.

I recall one time in Korea spending some time with a rather highly placed Korean official, with advanced degrees equal to my own and of about my own age, who constantly called me "Dr. Downs" and deferred to me in every way. It happens that I wear a beard that has been white since my early thirties, so I looked to him like a much older man than he (in Korea beards are reserved for respected elders). In the course of a dinner party I mentioned my age, which was in fact two years younger than his, and in midsentence his demeanor changed, and he began to use my first name and treat me very familiarly. In Korea, the use of the given name is a sign of great intimacy and is invariably initiated by the superior or elder. Once again, the Korean gentleman did not repeat to himself that little rule; rather, he simply shifted to behavior which was more appropriate in his mind.

The concept of cultural pattern is certainly less rigorous and more difficult to deal with than the cognitive approach outlined in the last chapter, but the two are not related. The way people classify things is in itself determined by cultural patterns. Americans and most people of the Western or European tradition, for instance, tend to see things in groups of three—every play has a beginning, a middle, and an end; three strikes you are out, and so on. Other cultures do not necessarily find these natural and meaningful divisions by three. Things are apt to appear to many American Indians as falling into natural sequences of four. While I was conducting research on the Navajo reservation, I attended many ritual–social observances called "squaw dances" and from my observations saw them as events which lasted three nights. I was surprised to learn that the Navajo with whom I lived always considered them as lasting four nights, although to my way of thinking the fourth night was hardly part of the observance at all. They were equally puzzled, thinking that anyone would not see that in fact a squaw dance was four days long. Irrespective of our points of view, the same things happened at the same time in each squaw dance. How many days we counted was a product of the cultural perspective of the viewer. Similarly, when American Indians describe ceremonies of the past they not infrequently say they lasted four days even though there is evidence to the contrary. One Washo informant of mine once said about another informant's description of ceremony no longer practiced: "Oh, sometimes they was two days, sometimes three. Don't believe them other guys. They say four just to make it sound important." Why should saying something lasted four days make it more impressive than three or five?—for the same reason that Christian theologians who stubbornly insist they are monotheists have developed the Holy Trinity: because solving things in fours is satisfying to Washo Indians just as explaining things in threes is satisfying to Europeans.

Similarly, Americans like to organize and vote on things. Alexis de Tocqueville, traveling in America in the 1830's, described with puzzlement the willingness of Americans to organize, meet, debate issues, and tally votes. This is not true of many other cultures, which

There are many editions of de Tocqueville's famous book, *Democracy in America*, both hardbound and in paper; many of them are in two volumes. One reliable edition, with translation from the original French by H. Reeve, was issued by the Oxford University Press in 1947.

find voting an embarrassing process that makes people take sides and creates the possibility of schism in the society, or in which the idea of *one man, one vote* is abhorrent—how can the vote of a beardless youth mean as much as the vote of a wise elder? For yet others, voting is tyrannical because a small majority can force its will on a large minority. Many American Indians saw the imposition of "democratic principles" as a terrible restriction of their freedom. To them freedom meant just that, the freedom to decide for themselves whether they would follow one leader or another, go to war or stay home, observe an agreement or break it. For Americans, on the other hand, the tendency is to organize committees or meetings and have votes about things which cannot possibly be decided by such means. Many universities are bogged down in administrative inefficiency because they insist on observing the form of democracy and establish committees to govern all sorts of administrative procedures. In the final analysis, the committees are seldom able to make decisions fast enough

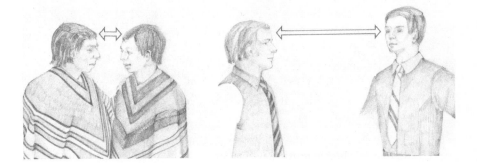

Figure 67. *Social distance*—the "comfortable" space between an individual and another person—is determined by the individual's cultural heritage.

or clearly enough to get the job done. But Americans would feel distinctly uncomfortable were they to admit that the democratic principles were applicable only to certain situations. Despite a so-called generation gap between students and their professors, we find that most of those who protest the inefficiency and lack of response of American universities seem mollified if they are but admitted into the process of making cumbersome decisions through boards and committees. As often as not, the basic problems remain unchanged.

Patterned behavior is demonstrated constantly in our daily lives. The fact that we do observe patterns of action and reaction makes it possible for us to anticipate other people's behavior and get on with the business of the day. Thus, our most minute actions are apt to be those shared by most people in a culture—the things none of us think about as we go through the day. To test this, resolve for a time to stand no farther than one foot away from anyone you talk to. You will find that people begin backing away from you, trying to maintain the somewhat wider space that is a patterned part of American social interactions. If, on the other hand, you were in Brazil, you might resolve to remain at least eighteen inches away from everyone you spoke to and find that people kept pursuing you because the patterns of Brazilian social discourse call for very short distances between people who are engaged in conversation.

SYSTEMATIC PATTERN AND STYLE

There is yet another way to apply the concept of pattern to the study and understanding of culture: that is to analyze a specific set of culture material—actions, technical traits, religious beliefs, or what have you—that seem to always appear together. This is most obvious in the technical side of culture. A. L. Kroeber has called these "systematic patterns." The automobile is an interesting case in point. Since its invention, the automobile has developed an entire system of technical and behavioral supports for its existence. The automobile is not really part of a culture until there are roads, places for obtaining fuel and service, and some means of obtaining spare parts and repairs. Invariably, cars are licensed and taxed, drivers are licensed, and laws are passed concerning driving behavior. These constitute a core of traits which have spread with the automobile across the world.

Kroeber illustrated the same point by discussing plow agriculture, which "Comprises the plow itself; animals to draw it; domestication of these beasts; grains of the barley or wheat type sown by broadcast scattering, without attention to the individual seed, seedling, or plant; fields larger than gardens and of some length; and fertilization with dung, primarily from the draft animals." Without any one of these components, the plow agriculture system would collapse or could not be adopted. We can see this in our agriculture today, in which the draft animals have been replaced in large part by machine. This replacement took place very rapidly after 1930 in the United States, and it almost totally transformed agriculture culturally and socially. Only the plow (in greatly modified forms) and the broadcast seeding of plants remain. There are other systems of agriculture that do not include all these elements that have developd in Asia and in the New World—each with different processes for breaking the ground, different plants, and different social systems rising from the technical systems.

Kroeber also devoted a great deal of attention to the question of pattern and the associated idea of cultural style. He said that we can sometimes observe the systematic patterns of an entire culture coming to some sort of a climax—achieving the logical conclusions of the directions indicated by adherence to certain patterns of thought and behavior. After these conclusions have been arrived at, there is little more that can be done which is original or meaningful within a given system. Many primitive or tribal societies are examples of this: we can see the development of a style and then the continuation of that pattern for a long, long time with little change. It is as if nothing new can come out of that way of doing things. Perhaps this explains the long sequences in the archaeological record of the Great Basin and parts of California, where almost no difference between the earliest and the latest artifacts can be found. Perhaps these cultures developed a specific adaptation to the environment and, having done that, could do little more than repeat and repeat and repeat. Any change meant almost the total disruption of the entire system, followed by the rapid disappearance of the original cultural pattern and its replacement by another.

See A. L. Kroeber, *Configurations of Culture Growth* (University of California Press, 1944).

This, Kroeber suggests, is what happened in Greece between 600 and 300 B.C., the period of Greece's classic greatness. Politics, the military arts, medicine and the sciences, philosophy, drama, sculpture, architecture, and the social system that was uniquely Greek had gradually developed for several hundred years before 600 B.C. Then suddenly all these areas produced discoveries and successes that have been revered by the world ever since. After 300 B.C., however, Greece ceased to produce the original and innovative, and fell rapidly into eclipse in the shadow of Rome, which was developing another distinct cultural pattern.

There are those today who suggest that perhaps the patterns or style of American culture has climaxed and that we can be expected to produce little in the way of cultural advances without drastic departures from our past patterns. History will tell us whether this is right or not, but we must consider that perhaps the very patterns that helped us solve many problems are not useful today except to reproduce the past with its achievements and failures without improving on one or correcting the other.

One other use of the idea of pattern has been made by Clark Wissler, who suggested that there is a universal pattern for all cultures, composed of those traits possessed by all cultures— social organization, religion, the family, warfare, etc. However, this was so broad an approach that those who followed could do little more than nod their heads in agreement. True, in order to include the religions of all cultures, some widely varied phenomena had to be included under the same rubric (see Chapter Sixteen). Some authorities would suggest that war did not in fact exist among certain very simple peoples. But in general very little has been done with the idea, because it is simply too vast and too general to lend itself to examination and elaboration. Nonetheless, it or something like it has been the basis of the tables of contents of most ethnographic accounts of the world's cultures, with each part of the "universal pattern" used as a chapter heading.

CULTURE AS A COMBINATION OF TRAITS

12

TRAITS AND TRAIT COMPLEXES

In the last chapter I used the word *traits,* and I felt oddly old fashioned and out of date as I wrote it. Modern anthropologists do not use the term much anymore, but once—really, not long ago—it was central to anthropological theory. The development of the idea of culture traits was, like the concept of ethnoscience, an attempt to make anthropological research systematic and more scientific. It is helpful, when confronted with a phenomenon or a problem, to divide it into its components; this was what the culture-trait idea was all about.

The trait was conceived of as a kind of cultural atom—a unit of description which could be useful in the analysis of cultures, just as the idea of

the atom or molecule is useful in analyzing chemical and physical elements. We can describe a molecule of water as being composed of one hydrogen and two oxygen atoms. Although atoms are grouped in different molecular arrangements, they comprise a single class of things and thus can be compared. Would it not be useful and convenient to describe cultural phenomena in the same way? Indeed it would, and in fact such work was done; the trait concept was very useful in the compilation of cultural facts.

A culture trait was conceived of as anything people did, thought, owned, made, or believed. The fact that the Navajo believe it is bad luck to speak directly to a dog is a culture trait. So is the presence in a culture of the bow and arrow. It is a culture trait to believe in one god or two, practice polygamy, or build square houses. Field work, then, could be considered the job of compiling a "trait list"—that is, a complete inventory of the traits present in a culture. At the University of California, anthropologists devoted many years to the compiling of trait/distribution lists for various western American Indian tribes, particularly in the 1930's and early 1940's.

Not only could one list the individual traits present in a culture, but one could see that certain traits—that is, *complexes* of traits—always appeared together. We have spoken of this kind of thing when we talked of systematic patterns. The Sun Dance, a ritual practiced by virtually all the tribes on the Great Plains, was viewed not as a single trait but as a very complex collection of traits. In some tribes the trait complex, as it was called, might contain more or fewer single traits; that is, one or more parts of the ritual might be carried out among the Cheyenne and not among the Comanche. The Cheyenne, in fact, had a more elaborate Sun Dance system than any other tribe on the Great Plains, and it served in the minds of ethnographers as a kind of model of what a Sun Dance ought to be. Other tribes' rituals were compared to the Cheyenne system in terms of whether or not one trait or another was present or absent.

See Leslie Spier, *The Sun Dance of the Plains Indians: Its Development and Diffusion* (American Museum of Natural History, 1921).

Now, as a descriptive device the concepts of the trait and the trait complex were very useful, but as an analytic device they proved to be less so. One of the problems with the trait was that it would never stay in one piece. Any trait could be endlessly divided, depending on the interests of the investigator or the point of view of his informant. For instance, is the bow a trait? Some would have said yes. But on the other hand, when one knows something about bows, there are all sorts of subdivisions one can make in the category, "bows." Is it a *simple* bow (that is, a single piece of wood, shaped and curved); is it a *complex* bow (made of two or more materials)? Or is it a *reflex* bow (made so that it is curved against the pull of the string)? And the string itself—is it made of sinew or fibre, and how

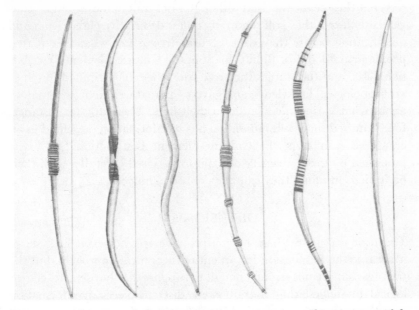

Figure 68.   American Indian bows: great variety in sophistication to fulfill the same basic function.

is it made (braided, twisted, and so on)? With each of these subdivisions, new questions rise.

In fact, then, each "trait" could become a "trait complex," and the subdividing never ended. It was as if each atom could be analyzed as a combination of other atoms. The problem is, of course, that until one can make one's categories stand still and remain on the same level of classification, one cannot compare them. To say, for instance, that the Hopi Indians and the Navajo Indians both possessed the trait "bow" was just not enough. The Hopi made and used a very simple bow, whereas the Navajo brought into the American Southwest a far more efficient and complex weapon that required different materials, and different skills to manufacture; the Navajo bow was simply not the same thing, save in the most general way.

Thus, to say that the Hopi and the Navajo cultures are the same, in the sense that they both possessed "the bow," would be an untrue "truth." They do indeed possess the bow, but that fact itself reveals differences and not similarities. The two bows could not be compared in any meaningful way—nor could a host of other "traits" which, on the surface, looked very similar, once a persistent investigator began to prod and analyze.

What this meant was that although brief trait names could be conveniently listed, they still required endless descriptive elaboration and qualification before they were accurate records of what this or that people actually did or didn't do. Still, the Culture Element Distribution Lists, and the studies that rose from them, contributed much to anthropological knowledge and gave us a great wealth of information about what various people did in their lives. There are, for instance, four hundred thousand individual bits of information presented in an organized fashion in the Culture Element Distribution List Series published by the University of California. Used carefully, with their limitations in mind, they can be very useful indeed.

DIFFUSIONISM

The trait was more than a descriptive device, however, in a sense, it became the foundation for an entire theoretical approach—but the trait was simply not strong enough to support that burden. It seemed logical to suggest that if traits were discrete pieces of information about practices or beliefs, and if one could find them in various cultures, then perhaps one could reconstruct their movement from one culture to another.

Under the leadership of Franz Boas, American anthropologists had rejected the theories of cultural evolutionists; that is, those who purported to outline the laws of cultural evolution for all time. Boas had argued that we simply didn't have enough information about culture to make general laws. His students were taught to devote themselves to less flamboyant tasks than theory-making and to collect, collect, collect. And, indeed, they did—which may be why so much emphasis was placed on the trait as a device for recording comparable data. However, abandoning the idea of cultural evolution, even temporarily, left a vacuum which was filled by what was then conceived of as an anti evolutionary theory: *diffusion*.

There were those who argued that most cultures did not develop internally, but mainly by borrowing from other cultures. No one can seriously argue that cultures do not borrow from each other. Our language is full of words from virtually every other language—our material lives packed with objects, materials, and ideas which originated outside our own system. Our essential beliefs are not in any sense purely American, having had their origins in the ancient Near East, or classical Greece, or Rome, or somewhere else. No one has made this point more clearly than Ralph Linton in his famous essay on the modern American man. But to assume that human beings are simply not smart enough to invent something more than once—so that the appearance of any trait in two places automatically implies diffusion from another culture—is hard to swallow, at least today.

See Ralph Linton, *The Study of Man: An Introduction* (Appleton-Century-Crofts, 1936), pp. 326–327.

Nevertheless, the idea of traits and trait complexes, combined with the idea of diffusion, apparently gave anthropologists a way to study the history of people who had not written any history—and in the nineteenth century and for most of this century, history was a major focus of anthropology. To be sure, scholars were looking for the universal principles that shaped history and cultural development, but they largely devoted themselves to the question of what had happened in the past. Often, this amounted to asking how such and such a trait had diffused from one people to another. At this point, the question being asked was not about the process of diffusion—that is, how does one people adopt an idea or a practice from another—but about the time-sequence and direction of diffusion.

Now there is a logical problem in all this. If fifteen tribes all practice the same basic dance ritual, we can assume that the idea passed from one to another of these people. That is, someone probably invented the dance and other people borrowed it. (There are those who would argue that that is not necessarily so, but for the sake of argument let's assume that it is.) How can one determine by looking at this phenomenon who invented it and in which direction it spread, and what was the sequence of adoption? In short, how can one turn space (the distribution of a trait) into time (the history of a trait)?

A rather elaborate and, on the surface of it, logical scheme was developed which attempted to do this—turn space into time. The argument went something like this: If something was invented—a pottery form, design element, dance, ritual, or what have you—it would, in the beginning, be simple. In that form the trait or complex would be borrowed. At the same time, the inventor culture would be elaborating it. While this elaboration was going on at the point of origin, the first borrower would become the donor to the second borrower—at the same time borrowing the *elaborated* form from the originator. Thus—to follow the logic—we need only discover where the trait or trait complex is most elaborate to know where it originated; we then explore the geographical distribution in terms of relative elaboration in order to know precisely in what sequence a trait or an entire complex of traits diffused through an area—or, in fact, the world.

Now, one can examine that premise for a long time without finding fault in it. However, the evidence simply doesn't support the theory, when the evidence is known. The theory was developed to deal with situations where written historical evidence was lacking. The Great Plains of the United States was an important focus of this kind of work. The elements of a general Great Plains culture were worked out in great detail by students of the area. The basic elements were the horse and the pursuit of the buffalo, the unique skin tepee, certain rituals and religious ideas, patterns of clothing and costume, the emphasis on warfare and individualism. One seldom makes mistakes in identifying a material object that originated on the Great Plains, as compared with other objects made in the West, or Northwest, or Southwest.

The most elaborate form of the Plains culture—where all the identified elements were present, plus many not found in other plains cultures—was felt to be that of the Cheyenne, who lived in the Dakotas and Wyoming and in parts of Colorado. Earlier books on the American Indians state this very clearly: the Cheyenne were the typical Plains Indians. However, when archaeologists began to dig on the Great Plains, and when tribal mythologies were closely examined, and the accounts written by early travelers, trappers, and explorers on the Great Plains were studied the diffusionists' conclusions turned out to be the reverse of the truth.

THE AGE–AREA HYPOTHESIS QUESTIONED

Far from being the first people to take advantage of the horse and to turn to the pursuit of the buffalo, the Cheyenne were among the last. How then did they develop such a "typical" Plains culture? Rather than being the great originators, it would seem they were the great borrowers. Much of what was distinctive on the Great Plains had already been elaborated by others—the Sioux and Shoshone, Comanche and Lipan-Apache, Kiowa and Arikira, the Cree and Blackfoot—and still others. The Cheyenne had simply to adopt from many sources what others had done.

Ralph Linton—who had the ability to see the illogic in the seemingly logical schemes—"proved," using the diffusionist theory (called the age–area hypothesis), that corn and tobacco originated in Africa when we know that they developed in the Americas.

The fact that studies of the distribution of some cultural practice cannot be made to yield infallible historical results does not mean that such studies are useless, however. They reveal to us many of the facts about human behavior and history which are essential for scientific analysis. The superstructure of theory built upon the concept of the culture trait was truly enormous, and to a degree we still live with it, long after the concept itself has fallen into disuse or more properly found its rightful place in the science. Not only could entire cultures be described in terms of the traits and trait complexes practiced by the people, but also entire areas were defined in terms of common traits.

The Great Plains of the United States was one of these—perhaps the most thoroughly studied, and the region which appeared to support the idea most completely. The rest of North America was divided into culture areas: the Eastern Woodlands, the Southeast, the Prairies, the Great Basin and Plateu, California, the Northwest Coast, the Southwest—and so on. Each area was defined by a series of culture-trait complexes—social, material, religious, even psychological—which seemed to distinguish them one from the other. Anthropologists also set out to divide and define the whole world in culture-area terms; such attempts were made for South America, Africa, Asia, and the islands of the Pacific.

Now it should be remembered that there are indeed geographical areas within which societies tend to share many culture traits. However, when this obvious fact is explored and systematized—particularly in the Old World, where cultures were more complex in many ways than they were among American Indians, where cultures had been in contact through war and diplomacy and trade and migration for thousands of years and where written history was often available—the problem became more and more difficult. Decisions tended to be made upon geographic, environmental, economic—even racial or linguistic—evidence rather than purely in terms of culture traits.

Nonetheless, it was during the heyday of the culture-trait kind of thinking that most anthropology departments were established, and the curriculum of most of them tended to be divided into courses devoted to exploring in detail the various culture areas. Many departments today still retain remnants of culture-area thought. This continues even though we no longer use the trait idea as a primary conceptual tool in modern anthropology. In many departments, the culture area has simply been replaced by geographic areas, because no distinct culture area has been defined for every part of the globe. Anthropology departments still often feel that they should have a faculty member representing each of the "cultural–geographic areas" of the world. Only recently have they begun to think in terms of the theoretical or topical areas of the discipline as a point of organization rather than culture–geography.

> Until recently, anthropology curriculum tended to be organized around a core of "Peoples of _____" courses, each dealing with a different cultural or geographical area ("Peoples of Africa," for instance). Anthropology faculties tended then to be composed of professors who each specialized in one cultural geographic area. Today, theoretical or topical interests are increasingly reflected in anthropology curriculum: pastoral peoples, applied anthropology, social organization, or war, for instance. Faculties tend to be less concerned about having complete geographic coverage, and may indeed prefer to have several professors who have different theoretical interests although they have worked in the same general geographical area.

It is often fashionable in scholarly circles to decry the work of previous generations, particularly those aspects of their work which are today out of fashion or appear to have been in error. It would be a great mistake to do this in case of the work based on the idea of culture traits and all the ideas which sprang from it. First, the trait list—as inadequate as it might be—gave us a systematic approach to the collection of a great deal of information about many cultures. Moreover, in the discovery of the weakness of the trait idea, we can see, I think, the beginnings of lines of thought which led to today's methods of anthropological investigation. The realization that how one defined a trait depended in large part on the context in which it appeared led to the formulation of a number of useful lines of thought, including the idea of cognitive anthropology. The twin ideas of form and function, which are very important in understanding other peoples, are a product of problems discovered in distribution studies and comparisons arising from them. Finally, from the culture-area theory there developed what we now call cultural ecology, which we will discuss in the next chapter.

CULTURE AND ENVIRONMENT I: INTERRELATIONSHIPS

13

ENVIRONMENTAL DETERMINISM

The relationship between the behavior of a people and the environment in which they find themselves has long been acknowledged. Often, simple one-to-one linkages are part of common "knowledge." For instance: people from the tropics are supposed to be lazy because it is so hot that it is too much trouble to work, or because nature is so bountiful that they don't ever have to work hard to get enough to eat. Of such ideas as these are made very elaborate theories about the nature of human history and the factors involved in the development of cultures and civilizations. Many of these ideas once had strong influence in anthropology, probably because some of our earliest academic ancestors were geographers and we inherited much from them— perhaps including the urge to study the distribution of culture traits as described in the previous chapter.

Around the turn of this century, when Darwin's idea of natural selection was widely accepted, social scientists saw many analogies between biological and historical processes, and became even more involved with biological or environmental explanations of human behavior. At the same time, evidence about past civilizations was beginning to accumulate through the efforts of archaeologists. And we cannot forget the influence of Karl Marx on social thought; his theories about society insisted on a close relationship between the economic production system and social attitudes and behavior. Inasmuch as economic systems are a link between man and environment, then, it follows that many people—who were not in any sense political Communists, but who were influenced by Marxian theory—also became interested in man–environment relationships. (It is important to remember that Marx was primarily a social theorist, not a revolutionary.)

> For further discussion of the influence of environment on heredity, see Downs and Bleibtreu, *Human Variation: An Introduction to Physical Anthropology*, revised edition (Glencoe Press, 1972), chapter nine and pp. 77, 206–207.

One of the outcomes of this kind of interest was the florescence of very elaborate theories that lacked the evidence necessary to support them. One such was that of Ellsworth Huntington. He argued that men responded mainly to environmental challenges and that great civilizations and cultural advancement always appeared in those areas that challenged man's ingenuity but did not create impossible barriers against further attainments. Such areas, he felt were the global temperature zones—exactly the zones in which modern civilizations existed in Europe and North America. Most of the rest of the world was at that time (around the turn of the century) under the control of European empires. Environmental determinism, as such thinking was called, very usefully explained the existing political and social facts of the world: Europeans had no need to feel guilty about their colonial and imperial adventures, because nature had set the stage in the first place.

Environmental determinism was rejected because as the evidence piled up it did not fit the theory. Civilizations were uncovered in places they should not have been—in the tropics, in black Africa, and in the Indies. So-called savage cultures proved to be far more creative and elaborate than most Europeans wanted to admit. All in all, very few of the hard and fast rules of the environmental determinist held hard and fast. So for some time cultural anthropologists rejected the idea that there was any relationship at all: culture was culture and environment was environment, and the two were forever separate. Admittedly environment created limitations, particularly for tribal or preliterate cultures—but nothing more. One could point to endless examples of environmental opportunities (like the presence

Figure 69.   The stereotype of the indolent dweller of the tropics. In fact, the tropics are not a particularly benign environment, and most inhabitants work as hard as anyone else. Those who do not may have little energy because of endemic disease or poor diet.

of gold in aboriginal California) being ignored. Quite probably this period of disciplinary isolation was necessary to get anthropology's own house in order—to explore the phenomena of culture without distraction, and to develop field methods and analytical systems suited to its own particular quest. When I was an undergraduate, my most respected teacher stated flatly that there was little or no relation between environment and culture.

However, as we saw in the previous chapter, the linkage between geographical areas and the distribution of culture patterns was explored and culture areas were gradually delimited. For some, this was almost a mystique; culture patterns were felt to develop and remain in an area like some miasma or fog. Other scientists, notably A. L. Kroeber, asked why the cultures of the Great Plains should be different from those of the Plateau. Obviously there were environmental differences, so why not explore them? In his carefully researched book, *Cultural and Natural Areas of Native North America,* Kroeber explored the correlations between various patterns of culture and various environmental zones. In doing this he had to move himself out of the subject matter of anthropology into sciences like climatology, forestry, botany, and zoology.

See A. L. Kroeber's *Cultural and Natural Areas of Native North America* (University of California Press, 1939 and 1953.)

The need for such broad knowledge has been the biggest impediment in the development of meaningful studies in human ecology. The social scientist, like man in general, hates to find himself in unfamiliar territory. Yet if one is going to relate two phenomena he cannot expect to be completely familiar with both subjects at the beginning (although perhaps he should expect to be when he is done). Kroeber's pioneering gave respectability to such eclecticism and opened the way for an expansion of the question of precisely how human history did relate to environment. Since Kroeber's work was published a sound foundation for further exploration has been built. Some idiocies have been committed, and we will explore a few, but we have begun to develop a meaningful set of ideas to use in investigating this question.

FORM AND FUNCTION

For a few pages we must digress to discuss two very important concepts in anthropology: form and function. We could have dealt with them in detail in virtually any chapter of this book because they are germane to every aspect of social and cultural anthropology. (In fact, it might be a useful exercise to run back through the book when you have finished this section and point out to yourself where I have used illustrations of these twin concepts.)

See Ralph Linton, *The Study of Man: An Introduction* (Appleton-Century-Crofts, 1936), chapter twenty-three.

In essence the idea involved is simply that things in different cultures often look very much the same, but serve very different purposes or functions. That is, the outcome of such and such a custom is different in one tribe than it is in another, although the custom looks very similar. That, of course, is *function*. *Form* is the appearance of a custom or belief or material item. Here we might simply reverse what we just said and point out that things that appear to be quite different often perform similar functions in different societies. Thus, when we look back on the discussion of marriage forms in Chapter Seven, we see that they all—no matter what else they might do—serve to provide a regularized environment for the production and education of children. (We also mentioned the possible function of polyandry as a form of population control. In the United States the same ends are sought by using chemical and mechanical birth control devices.) We speak of these ideas now because in studying man and environment we are often studying technical operations and material culture as well. It is important to be sensitive to possible differences in function of things that look the same, or one's conclusions can be very wrong indeed.

For example, let's take the case of pigs in the Pacific Islands. A great deal of attention has been given to them. One reason is that, by and large, people prize pigs but they don't seem to have much use for them. Now, pigs in America and Europe are purely utilitarian animals; one raises pigs to eat them, or at least to sell to others who wish to eat pigs. But Melanesians and Polynesians seem to like to have pigs around. Owning a number of them brings prestige and social status. Therefore a number of scholars have concluded that pigs are not important economically to Pacific islanders but are kept as social symbols. Admittedly, pigs are eaten at feasts, like turkeys in the United States, but that is special and the feasts themselves are social events.

Finally, some investigators began to count the number of feasts and realized that although individual families seldom kill a pig and eat it, their diets contain a relatively large amount of pork because of the share which always falls to them at numerous feasts. In short, the form of pig use and consumption is very different from European and American practices. It is difficult for a single family to eat an entire pig before it spoils; but, by having pig feasts on a more or less regular basis, a large number of people can share and consume all the available flesh. Pigs, in fact, are very important in the economic or subsistence activities of these people; it is simply that they are consumed in a different context than is the case in America. A case of different forms, similar functions.

Cattle-herding people in Africa provide another example. Many East African peoples keep large herds of cattle—fight over them, steal them if possible, name themselves after them, praise, love, and appreciate them. But the cattle are never eaten. Their milk is used, and so is the blood—but meat seldom, if ever. To most Americans this is waste and wrongheadedness. Cattle are to be milked and eventually slaughtered and turned into beef. They have hard cash value. The quality of their beef is important, and how fast they fatten, and how much milk they give. To the Masai and the Nuer and others, the color of the coat and the shape of the horns are vital—and the number of cattle a person owns is much more of a concern than the quality of the animals. In short, the cow in these societies has an entirely different function, and it has to do with social status rather than subsistence. Of course, large numbers of poor cattle still produce milk and blood for food, but this is a secondary consideration. Cattle simply have a different place in the minds of these Africans; perhaps we could say they are placed in a different category in Africa from the one in which we place them in America.

One more case and perhaps we can go on. Hunting and fishing are leisure time activities to most Americans. They are hobbies to be carried out when one isn't working. Most American fishermen and hunters readily (if somewhat sheepishly) admit that whatever flesh they bring home could have been obtained much more inexpensively at the corner meat market. In short, the function of hunting in the United States is to entertain, relax, interest, or amuse.

In the small towns of Hawaii, hunting is a very important activity. Scarcely a weekend goes by without parties of men going into the rugged hills to kill wild pigs, goats, or sheep—or, on some of the islands, deer. Many people spend much of their spare time fishing. Yet if anyone were to interpret these activities as purely recreational he would be mistaking the function because of the form. The pigs, deer, sheep, and goats killed and the fish caught are important components of the local diet. Without them, families would have to spend much more money on meat and fish than they do today. In short, hunting functions quite differently in Hawaii than it does in the mainland United States.

THE STUDY OF CULTURAL ECOLOGY

The study of evolution has proven that the interaction of our prehuman ancestors with their environment produced the first humans— that is, creatures with a capacity for culture. This capacity then created the greatest selection pressure on the species. Man has constantly selected for a greater ability to think and use symbols and language, to form social units, and to manipulate objects in technical systems. That is, the creatures best able to perform these "human" tasks produced more offspring, in the long run, than those less capable. In short, environment created man.

We must now ask how man has related to environment since culture, not environment, became the primary factor in human existence.

The study of culture–environment relationships has been called *cultural ecology*. In contrast to biologists who study ecology, the concern of the anthropologist is with the cultural consequences of specific environmental situations. To understand these relationships he may well have to take into account biological factors, but his main concern is with culture.

Defining the Issues

Thus, the fact that an environment contains mosquitoes and this means that malaria is endemic, which in turn means a high infant mortality rate, is only part of a line of investigation for the cultural ecologist. His concern is how that series of facts influences the patterns of behavior or the cultural categories of the people who live in the malarial region. How do these people deal with malaria? What explanations do they give for it? What adjustments in their behavior and attitudes have they made because of it? Or, conversely, how does the presence of men living in a certain way influence the existence of malaria? Livingstone, for instance, has suggested that malaria in parts of Africa was a consequence of the spread of agriculture, which opened dense jungle regions and created more hospitable environments for mosquito breeding. The anthropological issue is culture, not the disease or the mosquito.

See F. B. Livingstone's "Anthropological Implications of Sickle Cell Gene Distribution in West Africa" (*American Anthropologist* 60, pp. 533–563).

Studies in cultural ecology have generally fallen into two types. The first and perhaps oldest type includes studies devoted to an exploration of the origins of a custom or practice, or material culture trait or complex. The search for the origins of domestic wheat, maize, animals, and the like, has of necessity focused on environmental questions. It is clear that man would not have domesticated wheat or corn or cattle had not the predomestic ancestors of those plants and animals been available to him in his environment. However, we should remember that simply because something exists in an environment does not mean that man will make use of it. Thus, the study of origins becomes the study of the environmental and cultural conditions that occur to encourage an invention—which of course is what the domestication of animals was.

Some scientists have argued that cattle, for instance, were domesticated first because the peoples of the ancient Near East wanted bulls available for religious reasons. That is a highly suspect argument, but one that was accepted for a long time. It does, however, show the tendency to emphasize cultural reasons for domestication rather than assuming, as many people did in earlier times, that the domestication of animals was simply a natural event—of animals destined to be domesticated finally succumbing to their fate.

The other kind of ecological study attempts to explain why some custom or practice continues to exist—that is, what is the environmental basis, if any, for the existence of patrilocal hunting bands, or polyandary, or regular feasts in which large numbers of pigs are killed and meat eaten, or the sacred status of cattle that are not killed or eaten.

While one might well have to discover the origin of a given custom before he can comment on why it continues (its function), the two kinds of questions are distinct. As we noted in Chapter Five, a practice may continue long after its initial function has changed. In common thinking, the answer to the question of why we do something is often best answered by reference to its origin. Thus we can ask: Why do soldiers salute each other? The answer most frequently given is that in medieval times knights lifted their visors to reveal their identity and show respect, and that the act of lifting the visor evolved into the salute. That may or may not be true, but it gives us no explanation of why modern soldiers salute. To understand that, we must study the modern army and its system of ranks and discipline, and see how saluting serves to keep the modern military system working. One does not have to know how or when sheep were domesticated to study how the Navajo Indians shape their lives in order to keep sheep, nor the origins of steel-making to understand how the production of ore and steel affects the lives of modern Americans.

Figure 70.   The military salute originated with the medieval practice of one knight's raising his visor so another could identify him. That does not explain why the modern military continues the practice. Can you suggest a reason?

Thus, origins and continuity are two different questions, both of which often yield to cultural ecological studies.

Navajo Sheep Raising

Ecological studies frequently reveal that some practice of a tribal people has its roots in the environment—though as often as not, on first examination, Americans or Europeans cannot understand the reason for practices which to them appear inefficient or unwise. For instance, among the Navajo, sheep are traditionally bred early in the fall, even in late summer. This is contrary to European and American practice because we wish to avoid lamb drops in the midst of winter when it is hard to care for young lambs and hard to feed their nursing ewes. So for several decades, American experts have been lecturing to Navajo sheepherders about the late breeding of sheep. In many places they have convinced the Navajo that they should change their ways. In others they have not, so that one can now compare the two systems in the Navajo natural and cultural environment. It turns out that, despite the certainties of American animal scientists, areas which adhere to the older system have larger lambs the following fall when the lambs go to market. This happens in spite of severe winters and sparse food, which often has to be scraped from under the snow in order for the sheep to eat.

> See J. F. Downs, *Animal Husbandry in Navajo Society and Culture* (University of California Publications in Anthropology, Volume I, 1964).

What the animal scientists did not look at was the way the Navajo social and cultural system related to the nature of sheep and the environment of northern Arizona. Traditionally, when the Navajo were great warriors, and today when many people go off the reservation to work in the summer and fall, the winter is a time when the Navajo remain close to home. In small winter camps tucked into the protective folds of the mesas and hills, all the people of a homestead group are present. Thus, in the winter there are more people to care for sheep than at any other time of the year. There are hands to do the extra work involved in raising newborn lambs in the bitter winter. There are people to build little houses for them to live in, to keep fires burning all night to warm the lambs and to rub and massage them if needed. There are a number of men to gather wood, and both men and women to divide the job of herding. There are always people in camp who can respond to the herder's mirror-flash signal to come and pick up a newly dropped lamb. And by having the lambs drop early the Navajo can take advantage of every bit of new growth in the spring to feed nursing ewes and to properly start the new lambs.

Moreover, the winter struggle against the elements to save the lamb crop is one of the experiences which unifies the entire Navajo family each year. The welfare of all is dependent on cooperation, and the forced cooperation to save the lamb crop in December and January and February and March is a constant reminder of how important the family is to each individual. It is not likely that the Navajo sat down to figure all this out. Rather, they let nature take its course among the breeding sheep and then adjusted their lives to nature's course.

Americans, on the other hand, seldom have available two dozen adults who could cooperate in the lambing of a single herd. Thus American culture, confronted with the same problems, developed means of delaying breeding so that the demands on their labor would not be so high. These two ways of dealing with the nature of sheep and bitterness of winter stem from two different styles of family life, concepts of ownership, and sets of aspirations. In their particular context the Navajo get the most from their sheep, and other systems are less effective. In Vermont or Missouri the American system works better, given the basic assumptions of American culture. Both represent adjustments to the environmental realities that confronted man in different places at different times.

ADAPTING TO ENVIRONMENT

In previous chapters I have spoken of social systems as man-made machines used to get the job of living done. Man has often used his social organization as a device to make adaptation to his environment more effective. Julian Steward has suggested that the type of social organization commonly found among hunters and gatherers is a direct adaptation to environmental needs. This system—the patrilocal hunting band—consists of a number of males, their wives, and their offspring. Young men, when they marry, bring their wives into the band of their father.

See Julian Steward, *The Theory of Culture Change* (University of Illinois Press, 1955).

Kinship Structure

Steward pointed out how this patrilocal system serves to make hunting more efficient. If, he said, a young man grew up in one area and learned to hunt there, but then went to the region of his wife's family when he married, he would have to relearn much of the lore or hunting to fit the new environment. If, however, he stayed in the region where he had learned to hunt and where he knew the lay of the land and the habits of the game, he would be at the peak of his efficiency at the time he married and began to produce offspring for whom he had to provide food.

It is generally true that matrilocal and matrilineal societies tend to be those in which women have an important and recognized role in the subsistence life of the tribe; that is, descent and postmarital residence are partly determined by economic factors, as witnessed by the male orientation of many hunting societies, and the female orientation of societies at certain levels of agricultural technology. This is not always so, however. In much of Africa, where women do the bulk of the farming, the kinship systems are patrilineal. In most such cases, though, the importance of farming is simply not recognized in the cultural system, and stress is placed on the cattle-owning and warfare activities of the men. Cattle raising, in parts of Africa, is inefficient and cattle not well suited to the environment. Cultural adjustments to this problem include special attitudes about the loss of animals and special explanations of disease, witchcraft, etc. Not infrequently, an elaborate system of cattle stealing provides a means of getting replacements.

This makes the important point that few if any cultures are in total balance with their environments. The simple hunting and gathering cultures are perhaps mostly closely tied to environment. Cultural practices that drive away game, ignore the time of ripeness of important plants, food, and the like—or that prevent people from moving quickly to take advantage of the opportunities offered by the environment—would soon eliminate the people.

However, as culture—including material culture—becomes more elaborate, it tends to impose itself between the surroundings and man, to provide a certain amount of protection from man's own mistakes. Those who seek environmental explanations for every practice of mankind find this hard to accept, but we can never understand man's relation to environment if we do not accept the fact that culture permits man to make choices based on the situation as he sees it, and sometimes these choices are wrong in environmental terms. We have only to see the freeways and polluted streams of America to recognize this fact—and yet many respected students of cultural ecology will not. Let us look at a well known example of purely environmental or ecological determinism.

The Cattle of India
Professor Marvin Harris, a few years ago, took up the question of India's sacred cows. Most agricultural scientists had long decried the Hindu custom of not killing useless cattle; they argued that millions of surplus cattle that were not giving milk or producing offspring often too old and sick to draw the plow—were a drain on India's agricultural resources and contributed to a degradation of India's cattle by perpetuating undesirable traits. Despite these criticisms, Hindus still refuse to consider eating beef and Indian law makes it

generally illegal to do so. Moslems and Hindus have fought in bloody riots hundreds of times because of the objections Hindu Indians have to the slaughter of cattle. Gandhi himself abjured beef and urged that cattle be protected.

See Marvin Harris, "The Cultural Ecology of India's Sacred Cattle," *Current Anthropology* 7 (1966), pp. 51–66; and "The Myth of the Sacred Cow," *Natural History* 76 (March 1967), pp. 6–12.

Most anthropologists have pointed to this Hindu attitude as an example of how culture is in many cases independent of environment. Professor Harris challenged this view and said, in effect, that Hinduism and its principle of *ahimsa* (nonviolence) was in fact a means of conserving a scarce resource—that is, cattle—and that it made ecological sense. He pointed out what most people knew already: that Indians raise cattle in order to have bullocks to pull plows. The cows do produce nearly half of India's milk supply (buffalo supply the rest), but the total is still only one-third of the needs of the country. Thus work, not food, is the most important contribution cattle make to India's agriculture. There were no really useless cows

Figure 71.   Cattle play an important part in Indian agricultural life. But the religious symbolism of the cow prevents farmers from eliminating useless animals that draw on resources without making any adequate return.

in the system, according to Professor Harris. Every cow *might* have a calf and that was what the Indian culture gambled on. Moreover, he pointed out, even a cow that does not produce a calf does produce dung, which helps refertilize the soil. Thus, every cow makes a positive contribution.

The argument was good and the paper well researched, but Harris' work gives an example of the biggest danger in cultural ecological studies. If one is to step out of the world of religions and customs and kinship systems in which anthropologists have lived for several decades, and involve himself in questions of soil and animal fertility and agricultural techniques, he must know as much about the new subject matter as about the old. Harris missed two important points. One is that the average Indian cow produces a calf only once in every three years. By improving the cows' fertility, India could have the same number of calves each year with only one-third the number of cows. This paradox of animal husbandry is well known to farmers and animal scientists: a small herd of healthy cattle will produce as many calves as a large herd of unhealthy and infertile cattle. India could have as many plow oxen as it has today if it eliminated the barren cattle and fed the food they consume to the remaining cows.

It is true that culling the herds would also reduce the amount of dung available for refertilization and for fuel (as it is often used in India). The problem here is even more simple. A cow does produce in a single year about enough dung to refertilize an acre of land, but to produce that much dung, she must be fed from ten to twenty acres. Thus, if a barren cow is contributing only her dung to the system and half of that dung is used for fuel or to plaster house walls, she can replenish only one-half an acre—while she grazes over ten acres to do so. That means the loss is in a ratio of twenty to one. Of course, cattle do produce milk and calves and thus the loss to the system is not in such a shockingly high ratio. Nevertheless, Harris' failure to see these two important points invalidates an otherwise intriguing article.

The article thus illustrates how complex the relationship between environment and man is, and how much one must know, or learn, before making conclusions about this relationship. In its failure, the Harris article also points out how influential are cultural considerations in man's life. I have known Indians who despaired at the economic burden of infertile cattle, but who would never slaughter one—

and who were grossly undernourished, but would never eat beef. To do so would be to lose one's total identification as Hindu, to risk the ire of one's neighbors, to preclude going to the temple or requesting the services of a priest. One's daughter could not find a respectable husband, nor could one's son find a good wife; neighbors would not associate with you or cooperate in work. In short, the burden of keeping useless cattle that give so little milk that one must buy it to put in the afternoon tea was not as great as the burden one would carry in violating the special rules of the culture.

One might ask: What, then, is the useful function of such a practice if it is detrimental to the environment by causing overgrazing and soil erosion? Even without prolonged investigation, we can see the function of Hindu cattle protection at the symbolic level, perhaps the most important level for men. There are people of a number of different religious persuasions in India, and Hindu society itself is divided into many castes and subcastes—each marked by special rules of behavior, including diet. By some accident of history, or perhaps because there was a need to preserve cattle in the past, the protection of cattle took on special symbolic significance in Indian life that it did not in other cultures. Symbols are often more important to men than life itself, so it is easy to understand Indians continuing to practice cow protection over many thousands of years, as their environment slowly ran down. Keep in mind that until recently India had open lands which could be settled and did not have the terrible press of population she has today. Thus any small, regular loss of fertility in the soil could be masked or compensated for by opening new lands and was not as apparent because the demands of population were not so great.

India provides another interesting issue in environment-culture studies. Professor Harris argues that because man and cattle are not in competition, the number of cattle does not really threaten the human food supply, cattle eat things which men cannot eat. However, cattle also eat things men use to produce food. Grasses that are inedible to man can be turned under and thus produce more soil fertility than dung. Small trees and dried grasses can be burned to cook food and make it more digestible—but small trees are invariably destroyed by wandering cattle unless man devotes money and energy to their protection. During World War II, when the high price of food made it profitable to use cottonseed for fertilizer, milk production fell off throughout India. Usually, cottonseed was given to cattle as a concentrated feed. Thus, in a sense, man competed with himself through the agency of his cattle.

Native American Ecology

All of this discussion simply goes to prove that studies of culture-environment relationships are complex things and one cannot leap quickly to conclusions. This is an important lesson today when the question of environment is on everyone's mind, and answers to environmental problems spring to the lips of everyone with great ease. Another example of a problem that is more complex than it appears is connected with the erroneous idea that primitive or tribal or oriental peasant peoples had a better understanding of the environment than our own, and thus were better at preserving their resources. It would be nice to believe that somewhere there are people who could simply reveal their secret to the rest of us and solve our problems for us. The famous historian Lynn White, Jr. blames almost the entire problem of pollution and environmental degradation on Christianity and its lesson of the earth's denomination by man. For Americans, there also seems to be a special pleasure in castigating ourselves for the sins of our grandfathers.

Unfortunately, the facts don't really bear out these views. If we believe some speakers and writers on the subject, American Indians, for instance, were the founders of some kind of aboriginal Sierra Club; each move they made, we are told, was in careful and conscious harmony with the universe and the balance of nature. Would that it were true. In fact, however, American Indians were quite ordinary people, very much like you and me if we lived in the same circumstances.

See Harold Driver, *Indians of North America* (University of Chicago Press, 1961).

Over most of North America where agriculture was practiced, Indians had to move frequently because their method of farming wore out the soil and it took many years to rebuild lost fertility. Once crops had begun to diminish—in some places, one or two years after the field was cleared, in some other regions a bit longer—the farmer moved on to another piece of uncleared forest. He girdled the trees and when they had died, cut them down. He seldom made use of all the wood he felled, and wood and brush were burned to clear the land. The burning itself is damaging to the topsoil but the Indian had no other effective means to remove the clutter.

Once cleared, the new land was opened with digging stick and primitive hoe, and corn, beans, and squash were planted. When the crops dropped off again the cycle of clearing began once more, and when the clearings were too far away from the village for convenience, the village was moved. Among the Iroquois of upstate New York this happened once every fifteen years or so, suggesting how long it took a field to recover from Indian agricultural exploitation. For the Indian, however, this system (called slash-and-burn agriculture) worked well, primarily because there were so few Indians and so much land. If our society reverted to this practice, however, available land would be exhausted very quickly, long before the initial fields had recovered.

In hunting, the Indian's practices were much the same. He killed for food—food he had to have in order to live. He was a good hunter, and he did tend to use every part of the slain animal—meat, bones, intestines, sinews, hair, and horn. (However, compared to the utilization of a beef carcass by a modern slaughterhouse—where blood, urine, glands are saved—the Indian was a wastrel.) His careful use of animal resources was not the result of scientific wisdom, though—the Indian simply had to be this thrifty. As much as we wish to romanticize it, necessity forced the Indian to use everything he could. Hunting was not easy work; game animals were not always plentiful. He killed as many as he could, when he could, and used everything he could, in order to survive. However, when he was able to kill more than he could use, he did so, and he was sometimes as callously wasteful as the white man who came later.

Entire herds of bison were driven over cliffs—some to spoil before they could be butchered. The Washo Indians often set fire to entire forests in order to drive out the deer. Studies of the consequences of fire made by Professor Henry T. Lewis, an anthropologist who was once a forest ranger, suggest that the damage done to the forest was not as grave as we might suspect—but the Washo wasn't too concerned, one way or another. What he wanted was food, and he got it the best way he could. The Pomo Indians in California not infrequently diverted streams to strand large numbers of fish, which could be picked up easily. The spawn, minnows, tadpoles, and other riverine life that died did not trouble them. Once again, the damage they did had no great effect because there were so few Indians. A section of stream stripped of life was not an area-wide catastrophe; there were many streams and nature soon mended the damaged ones.

When the Indians of the Plains obtained guns and made contact with traders who would pay—in beads and iron pots and more guns and steel knives and mirrors and whiskey—for the hide of the buffalo, they slaughtered the huge animals with abandon. The often-condemned white hidehunter was, in fact, a Johnny-come-lately who barely got in on the final chapter of the great buffalo slaughter. Indians alone wiped out most of the buffalo west of the Rockies before white men in any numbers penetrated the region.

The lesson here is that while Indians had lived in some sort of balance with the supply of buffalo using their aboriginal technology, once they obtained a new hunting device their ravages were as thoughtless as the next man's. And they no longer utilized the buffalo as had their ancestors. The hides were stripped off and the hump meat, fat, and perhaps the tongue cut away, and rest of the carcass was left to rot. What need of bone needles or arrow heads when the hide one had just taken could be sold for steel needles? Why bother with cutting up all the meat when with a gun a man could kill five times as many buffalo and feast on only the choicest pieces? A man of today would turn aside from ground beef if he had what appeared to be an unlimited supply of filet mignon.

All of this is not written to condemn Indians, but simply to humanize them. They had developed a technical system admirably suited to the environment. It was a crude system, but there were few Indians and the overall impact on the vast ecosystem of North America was not beyond the ability of nature to repair. However, the Indians were not in any sense any better men or more sensitive men than we are today. Given the opportunity to use a technical system that could kill faster than nature could replace, they helped eliminate the very basis of their subsistence, the bison. Today, giant corporations and individual men foul their environment and use up their resources as mindlessly and carelessly. We have learned little— but neither are our attitudes much worse than those of the Indians.

Problems with Technology

It is true that the philosophies of some oriental nations do not place man in the same dominant position as does Christianity: there is a philosophical basis for conservation and ecological planning. However, if we look at what men do and not what their philosophers say

Figure 72.   In Korea and China, despite philosophical attitudes that hold reverence for nature, the common people have virtually destroyed the forests of their countries in their search for firewood. In modern Korea, armed soldiers patrol the hills to prevent farmers from pulling up newly-planted seedlings.

they ought to do, we find a very different picture altogether. In Korea the peasants have stripped the hills of vegetation in order to obtain fuel. The government finds it necessary to patrol newly forested regions with armed soldiers in order to protect the young trees from the villagers in the valleys below. Similar deforestation has caused misery in China for hundreds, perhaps thousands, of years. In India the land is often ruined by poor farming methods, leading to erosion. The cattle spoken of a few pages back strip away the tiny new trees and graze the ground to the surface. Throughout the Mediterranean basin as well, people have historically herded too many sheep and goats on inadequate pastures and stripped away the cover and ruined the topsoil. The religions of the Buddhist, Confucian, Hindu, Muslim, Jew, and Christian—not to mention Sikh, Copt, and Parsi—none of them allows consideration for the ecological balance of their environment to override their own needs, or greed. Men, unfortunately perhaps, are men, and any new approach to nature must be made by all of us.

The problem of today is that our technical system consumes so much soil fertility, timber, fossil fuels, water, and minerals—and there are so many of us demanding the products of that technical system—that we apparently have begun doing damage at a rate beyond the capacity of nature to repair. A stream could purify itself when one small factory dumped pollutants into it. But when each factory has grown by a hundredfold and the single factory has become a thousand, the purification system of the stream is overloaded and collapses.

But this chapter is not about pollution; rather it is about cultural ecology. One point raised above must be elaborated. What men say they do, or say they should do, is not always what they do. We have mentioned this before. Technically we speak of the difference between *overt* (what we should do) and *covert* (what we really do, often without realizing it) cultures. We must always remember that these two levels of culture are separate. Culture is, in a way, a set of rules or patterns or categories, but every culture has room for individual variation. Most cultures simply accept the fact that people can't always do what they should and that variations on the theme are perfectly acceptable.

When we study cultural ecology, then, we should not expect every action of a man to be based on his environment. It is doubtful that there is any causative relationship at all between which of the universal religions a man adheres to and the kind of natural environment he lives in. To be sure, these religions—Christianity, Buddhism, Hinduism, Islam, Sikhism, and others—tend to occur in contiguous areas. But in many places they occur intermingled. And, in any event, historical and cultural factors would seem to be more important in explaining the spread of Islam than environmental factors.

However, certainly some of man's behavior is rather closely related to his environment. In general, it appears that the simpler the technical system, the more closely related to the nature of the environment are the social and cultural systems. As technology becomes more and more complex, social and cultural behavior becomes more attuned to the technical system itself, which acts as buffer between man and the environment.

It would appear that these three elements—technology, society, and culture—do not change at the same rates. In times of rapid change, this fact is extremely unsettling for mankind. For instance, many of our cultural attitudes are rooted in a past when most Americans lived in the country and worked on farms. Our social institutions are in many cases in much the same state. Of course, social behavior has altered faster than cultural attitudes; new technology means new jobs—that is, new roles and new organizations to accommodate them, such as factories, unions, management corporations, government bureaus, and the like. But, at the same time, society hasn't altered with each alteration of the technical system, which changes most quickly of all. Municipal governments still exist as if there were not another city for many miles, although the division between one city and the next may be simply a line on the map. We don't, in many cases, have the social-political tools with which to deal with our technical tools. And our cultural attitudes, rooted in an individualistic, agricultural past, resist the common-sense changes many people feel must be made. Thus we produce industrial wastes we can't get rid of, auto exhausts we can't control, because our ability to produce them has exceeded our ability to govern them. Our attitudes, too, resist changes, and therefore we have tensions within our social structure, reflected in many ways.

Numerous tribal peoples facing these kinds of technological–social–cultural mismatches—particularly when they were suddenly introduced by the appearance of another and more technically advanced culture—have attempted to relieve tensions through recourse to ritual and supernaturalism. The Indians of the Great Plains, during the years 1889–1890, were possessed by a prophecy that offered them a return to the old ways of life if they would perform certain dances and sing certain songs. In that case, the Ghost Shirt movement ended in the bloody massacre at Wounded Knee, South Dakota. In many other cases of cultural confrontation, similarly inspired rituals proved unsuccessful or adjustments for better or worse were accomplished; one way or another, however, the movements died out.

In Melanesia, though, an awareness of the material riches of the European world and the upset of traditional societies has been the basis, in various parts of the islands, for seemingly endless movements called Cargo Cults. Whatever the ritual prescriptions have been (and they often include the building of wharves or even landing strips), the aim is to catch up with the Western world by inducing ships or planes loaded with cargo to deliver their burdens to the disadvantaged tribesmen.

Those movements that in a sense look forward are often called Revitalization movements. Others, which seek a return to the simpler older ways (like the Ghost Shirt rituals) have been called Nativistic movements. There are those who suggest the sudden nostalgia in the United States for a simpler past—the renewed interest in simple agriculture, "pioneering communes," woodlore, cowboys, American Indians, and the like, as well as a fascination with the occult—may be a form of this kind of response expressed in a modern complex culture. Whether this is true or not, it is clear that disruption of established relationships with the environment, whether caused by outsiders or by internal developments, causes great tensions within a culture and sets the stage for new adaptations.

Anthropologists interested in the question of cultural evolution have always been concerned with the culture–environment relationship. The questions of how important technical inventions came into being, why cities first developed, and why and how agriculture was invented, are in large part environmental questions—or at least questions that have environmental elements.

For many years in American anthropology, the question of cultural evolution was dormant. However, some anthropologists continued to explore the question. The foremost of these is Leslie White, who has suggested (perhaps *insisted* is a better word) that culture has developed through a series of stages, each marked by a more elaborate use of energy and new sources of energy. From using the simple power of human muscles, man progressed through the harnessing of the wind and domestic animals to the use of fossil fuels for powering more and more complex machines. And finally we have crossed into a new stage, he argues—the stage of nuclear power. White's arguments have been considered too simplistic by many. But a number of his students, using his basic idea, have explored specific systems—the Indians of the Plains and their horses, various societies in the islands of the Pacific as well as phenomena such as warfare—and produced insightful and useful work. In each case, the question of energy-employment takes the investigator to the level of environment as a starting point, and thus the entire line of reasoning is part of the diverse subject of culture and environment.

> The essentials of White's evolutionist argument are embodied in his *The Science of Culture* (Farrar, Straus & Giroux, 1969).

Dynamism in Environments

The title of this chapter speaks of culture as an adaptation to environment, and so it is. Man has made innumerable social, cultural, and technological adjustments in order to survive in one environment or another. However, we are becoming increasingly aware of the effect man has on his environment, and the role of culture in shaping the environment to which it responds. This requires an alteration of our view of environment, which has often been seen as a static factor.

There it was—topography, weather, soils, and plants and animals—a stage on which man played out his cultural destiny. However, largely because of the interest of cultural geographers, we have increasingly come to realize that environment is a dynamic, rather than static, force. Environment changes through the course of the day, and from season to season; it delivers crushing natural calamities and benign years of abundant crops. Game animals grow fat and expand in number, or they sicken and disappear. Fish are plentiful and then sometimes are suddenly gone. Man's relation to this dynamic situation is much more complex than we had ever allowed ourselves to think—and one of the major elements of dynamism in the environment is man himself. We mentioned a bit earlier the work of Henry T. Lewis, who has examined in great detail the use of fire in aboriginal cultures in California and elsewhere. Fire was regularly used to burn off brush that was unpalatable to game animals or to encourage the growth of edible plants for later human harvest. Such fires, it would appear, helped preserve the forest by clearing out the underbrush and thus preventing later, larger, and very destructive fires. Vast areas of the world's surface may have been cleared by man using fire to open up farming and grazing areas in what would otherwise be impenetrable forest.

We have mentioned the effects of overgrazing on rangelands in the Mediterranean. The result of such overgrazing is not simply the absence of edible plants; what happens is that domestic animals eat so many of their feed-plants that the inedible plants they ignore are allowed to prosper until they have taken over the area entirely. Such transformations may encourage other animals, wild ones perhaps, or they may discourage them; uneaten brush may be left to accumulate and perhaps burn up, exposing the land erosion by wind and water.

The imposition of livestock always has some effect on the environment. That change becomes part of the environment to which man must react. Much of southern Arizona has gradually been covered with brush because cattle ignored it but ate the grasses faster than they could replenish themselves. The change in ground cover meant changes in animals, changes in the number of cattle

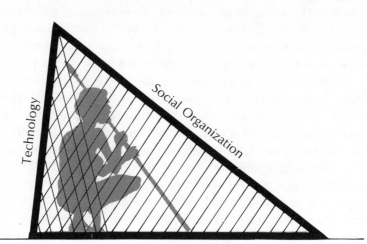

Environment

(a) Hunting and gathering societies

Societies based on hunting and gathering are (in general) most directly affected by their environment. Their technical inventory is usually small—merely sufficient to accomplish those tasks that would otherwise be impossible. Generally, hunters and gatherers tend to make adjustments in their social and cultural lives to suit the environment in which they exist. The lines drawn perpendicularly from the technology and social organization sides of the triangle intersect in relatively few places. Thus, social behavior and organization is less affected by technological considerations than it is by environmental factors. It is within this rather acute triangle that hunting and gathering cultures will develop.

Figure 73. Hunting and gathering, agricultural, and industrial societies. The three diagrams on these two pages represent the relative importance of social organization and technological efforts in various kinds of societies, indicating how each relates to its environment and surroundings. The relative length of the lines labeled *technology* and *social organization* shows how far each is developed. If the area inside the triangle is understood to represent, loosely, the society's culture, we can see about how much room for cultural development exists in that society. If lines directly connect technology to environment, or social organization to environment, then that society's environ exerts a high degree of control over the culture's technology or social organization.

(b) Agricultural societies

To a very large extent, agricultural-ists are affected by environmental considerations. But in order to carry on agricultural tasks, distribute pro-duce, and accomplish the necessary work of the society, much of the social organization must relate in part to technical abilities in the soci-ety. Specialists and social differenti-ation appear among these people. The perpendicular lines in this dia-gram intersect with each other *and* with the environment.

(c) Industrial societies

Industrial societies tend to organize their social and cultural life around technology, and are relatively free of *direct* influence by environmental fac-tors. The enormous superstructure of technical development requires major social adjustments to meet techno-logical needs. Thus, very few lines of either the social or technology sides of the triangle are tied to the envi-ronment. Rather, they intersect and end with each other.

CULTURE AND ENVIRONMENT I: INTERRELATIONSHIPS   259

that could be pastured, alterations in patterns of livestock raising and the way of life that went with it. Oddly enough, even though this change has taken place relatively rapidly, each generation has tended to accept its environment at face value and think of it as unchanging, and in a sense unchangeable.

THE CULTURAL ECOLOGY OF SOUTHERN ARIZONA

Much of Southern Arizona is dry, and all of it is hot. Rivers tend to alternate between being bone dry and flooded. Springs are not infrequent, but they are widely scattered. Before the coming of the white man, Indians—primarily Papago—occupied the area. They lived in semipermanent villages of houses made of easy to acquire brush, that

Figure 74.   The impact of three cultures—Indian, Spanish, and modern American—on the southern Arizona desert, illustrating the relationship between man's technology and his environment. The Indians lived on the desert with few alterations of the environment. The Spanish built courtyards and took afternoon siestas to combat the heat. Today, Tucson has lawns, air conditioning, and swimming pools, which not only help to make the heat bearable, but are also actually changing the desert climate, making it much more humid.

provided shade from the terrible sun and allowed the circulation of air. They hunted the jackrabbit, antelope, and deer in the mountains, and the shy, small desert whitetail deer. They also farmed, usually on alluvial slopes, taking advantage of short, hard rains to irrigate their crops. They gathered a great many desert plants as well. Their life was limited by the dryness, heat, and lack of water, but the possibilities of the environment were as fully exploited as possible with the technical equipment on hand.

When the Spanish came to establish missions in the 1760's, they brought new technology, notably domestic animals and architectural techniques unknown to the Indians. With the horse and the ox they could create irrigation systems of a limited scope and farm in small areas; most importantly, however, horses and cattle allowed them to transform the energy of the grass into energy useful to humans. They introduced cattle to the country and to the Papago. They dealt with the aridity and the heat by digging wells, thus assuring a somewhat more dependable flow of water, and by building with adobe. Walls several feet thick insulated them from the sun, and long midday siestas were their response to the worst of the heat.

For over a century, very little change took place in this living style. Even when the Anglo-Americans took over the region, they could make only minor modifications in the way of life dictated by the heat. Silver and copper mining became important in the late nineteenth century, but all in all, heat and aridity held the area in a vise. Until World War II, Tucson, Arizona remained a relatively small and sleepy town. To be sure, it was the site of a university and the commercial center for mines and ranches, and some farmers fortunate enough to have water; but the pace was slow, the population small, the way of life in a sense not greatly different from that of the Papago—even less different from the Spaniards and Mexicans.

However, the war and new technology made possible the exploration for water on a large scale, and air conditioning using that water made it possible to cool homes, office buildings, and automobiles in such a way that the heat could be neutralized. The eight-to-five business schedule of most American cities could now be duplicated in the desert, and the sun ignored. A man could drive from his air-conditioned home to his air-conditioned office in his air-conditioned car, and seldom really face the intensity of the desert sun. The new American-style houses had front and back yards— lawns, trees, and gardens—where, in the Mexican style, they had had courtyards with paving stones and shade. This new housing pattern required water; the urbanized desert was made green with plants which never before had grown in the desert.

The building of houses and roads, however, causes the delicate desert surface to crumble into dust. Evaporation from thousands of trees and front lawns sent moisture into the once-dry air, causing a humidity unknown before. Thus man, in fighting, the heat, has created humidity and this becomes part of the environment to which he must adjust. The demand for water to make the air-conditioned, swimming-pool-dotted city of three hundred thousand operate has made farming more difficult, because water is too expensive and the water table is sinking lower. Lands which once were planted now grow houses, and food is imported from California.

In reacting to an environment man has created a new one, and must adjust his culture to fit it. And yet, it is something of an irony that one can in minutes drive into the desert and find himself faced with the conditions that challenged the Papago—conditions which modern culture has not equipped man to meet. Each year, a few people sophisticated in the ways of modern technical culture wander into the desert—often only yards from the highway—and die of heat and thirst in the land which was hospitable to the Indians who knew how to live in it.

CULTURE AND ENVIRONMENT II: TECHNOLOGY AND ECONOMICS

14

THE ROLE OF TECHNOLOGY

We have seen how our need to adjust to environmental realities has been met by cultural and social adaptations that shape our society and our behavior in a complex interaction between environment, technology, and culture—each affecting and limiting the other.

When we look at the purely physical human being, it is somewhat amazing that the species has survived at all. Our ability to see and smell is not exceedingly well developed—at least not in terms of helping us compete for food with other animals. We hear well, but not exceedingly so. Our teeth are small and not very sharp; our fingernails, no substitute for claws. We walk well, but do not run as fast, particularly in a burst, as most of the animals we use for food. Our digestive system prevents the direct consumption of much of the plant life we encounter.

Man's substitute for "built in" tools and abilities has, of course, been technology—his ability to manufacture the tools, utensils, structures, and other artifacts he needs to survive—*in his own terms* (and that is extremely important) at any given time. The lion exploits his environment with his scenting and seeing ability, his size and muscular coordination, and his fangs and claws. He generally gets enough food to maintain life and perpetuate his species. The bison exploits his environment with his specialized teeth and a special digestive system which enables him to live on grass; and his senses and the collective sense of the herd protect him. Man exploits his environment by making tools, and by organizing himself and his fellows to use those tools. Technology wrests the necessary products from the environment and transforms them into a form useful to man. It protects him from the dangers, both natural and human, of his surroundings, and provides him with the satisfactions of beauty. Because he is a group-living creature, man must and does think of his group's survival; his young must be tended and taught, his old protected, his women—in whom the future rests—provided for.

The systems man has developed to distribute the things he wrests from the environment, and the products he creates from these materials, constitute what, in the broad sense, we call *economics*. The formal discipline of economics is mainly restricted to the study of distribution systems in large societies with money economies. Anthropologists, however, have explored economic behavior in many simple, non-Western societies to understand more fully how technology relates to our social and cultural selves.

Technology is, in its simplest sense, an enhancement of human strengths and abilities. Let us take a simple but basic example: driving a stake into the ground. Without any tools at all, one is at a distinct disadvantage. If the stake cannot be pushed into the ground or lifted up in two hands and driven into the soil, man has exhausted his immediate personal resources. A doubled fist will simply hurt, so the simplest effective act is to pick up a stone and use it. The stone does two things. It protects our flesh. It also is heavy, so that, swung at the length of the arm, it delivers more force to the end of the stake than we could deliver with our fist. If that stone is shaped a bit and attached to the end of a stick it can deliver—depending on the length of the handle—many times the force we could develop with the stone held in our hand.

The hammer we have thus made solves the same problem as the most complicated mechanical pile driver. The latter does nothing very different. It simply does it more. It delivers millions of times the force which human muscle, even the muscle of many humans together, could deliver—and it does it faster. In order to organize that force man has had to elaborate his technology, taking into account a number of principles, including methods of creating energy. Steam, gasoline, and diesel fuel—all are variations of the same principle of using fire to change matter, and in the process releasing energy. The pile driver is constructed so that the direct force of an internal combustion cylinder or a steam piston can be converted

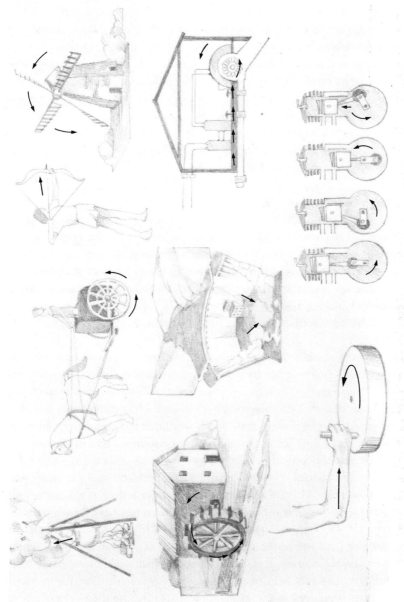

Figure 75. From a cooking fire that converts the energy of burning wood and releases nutrients in food through cooking, to a vast dam and its electricity-producing turbines, human technology is largely involved with conserving and storing energy, and converting it from one form to another.

into rotation and then transmitted through gears and pullies and the like to a point where it once again is converted into a direct thrust. To move from a simple hammer to a pile driver has required not only a million years or so of technical development; it has required a complex system of human interaction—mines for obtaining ores, mills for manufacturing steel, factories for fabricating machines; sales organizations to distribute them, contractors and construction crews of laborers, operating engineers, civil engineers, foremen, carpenters, welders, and the like to use them. All of this great elaboration is used just to drive a stake into the ground, albeit a very big stake driven by an enormous hammer.

Energy Storage and Use

Thus, in a sense, there are really very few important technical principles we have to consider, and they all deal with the conversion or storage of energy. An ostrich egg, blown empty and then used to hold water by a Kalahari Bushman, is simply a way of storing a substance essential to human energy expenditure. Dehydration is a most serious threat to man, who can go without food for relatively long periods, but who dies within hours in high temperatures without water to replenish that which he perspires away. The Bushman of the Kalahari desert stores water so that he can move away from the permanent water holes or survive during times when the water holes are dry. Without this device he could not survive in his desert. The immense Parker Dam also stores water, which is distributed into desert irrigation systems to grow food. Without the dam, the Colorado would simply flow into the sea and men could not live in the desert—at least not the way they live today.

In the utilization of energy, fire was perhaps man's most important discovery. Most of the foods man has come to use are not wholly digestible by us unless the cellular structure has been broken down. Parching, boiling, baking, and other cooking methods—aside from changing the taste of the things we eat—in fact begin a process which man's digestive chemistry cannot accomplish without external help. Similarly, fire can help man hollow out logs, it can keep him warm and thus preserve his energy, and so on. Thus, the discovery of fire at least a hundred thousand years ago, enabled man to utilize a much wider range of potential foodstuffs and tools than his ancestors had been able to use.

But fire must be planned for and controlled. Men must anticipate climate so that sufficient fuel supplies can be accumulated. And if every person in a human group maintained his own fire and collected his own wood, some would most assuredly be unable to take additional time to collect food, tend babies, and the like. From the beginning, therefore, the possession of fire has given men a need to cooperate in collecting fuel, tending the fire, and sharing its benefits. The hearth fire is a symbol of group life and continuity in virtually every society; for some it is a simple "feeling," for others, the center of ritual life. The perpetual fires of the temples of ancient Mediterranean civilizations were but an extension of the hearth fires burning for generations in private homes. During the 1930's, the Tennessee Valley Authority had to take special pains with hearth fires that had been burning for a hundred years, in moving them from old homes to new ones when families had to be relocated to accommodate the building of dams.

In this example, then, we see the linkage between technology, society, and culture very clearly. The maintenance of fire was a technical necessity which created certain social requirements and conditions. To keep his fires burning, man had to form cooperative groups. The fire itself provided a focus of sharing for people, and from this developed ideas, patterns of belief and behavior we call culture. Other technical activities—hunting, for example—probably placed similar social demands on man.

The storage of energy is another important result of human technical development. No animal, from the largest to the smallest, can store energy against the future beyond his physiological limits. He consumes food and transforms it into energy or fat; to a degree can he reconvert the fat into energy, but if that process continues too long, the animal starves and dies. Squirrels and other animals, including ants do store food and so does man, but man also stores other kinds of energy which he does not release by eating.

Take the business of projecting a missile. The simplest means of doing this is to take it in hand, draw back one's arm, and throw it— a spear or javelin, for instance. The velocity and striking power of the missile varies according to the skill, strength, and size of the man, and the weight of the spear. This can be enhanced by artificially extending the length of the arm with a spear thrower or *atlatl*. But whatever energy is there is expended in the forward rush of the arm. The invention of the bow, however, allowed man to exploit the energy stored in the tensions of a piece of wood bent back against itself. A bow can hurl an arrow many times faster than man can throw a dart, and because its velocity is higher, the mass of the arrow can be lower and the accuracy increased. The bending of the bow creates potential energy, which can be contained for a time while the man aims and perhaps even adjusts his position (moves a bit closer to his target, and so forth). A bow drawn too long becomes set and will not spring back into shape, so that it is not a long-term storage device; within its limits, however, it is like a hydroelectric dam, inasmuch as it stores the potential energy in the bent stave in a form to be released when man wants it. The dam holds water against the time when man wants more electricity and calls for the water to be run through a turbine, and the energy created by falling water is converted into light and heat.

Thus is man's enormous, almost unbelievable, technical development built on a very few basic principles. Man can store energy and use it in several forms. Direct forward motion can be converted to rotary motion, a principle on which all machines are based. Rotary motion can in turn be changed to forward or direct motion, which of course is the basis of the wheel and all vehicles. Energy can be created by converting matter from one form to another—fire, nuclear fission—and by containing the force of matter in motion—the bent bow or the stored water.

Technology and Social Structure

From the standpoint of the anthropologist, however, the effect that technology has on human organization and thought is as important as the details of the technical system itself. One generalization we can make is that the more complex the technical kit of a society, the more elaborate are its social and cultural forms. I can think of no real exception to this—although I imagine that some of my colleagues will, as anthropologists always do, pull an exception or two out of the hat. But I will wager that upon detailed examination we will find that they are not exceptions at all.

Without distracting ourselves with endless illustrations, let us simply say that a technology which allows a single productive sequence to be undertaken and completed by a single person is one that is part of a simple society. That is, if, in order to obtain meat, a man makes a bow and arrows and then goes hunting and, when successful, brings the game home and this is the normal course of events, we are dealing with a simple society. Now in fact he might borrow an arrow or two from a friend, barter a choice fur for some good flint pieces or some sinew for his bow. But the reason this was possible was because all other men in his society also made bows and went hunting. If, on the other hand, before he could go hunting with a bow he had first to go to a bowyer for the bow and the fletcher for the arrows, we are dealing with a much more complex means of achieving the same end: venison on the table. There would have to be some means for the hunter to repay the bowyer and the fletcher, in kind, currency, or service.

We earlier (Chapter Eight) discussed the *jajamani* system of India, in which the complex business of running the agricultural, social, and religious life of an Indian village is organized around occupational specialties. This division of labor is a marked contrast to that of tribal peoples, among whom work is seldom divided beyond different categories of tasks for men and women, and for young and old. There might be an expert in ritual who makes a special input into the technical system, but in most cases he must also earn his living in the same way as all other men. In such tribal societies, working groups—which usually means people working together to obtain food or products necessary to obtain or process food—are usually fairly small. Larger gatherings are dependent on a temporary plenty of resources in a single area, and, while they have important cultural and social functions, they are seldom the occasion for work. What project could a society that is normally divided into small bands of thirty or forty possibly undertake, using a thousand eager hands?

The Indian village and the medieval town (where the archer shopped for his bow) are examples of more elaborate technical systems in which the development of agriculture and animal husbandry have permitted man to expand his technical kit—in fact, required it. The resulting social structure and culture have provided man with new perspectives, and needs which can be supplied only by specialization.

DISTRIBUTION

The discussion of technology and man's responses to it has brought us to the threshold of the other face of technology: economics. A few animals do, we know, manufacture very simple specific-use tools; but no animal can be said to have a technology, that is, a system of tools and machines that serve as a core to his survival ability. Even less can we say that any animal has an economy. Some animals share food and specialize, in the sense that the female lion is most often the killer of game while the male is the stalker and driver, and the female musk-ox, threatened, withdraws with her young inside a

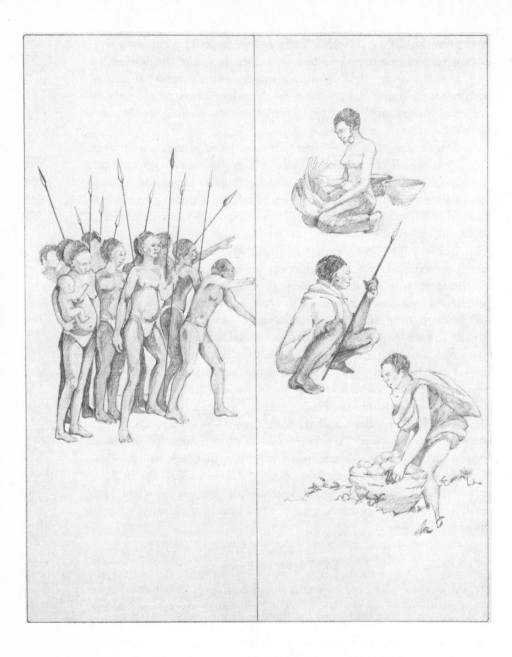

Figure 76. One way to classify societies is according to the number of different lifestyles incorporated within the single social framework. In extremely simple societies, the principal differentiation—in many cases, the only one—is between men and women. As the society becomes larger and more complex,

and must deal with an elaborate technology, members of the same social system will split into classes that have sharply differing lifestyles and expectations. In many important ways, the cultures of these different social classes will become quite distinct.

circle of males. The fox, in fact most carnivores, shares his kill with all his family group. But beyond those simple relationships we cannot speak of animal systems of distribution. And yet all human societies, even the simplest, have systems for distributing available resources to all members. In some societies, particularly the more complex and specialized societies, the distribution is far from equal; even the most inequitable, however, has standards of minimal requirements.

Subsistence Economics

Many so-called tribal societies, that is, those people who live in relatively small groups and use a relatively simple technology—whether they be hunters and gatherers or simple farmers—oprate at what we often call the *subsistence* economic level. This has often been misinterpreted or misunderstood, particularly in the case of hunting peoples. This term does not refer to a society scrabbling together barely enough to eat and subsist on. A great deal of theorizing has been based on this misunderstanding. Primitive man, we were and sometimes still are told, could not develop culturally until he had technical systems that produced a surplus, which could then support specialists who could devote themselves to the elaboration of their special areas. However, empirical fact does not support this picture. Most hunting peoples do or did produce a surplus, if that means more than could be consumed at the time of gathering.

The Washo Indians, for instance, almost always gathered more piñon nuts (a staple of their diet) than they could consume before the next spring. Often, stored nuts would simply be abandoned in the spring because they could be replaced by renewed crops of plants and by fishing; before the plenty of summer was exhausted, a new crop of nuts could be gathered. And yet this abundance did not lead to cultural elaboration. In southern California, without agriculture or elaborate technology, many tribes held ceremonies at which great amounts of food were burned. The surplus was indeed available but it did not lead to a burst of cultural elaboration. Similarly, one of the features of life on the Northwest Coast of North America was competition between prestigious men, in which they vied with each other in a series of parties to give away or destroy more than their rivals—thus accruing great renown.

If *subsistence economy* does not mean working simply to subsist, what does it mean? The term is more useful when used to refer to an economic system in which the participants directly supply most of their own food and other needs—whether it be much or little—and in which work relations are based on social and cultural considerations, rather than economic ones.

That is, in simple societies the productive units are seldom organized according to principles of wage labor in money or in kind. Rather, kin groups, large or small, tend to form the nuclei of working groups. To accomplish a given task, many kin groups may collaborate; but the principle of recruitment is based on the obligations one relative has for another, not on earning money or even food. Of course, the job is done and in fact the workers are fed, but these acts are incidental to the fact that men and women were cooperating as an expression of their kinship, not their economic relationships.

Among the Navajo, such a production unit is variously called an "outfit" or a "homestead group"—a mother and her daughters and their husbands constituting its ideal membership. The duties of herding sheep, gathering wood, hauling water, and building houses are not viewed as economic tasks for which one is paid. Rather, they are the kind of things one does for and with relatives. Naturally, when the day's work is done, food is prepared and served and shelter is always available for a relative. But not because he did this, or that, specific piece of work—rather, because he is a relative. The women of such a unit weave rugs which they sell at the trader's store; but there are no rug factories where the weavers go to work and get paid for their labor. Each rug is made as part of the total product of the outfit, rather than as the output of a specialized production unit.

Economic activity in such societies can be, if we convert it to dollars and cents, very great. Among the Navajo, the summertime is a period when a special curing ritual, popularly called the squaw dance, is held. The ritual, performed by a medicine man who is indeed paid for his labor in a truly economic fashion, is the center of a very large social event which lasts four days. The gathering is reckoned a success if many people (often hundreds) attend—and each guest must be fed. To accumulate the necessary food and the firewood, the family sponsoring the event activates its kinship obligations, calling upon distant relatives to contribute a sheep or goat or sack of flour, and expecting closer relatives to help in the building of shelters for the guests and in the preparing of food. At one such dance I attended in the summer of 1960, over forty head of sheep and goats were slaughtered and several hundred pounds of flour used to make bread.

Such an event, in fact, results in a major redistribution of property, including gifts for people who participate in the ceremony. Sheep and goats and food from widely separated sources are collected and then, in a very short period, parceled out to guests from all over the reservation. The Navajo are very aware of the magnitude of the effort; sometimes a poor family cannot accumulate enough food or call in enough obligations to hold such a dance. But if one were to tell them they were involved in a purely economic activity, they would laugh, just as you would laugh if you were told that giving a Christmas present to your mother was a purely economic activity.

An example of the economics of a subsistence society is to be seen in the fine film, *The Hunters,* which depicts in great detail the four-day pursuit of a giraffe by four men of a single band of Kalahari Bushmen. When the animal is finally slain, it is divided into five, not four, parts. Each of the hunters, of course, gets a share. But in addition, the man who made the arrow that first struck the giraffe and delivered the fatal poison to its system—he had loaned that arrow to one of the hunters—got a share. Now, in a more complex society the five men with meat could sell or trade it for money or goods. In a society of this type, however, kinship is the basic principle of distribution. Thus, each of the meat-owners passes meat to his nearest relatives, and they each divide their share to give it to other relatives, and they in turn pass some on to others until the meat is distributed fairly evenly through the band of people to which the hunters belong.

The Hunters, a film depicting the pursuit of a giraffe by the Bushmen of the Kalahari Desert, was produced by the Harvard Peabody Museum.

Often, very complex societies operate much of their economic life on principles of custom, as opposed to economic considerations. The complicated systems of the European medieval period, in which each piece of land and each master–vassal relationship was vested with a bewildering array of rights and duties and obligations, provide an example. One of the most profound and traumatic changes in English history occurred when the traditional use of the land—based on the customary and time-honored relationship between the manor and the village—was transformed to a purely economic use of the land. In this case, the landowners gradually succumbed to the lure of profits to be made by transforming farmers' fields into pastures and growing wool. The farmers were put off their fields, fences built, and villages abandoned. The uprooted countrymen fled into the cities to sell their services for wages instead of basing their security on their time-honored right to farm certain lands.

It should not be assumed that everything used and consumed by a subsistence society is produced directly by members of that society. Oftentimes, people need or want things which their own environment does not provide. Salt is one of the most necessary and common products of this nature. Peoples living near the sea or near salt springs may allow other peoples to gather salt as they want, or they may harvest more salt than they can use and exchange it for things the foreigners produce. Even the simplest of peoples appear to have trade relationships to supply some of their wants. Abalone shell and beads from the coast of California traveled long and torturous routes into inland America, moving from tribe to tribe, with each group trading something it produced that others did not. The Navajo and Pueblo peoples maintained regular trade relations (when they weren't at war) whereby the Navajo—more vigorous hunters and much wider-ranging—supplied deerskin, minerals for paint, and certain gemstones

Figure 77.   Indian trading patterns had an important effect on the spread on culture traits.

in exchange for agricultural produce. The ancestors of the Pueblo peoples appear to have traded with merchants from Mexico who, among other things, provided them with parrots—in exchange for products not available in the valley of Mexico.

Some tribal peoples, fortunately situated at a point of transshipment—a waterfall or rapids, for instance—made a living acting as middlemen, taking in goods from inland people and exchanging them downstream for coastal goods. As simple as their society and technology might have been, such tradesmen were businessmen in the real sense.

The distribution of goods according to social principles rather than economic ones is illustrated by the Plains Indians, who spent much of their time at war. For a young man, the road to leadership and prestige was through the theft of enemy horses and performing acts of bravery. A brave man could, through theft, accumulate a great herd of horses—but he would not by this means alone acquire respect and prestige among his own people. A wise warrior brought his horses into camp and distributed them. Ordinarily, such gifts were made to people who someday might be in a position to repay them. That is, it was a good thing to give a horse to a man with marriageable daughters so that one's suit would be heard, or to members of one of the warrior societies which one might want to be invited to join. But to gain truly high prestige, one gave his horse to the blind widow, or the crippled orphan, or the old man without surviving children. Since unfortunates like these clearly could never repay, such a gesture brought immediate fame. Perhaps, in today's industrial society, a wealthy man endowing an orphanage is in a similar position. He would not be blamed if he invested his money in stocks and bonds, or built a factory; but to support such an approved cause is considered a higher kind of act.

Complex Economies

A complex economic system is one in which work groups are organized at least partly according to principles of employer–employee relationships, and economic considerations are overtly recognized in the distribution of goods. Money is not used in all of these systems. Markets and trade centers can be established where barter is the principle means of exchange, but at least some production is aimed at sale or exchange; in other words, the link between production and consumption is not direct.

In such systems, the specialist appears. A specialist is a person who can exchange his product—ritual knowledge, medical services, pottery, woodwork, weapons, or what-have-you—for food and other necessities of life. On a broader level, entire villages or groups may be involved in specialized production. There might be a village of potters, each of whom works for himself and carries his productive process through from beginning to end—but in the wider society, production of the goods needed for general survival is based on occupational specialization plus the exchange of commodities.

An important aspect of economic development is the invention or use of some form of money—which is simply something to which a standard of value has been attached, and which can be used as a measure of value of a number of things. In many cases, "money" may have only specific, limited uses. This is sometimes called special use money. The dentalium shells and woodpecker scalps of the Indians of northern California are an example: they were used in paying for brides and settling damage claims, but not for buying food. Farther to the north, wealthy men had plaques of raw copper hammered into designs. These were exceedingly valuable and highly treasured, but were used to trade only for specific items. To suggest that they be used for something else would only invoke shock or laughter. Before we smile at the oddities of "primitives," reflect on your reaction to an offer of a thousand dollars for your girlfriend or boyfriend, or your college diploma. Some things are simply not for sale.

It is true, however, that in societies where a general-purpose money has been developed, such as our own, a much wider range of products and services can be assigned value and exchanged. For instance, it is possible to use money and promises of money to deal in the prospective value of next year's crop of wheat. Without money, we could not do this. Whether we *should* do it is another question—one we will not discuss. Money, in a sense, allows us to store value in a way that is difficult for a people without money. It also allows a person or group to accumulate wealth in a way they cannot if wealth is represented by a perishable commodity.

In the Trobriand islands, a woman is normally supported by food supplied by her brother. Her husband, in turn, lives on the food supplied by his brother-in-law and works to supply food for his own sister. Since the headman of a village is the only one who can marry more than one woman, distribution is fairly even. However, the headman receives food from four or five brothers-in-law and thus has more wealth than ordinary men. But the wealth is in yams, and yams perish. He uses his wealth to maintain his position in several ways. First, he is a source of loans of seed yams for young men who wish to get married and start a garden of their own. And it is to the chief that strangers and visitors are directed for hospitality, because he has the extra food to give them. In addition, he can help support the magician, who controls rain. This magician will assist the headman by withholding or encouraging rain at the proper time, and thus he enhances the power of the chief. In thus maintaining his power, the chief is expending his wealth, which cannot be accumulated indefinitely.

In our more complex societies, taxes serve in part to limit the ability of an individual to accumulate wealth indefinitely. Income and corporate taxes, death duties, and the like, are taken by the government and in theory redistributed by government spending to benefit all the people. How well this works in actuality is debatable, but taxes themselves are more easily administered when money exists than when they must be collected in services or in kind.

Certainly, money allows for an easier flow of wealth and perhaps contributes substantially to the uneven distribution of wealth in complex societies. We have seen earlier (Chapter Eight) that, despite restrictive laws and regulations and customs, the movement of money in feudal Japan resulted in the amassing of wealth by the trader class. This was in part possible because the value of rice harvests of the future could be expressed in terms of a general-purpose money and loaned to the nobility and *samurai*.

It should be noted that the business of loaning (or, in fact, renting) money has in many societies been considered immoral or unethical. European laws against usury were based on biblical injunctions. The more traditional nations of the Islamic world still view loaning money at interest as immoral. And in many societies, the moneylender has been an outsider, a person not bound to the rest of the population by ties of custom or kinship. Thus the Jews were permitted to become moneylenders in medieval Europe, and at the same time were thoroughly persecuted for it. It is inevitably the white store owner who lends money and extends credit to American Indians from southwestern reservations, and in India the moneylender is more often than not of a religious or social order different from that of the people to whom he lends money.

If we think of the simple, subsistence-level society as one in which most economic arts are motivated by social and cultural considerations, we can also postulate a hypothetical complex society in which most social and cultural decisions are motivated by economic considerations. Neither type of society exists in a pure form. Not all our decisions are made with profit and loss foremost in mind; nor is every decision made by a Bushman of the Kalahari completely social, without considerations of personal investment and return. But in some tribal groups, what we would call reasonable economic decisions are avoided because they do not coincide with social expectations. On the other hand, in our own society, many social decisions are not made because they do not make economic sense. Thus, the need to improve our courts or to deal with environmental pollution is often countered with an argument about the *cost* of such improvements. The opposite is when a simple society is confronted with an obviously more profitable system of production or organization, but rejects it because if it were adopted important social relationships would be changed.

In essence, we have explored the question of how man relates to the surroundings in which he finds himself. We have seen that culture and society can be viewed as adaptive mechanisms which allow man to exploit his surroundings. The human ability to develop technical substitutes for his own strength is the primary means of extracting human needs from the environment. But, in addition, man must distribute these products, and in the developing of distribution systems we have the basis of economics.

THE EVOLUTION OF CULTURE

15

ORIGINS OF EVOLUTIONARY THEORY

No subject has been more heatedly debated in anthropology than the question of cultural evolution. Good friends have become enemies, despite the rules of the academic game which forbid making personal issues of scientific ones. So strongly did people feel about the question during the first four decades of this century that the careers of promising young men who persisted in asking it were undoubtedly blighted by seniors who felt the issue was a closed one and investigation was frivolous or simply wrongheaded. Today, however, we can speak of the question without apologizing, and one sometimes wonders what all the fuss was about.

The problem is, *how did culture develop from its simplest beginnings*— and all of us know that these beginnings did occur and were simple—to the complex and varied forms we know today.

There have always been those who felt that general rules could be formulated—that we could understand the process of past evolution and predict the paths of present events. Others have argued that much of what has happened to man was random and accidental, "purely historic," as some people would say, and that attempts to regularize and generalize were hopeless. Those familiar with the history of science will see a parallel in this dispute with that of biologists, who formed the opposing schools of thought. One argued that physical evolution had some goal, some ultimate end which we could anticipate and which would explain the processes of the past as well as the possibilities of the future. Opposed to them were, and are, those who felt that the whole thing is random and without any predetermined purpose.

During much of the nineteenth century, the question of the evolution of culture was very much on a lot of minds. The early years of the nineteenth century saw a rather rapid development of archaeology, based on some interesting beginnings in the previous century. Europeans already knew of the ancient civilizations of Greece and Rome, and something of Egypt and Babylon and Assyria and Persia from the writings of classical antiquity and from the Bible. But European archaeologists began uncovering all sorts of interesting remnants of cultures from the earliest Stone-Ages and later—although in many cases the earliest evidence of man's physical and cultural evolution was not recognized at the time. Spurred by Napoleon's conquest of Egypt, French archaeologists began to uncover the ruins of that civilization. The civilizations of the New World, which had been flourishing when Cortez and Pizarro arrived, had been somewhat neglected; but new explorations in the jungles of Yucatan and the remoter parts of Latin America revealed that even before the Aztecs and Incas there had been complex civilizations in the New World. And, of course, the reports of exotic peoples contacted during the sixteenth, seventeenth, and eighteenth centuries had stirred scientific and popular imagination. (See the Introduction to Part One.)

By the middle of the nineteenth century, a number of scholars had begun to speculate on the process that had led to the modern cultures of Europe and America. Remember, in those days the ideas of racial differences and racial superiority were unquestioned by most men. The calm assumption that Europe and the United States represented the apex of evolution—the end product for which man had struggled—was completely reasonable in the context of the times.

In England, Sir Henry Maine, who had wide experience with the laws of India, began to write about the evolution of law, gradually developing the idea that law changed from a matter of custom, as illustrated in primitive societies and traditional civilizations, to a matter of contract, as found in modern societies. Today his work can be criticized for its methodology and its assumption of European superiority, as well as the hierarchical ranking of different kinds of social control mechanisms. Nonetheless the distinction between custom and law is a good distinction, and one that has assisted later scientists.

In *Ancient Law* (G. Routledge, N.D.), Sir Henry Maine discusses his ideas on the evolution of law from "custom" to "contract."

Lewis Henry Morgan, an American lawyer from upstate New York, became interested in the Iroquois Indians who lived near his home. Morgan's importance in anthropology cannot be overemphasized. Unlike some scholars who wrote about evolution, Morgan actually went among the people he studied and talked to them about their own cultures. Others depended on the writings of travelers and missionaries, and rereadings of classical writers, and seldom saw the primitive peoples who played such an important part in their theorizing. Not so Morgan, who gained his knowledge of the Iroquois from the Iroquois themselves. He thus unknowingly established the tradition of field work in anthropology, which distinguishes it from all other social sciences (although admittedly less today than a few years ago, since many social scientists are beginning to understand the value of intimate field work).

See **Morgan's** *Ancient Society* (World Publishing), and *The League of the Ho-De-No-Sau-Nee or Iroquois* (reprinted by the Human Relations Area Files, 1954).

Morgan published his report on the Iroquois in 1851, but continued his ethnological researches among other Indians in the Great Lakes area and in the prairies of the Midwest. He became fascinated by kinship systems, and assumed quite wrongly that they were evidence of past forms of social organization, distinctly and forever connected to the people who displayed them. Thus, in his reasoning, if the Iroquois used kinship terms in a certain way, and some other people—no matter how far away—also used this system, they must at one time have been closely related. This led him to send out questionnaires to missionaries all over the world, asking for the kin terms used by native peoples of whom they had knowledge. Much of the material he got was useful, some of doubtful validity, but it did establish even more firmly the idea of using comparisons in cultural studies, which has also become part of the anthropological tradition.

Morgan's work with the Iroquois and other Indians, and his familiarity with other exotic peoples, finally led him to speculate on the nature of cultural evolution which he outlined in his work, *Ancient Society* (1877). Evolution occurred, he argued, in a series of stages, each marked by a distinct social system, technical system, religious system, etc. Each society either had gone or would go, through each of these stages on the road to "civilization." Some peoples, he noted, were at the bottom of the ladder, scarcely started on their cultural climb. Others were at various higher stages on the ladder of evolution—but all were on the same ladder and therefore had the same ultimate goals.

One could, then, if we accept these assumptions, learn about the life of one's own ancestors by studying exotic and primitive peoples. The Australian aborigines (scarcely known in his time) represented the ancient Stone Age man of the past, and the American Indian a somewhat more advanced stage, etc; one had only to look to find each stage of our own culture's progress. Somewhere, Morgan and his followers were sure, must be the tribe as yet without fire, or religion, or morality, or the family, or the concept of property. Thus his work was of monumental scope; it discussed facts unknown to most intellectuals of the time and had a tremendous impact on the scholarly world.

Morgan's reasoning, and that of his followers (who for a time were practically the only scholars interested in the subject) was very simple when stripped to its essence. If Europe and America represented the upper end of evolution, then the lower end must be in every way the exact opposite of Europe and America. We believed in one god (Morgan was a Protestant, and one cannot help but think that he must have placed Catholics on a slightly lower evolutionary step) who is all-powerful; earliest man must therefore have believed in none at all, or in so many as to be undistinguishable. Since we marry only one woman, they must have been totally promiscuous. If we own property and hold that right above all others, then they held none. Of course, no society was ever found to fit the exact opposite position. But the line of reasoning was interesting and, given evidence then on hand, a totally reasonable proposition.

Morgan's impact went beyond the scholarly world. Friedrich Engels, patron and promoter of Karl Marx, took note of Morgan's work and directed Marx's attention to it. The relationship between property and family and evolution attracted Marx and greatly influenced his work and that of Engels. Morgan became something of a patron saint among Marxian socialists. Long after he had fallen from favor in his own country, his picture was to be found in remote railway stations in postrevolutionary Russia. For many years the only place his works were published was a socialist publishing house in Milwaukee. Old time union members of the first decades of this century often knew Lewis Henry Morgan more thoroughly than did the most prominent American anthropologists.

The weakness in Morgan's theory was primarily a lack of data. Ethnology was an infant science (not a science, really—*activity* is a better term). Information was taken catch-as-catch-can from the accounts of men who were not primarily interested in unraveling the questions of evolution. Missionaries, despite good intentions, were often prejudiced against the people they described because of what thy considered un-Christian habits. Soldiers who had to fight Maoris and Sudanese and Sioux and Cheyenne might be excused if their accounts were less than objective (although, surprisingly enough, accounts written by many military men were very good indeed). Moreover, vast areas of the world remained ethographically unreported. Siberia was virtually unknown save by the hardiest, who were

Figure 78. What biases would be likely to creep into descriptions of native populations by missionaries? Soldiers?

driven in search of furs, not knowledge. Likewise, the American West in the mid-nineteenth century was hardly a place for a man with a notebook. The islands of Melanesia were totally unknown, frequented only by slave hunters of the Pacific—"blackbinders." Polynesia was known to the whaler and seaman but not the scholar. Africa remained largely unexplored by Europeans.

However, as these places began to be subject to increasingly detailed ethnographic investigations, more and more peoples were found who simply didn't fit the scheme laid out by Morgan. Tribes practiced one system of agriculture, but did not have a corresponding kinship system. Pastoral herdsmen, who were supposed to be patrilineal, on many occasions turned out to be matrilineal. For a while the theory was kept alive in its entirety by developing new and corollary ideas to explain the discrepancies. Perhaps some peoples had suffered lags in evolution; others might have degenerated for a few generations. Soon, however, the weight of the data broke down the foundation of theory. The reaction to this was in part that described earlier—that of Boas and his students (Chapter Twelve). There were others who rejected the idea of evolution altogether, simply because Morgan's hypothesis didn't hold up in its entirety.

REACTION AND RESPECTABILITY

There were other reasons for rejecting evolutionary theory. It did run counter to accepted religious doctrine. Man, according to the Christians, has not risen but rather has fallen. From the perfection of Eden he had devolved into idolatry, promiscuity, greed, and avarice. Adam was a monogamist who worshipped one God. In Eden he appears to have been a vegetarian gatherer of fruits (which would be in keeping with evolutionary thought); once he was driven from the garden, he became a farmer and herdsman. Since then man's morality has disintegrated; he has in many cases abandoned a single god for polytheistic religions, sinned by committing polygamy, and so on. There were always those, even in the science of anthropology, who accepted that approach. Anthropologists who were also priests—and some of them made tremendous contributions to the science—particularly hoped to find a primitive tribe with a concept of a single god, to support the idea of man's fall.

But this antievolutionary school was perhaps not as effective in overriding evolutionary thought as were the diffusionists. Evolution as espoused by Morgan assumed that all men were basically the same mentally (which was, at the root of it, nonracist in assuming that all men could achieve the same things). According to Morgan, at the proper stage in evolutionary progress someone in each society would make the needed discovery or devise the required idea. The diffusionists, on the other hand, took a very dim view of man's inventiveness, we have said.

One extreme diffusionist school argued that all men wallowed in almost animal-like ignorance until representatives of Egyptian civilization went among them as missionaries and spread the good tidings of civilization; most cultures' belief in gods and angels and great saviors from the East (or West) was supposed to stem from a cultural memory of these Egyptian light-givers. Unfortunately scholars learned that, far from being the earliest of civilizations, Egypt did not develop a complex culture until after other places in the Near East, and perhaps even after India. A setback, but not fatal.

Some of the more convinced diffusionists argued that the real light-givers came not from Egypt but rather from Atlantis, a continent long sunk in the ocean, whose people possessed technical, intellectual, and spiritual prowess known to no one today. Others invented a wonderful place in the Pacific called Mu, which also sank and sent refugees into the rest of the world.

Many diffusionists, not quite so fanatic, simply assumed that various inventions appeared at different times and places and spread throughout the world to create the combinations of traits we know today. This last position was the one taken by the more reasonable anthropologist; the results of some of their distribution studies were discussed in Chapter Twelve. The important point here is that diffusionist thinking and diffusion studies replaced evolutionary theory in America for nearly forty years.

However, in the mid-1930's, young scholars began once more to ask the unaskable. Ethnographer Julian Steward developed the idea of multilinear evolution, a concept that does not presume that every society goes through exactly the same stages. Steward does believe, however, that there are distinct stages of cultural evolution,

Steward's evolutionary theory is outlined in his *Theory of Culture Change* (University of Illinois Press, 1955).

each with characteristics that can be considered separately from any specific society. A civilization is a civilization, wherever it occurs, because it displays certain characteristics; the process of getting to that stage involves necessary preconditions which must be met before the development can take place. Steward emphasizes that similar environments interacting with like technologies will result in similar, although not identical, social institutions and cultural patterns. He is seeking explanations for a number of different events in cultural history in order to find a common denominator among all cultures. His evolutionary theory is called *multilinear evolution*, by way of contrast to the unilinear theory of Morgan and Leslie White.

Leslie White, as a student, read and accepted much of what Morgan had said, and steadfastly held out against the weight of opinion and authority until his views once again became respectable, if not acceptable to everyone. In his views of cultural evolution humanity has progressed through a series of stages, each based on the control of different energy sources: muscle, fire, domestic, animals, wind organic-based fuels like coal and later oil, finally nuclear power. Each energy source requires a different technical system for efficient exploitation, and this in turn calls for new social institutions and cultural patterns. Because he thinks on a global scale, White tends to

Figure 79.   With each new stage of development of energy sources, a more complex society is required.

regard environment as a constant. He thinks environmental differences cancel out each other in determining a sequence of worldwide cultural developments. Much of the responsibility of a cultural anthropologist, he thinks, is to determine what cultural characteristics appear together in each stage of evolution. His theory suffers from the same weakness as all general theories: because it attempts to explain everything, it often explains nothing—that is, it is difficult to apply to specific situations. Many of White's students, however, have developed useful specific statements about the relationships between elements in single cultural situations or in cultural areas.

See **White's** *The Science of Culture* (Farrar, Straus & Giroux).

The new willingness of scholars to consider evolutionary theory made it possible for ethnography and ethnology and archaeology to share once again the same theories. Archaeologists had for a long time spoken of stages of human development, based on the kind of tools they found—chipped stone (Paleolithic Age), ground and polished stone (Neolithic), copper, bronze, iron, etc. As long as one was not supposed to speak of cultural evolution, equating living peoples who used chipped stone with the Paleolithic Age was dangerous business. However, once evolution was a respectable word, ethnographers could freely speculate at least about the relevance of information gathered from hunters and gatherers in Nevada for a study of evolution. Prior to that time archaeologists avoided drawing inferences about the significance of what they found by reference to the tools of living people, and ethnographers side-stepped comparing the tools they collected with anything found below ground.

THE PROCESS OF EVOLUTION

Now that the long and bitter argument is over, we can begin to unravel the process of evolution of culture. No clear-cut generalizations exist yet; after all, there has been nearly half a century of time lost. Or perhaps it is not lost. During that time we learned a great deal about mankind and how his society works. Much of this can be applied to studying the evolution of man with some certainty that it is truly relevant.

We know that human culture is cumulative. Very few skills and behavior patterns ever practiced by man have been lost, although they may have changed contexts considerably. Chipping flint was once a life-and-death matter; today it is a skill most frequently found among people who make arrowheads to sell to gullible collectors. This cumulativeness of culture also perhaps accounts for its growth in social complexity.

We know, too, that the evolution of culture—that is, changes in technology and attending social complexity—appears to have taken place at an increasingly rapid rate. It may have taken man a million years to develop skillfully made stone hand axes and the social system to go with them; less than half that time was required to progress from that level of skill to the fine art of flint-chipping as displayed in the Upper Paleolithic; less than half that time again passed before man moved into the Neolithic and the discovery of the technique of grinding stone. The first agriculture probably appeared only twelve thousand years ago. The first cities developed perhaps five or six thousand years ago, and writing about the same time. Everything we know technically, we have learned in the fragment of time since then. The first practical internal combustion engine was invented in the late nineteenth century, for instance, and in brief time since has come the tremendous technical and social development of modern society.

The first men, a million or so years ago, probably lived in groups of twenty or thirty. It is doubtful that any hunting and gathering people has ever exceeded a couple of thousand people in a single unit—and that, under the best of conditions. Agricultural villages usually contain a few hundred, at most a thousand or so people. The first city of a million inhabitants probably did not develop until about the beginning of the Christian era or later, and now eight million people live in New York City, eleven million in Tokyo, and so on. How all this occurred and what laws and generalizations we can discover from the examination of the process, we do not know. However, given the speed with which history seems to be traveling, the need to know its consequences is very great indeed.

One special note about evolution must be added here. Cultural evolution is not *progress* in the American sense of the word. That concept is an artifact of our culture, like Congressmen and hamburgers. The progress which dominates the American mind is a moral concept, tied to technological advances; there is no scientific proof of it. In technology we can, to be sure, see a continuous line of development toward increased complexity and efficiency in machines, extending back to the beginnings of human skill. That kind of progress does occur, but to assume progress in the other fields of human endeavor is simply a mistaken analogy.

Certainly our societies have grown larger and more complex, but ask a New Yorker, faced with a strike of vegetable-truck drivers on one hand and policemen on another, if all that complexity is better than what he knew or his father knew in the past. World War II was bigger and more mechanized and killed more people than World War I, but that is hardly progress—is it? Social Security, welfare payments, and a host of other social legislation may constitute an advance over our immediate past, but is this system really better than the security of the extended family and the responsibility of the traditional community to its elderly and unfortunate? In fact, are not these latter-day institutions really just replacements for earlier institutions that have collapsed? Of course, we no longer sacrifice living humans on an altar to our god—but fifty thousand die on the highways each year, and the highways, we are told, are monuments to progress. As for art, music, literature, and the other creative aspects of human endeavor, who is to say that one style is an advance over another? In short, evolution may not have given us progress, as we think of it, at all. Remember that the end of physical evolution for the dinosaurs was extinction. The evolution was a success, but the patient died. Parallels could occur in cultural evolution as well.

Figure 80.   Dinosaurs: an example of "successful" evolution that ended in extinction.

BELIEFS AND BELIEVING

16

THE POWER OF BELIEF

We have seen how culture can be viewed as a set of categories, a classification system used by a specific people to organize the phenomena with which they must deal. Cultural reality is different from objective reality in that things which are objectively "real" to us can be totally ignored by a different cultural system. The other side of that coin is that things which are objectively "unreal" can be considered very real indeed. In short, culture can make something out of nothing.

The result is that the human environment is not only full of other human beings and plants and animals, but is also peopled with a bewildering multitude of goblins, gods, angels, devils, jinns, menehunes, spirits, ghosts, werewolves, and so on. These beings are very real to the people who believe in them. All too often, we tend to shrug off the beliefs of other peoples as superstitions—interesting perhaps, but evidence of the lesser caliber of a people or a "primitive" cultural system. But remember that, even if you are a most devout Christian, you have no objective proof of the existence of God. You *believe* in God, and because you believe in Him you explain feelings and experiences in certain terms and treat your explanations as if they were scientific evidence. This is precisely what the Australian aborigine, the Tibetan Buddhist, the Caribbean voodooist, and the African witch do.

Our beliefs are constantly reinforced if the people with whom we live also believe. Perhaps a personal example will illustrate what I mean. When I first went into the field among the Navajo, I was aware from my reading that the Navajo people believed in a being whom they called, in English, the Wolf-man. This creature was supposed to be a Navajo who had obtained the power to change himself into a wolf—and, in that guise, to do harm to other people.

Jinns are powerful spiritual beings believed in throughout the Islamic world. **Menehunes** are a supernatural population of Hawaii, said to be extraordinary engineers and builders.

Now, no properly brought-up American anthropology student believes that sort of thing. He has been trained to respect the sincerity of such beliefs, but certainly none of his professors has ever said that he must believe the same things as the people with whom he works. So, when my Navajo informants spoke of the Wolf-man, I took them seriously. That is, I accepted the idea that *they* believed, and this

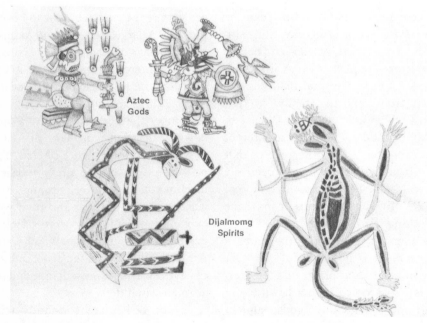

Figure 81.   The human mind is capable of inventing a fantastic array of creatures to inhabit its supernatural world.

explained to me why they were reluctant to wander alone in the darkness, and why they avoided certain people and took certain other precautionary measures. But at first I behaved as a disbeliever. I went out in the evening, I drove alone at night, and so on.

After several weeks, during which I associated entirely with Navajo, they changed very quickly from being "informants" into people. They knew many things I did not know, including how to speak Navajo, where to find water, how to tend sheep, how best to deal with the trader, and so on. Like any anthropologist in the field, I became increasingly dependent upon them, not only for knowledge but for human company and support. As my acceptance of them and their acceptance of me grew, I found myself less and less willing to go out at night. When I did, a sound in the brush set the hair on the back of my neck aquiver and my heart pounding. Soon, my pattern of living was even more like theirs. I avoided going out at night alone, and when it was unavoidable, I had to acknowledge that I was afraid.

Since that experience, I have discovered that similar things have happened to many of my colleagues. What it amounts to is that the social system in which one lives defines reality far more than any set of abstract ideas or any amount of objective knowledge. If perfectly normal and rational Navajo believed in the Wolf-man and patterned their behavior to accommodate that belief, it was easier, perhaps unavoidable, that I too began to believe.

Now, I did not abandon all my cultural training and beliefs. Men can't become wolves. But was it not possible that there were people who disguised themselves as wolves and wandered about at night? Thus, I was able to adapt my Anglo-American beliefs to the reality of my Navajo experience. I later found that very much the same thing is done by educated Navajo, who otherwise could not reconcile the things they learned to believe in childhood with the things they learned to believe in later life in school and college.

The important point in all of this is that if one is to try to understand the beliefs of other people—or in fact his own beliefs—he must understand that belief is a unique potential of human beings, and that by definition, if one can prove a belief, he no longer believes; rather, he *knows*. Thus, a scientist does not believe the equation $E = MC^2$; he knows it because he can prove it. Belief, in a sense, is a way human beings have of handling problems for which there are several possible (or no known) explanations. How was the world formed? Until the sciences of astronomy, geology, and paleontology began to develop provable hypotheses, there was no way for anyone to say unequivocally how the world, as we know it, was formed. Any number of explanations developed in different cultures and were accepted—believed.

This human ability to believe is the basis for a great deal of work done by anthropologists: the study of religion. There is no logical reason for the heavy emphasis on studies of religion as contrasted to other aspects of human life, save that the strange ritual activities of foreign peoples, as well as their unusual beliefs, were fascinating to many men of the nineteenth century, for whom organized Christianity was a focus of their social, if not their intellectual, lives. Nineteenth-century evolutionary theory held that Christianity marked some pinnacle of cultural development, and thus many scholars puzzled over the questions of precisely how religion developed, whether all men were religious, and so on.

This concern was important even to men who were personally agnostics or atheists. For many years, lines of argument were drawn between science and religion, each side arguing that the other was somehow in error. As the battle itself waned, scientists increasingly began to study religion in a systematic way, seeking rational explanations for universal behavior patterns that were based, seemingly, on nothing—that is, beliefs. By the early decades of this century, theories of the origin of religion were many and ingenious. From then on, the ethnographic reports of the religion of various peoples became more objective, and more and more subject to scientific analysis.

RELIGION

If we define *religion* according to any specific cultural system—that is, accept as a standard the elements of behavior and social organization which we define as religious in any given society—we can say (and many people have) that certain peoples do not have "religion." Some have argued, for instance, that Buddhism is not a religion because the Buddha was not a divine being, nor did he claim divine revelation or infallibility. But by examining other cultures, we have been able to formulate definitions of a more general nature. Gradually, anthropological definitions of religion expanded to fit a wider and wider range of reported beliefs and behaviors. It is well to remember, however, that this is an anthropological or scientific definition; for many people, beliefs and practices too different from one's own are simply called superstition.

At least informally, many anthropologists will say religion is simply a category in which we include behavior for which we have no other explanation. For instance, if we were to observe a Catholic mass in detail and ask why the priests did certain things, we could not point to social-structural, economic, or other reasons. We could only refer to statements made by Catholics as to what they believe. To a person who does not believe the same things, such explanations would make no sense. The same thing can be said about the beliefs and practices of any religious system. A Tibetan Buddhist, for instance, constructs an elaborate water-driven drum full of written prayers because he believes that each turn of the drum sends all those prayers to heaven to be recorded to his favor. To an austere and conservative Buddhist from Ceylon, the Tibetan's act is silly—and so on, and on. The only reasonable way a person can react to this is to accept the fact that human beings can and do believe things that cannot be proven or disproven by "logical," "scientific," or "objective" argument. Accepting this, one can then develop a respect for man's ability to believe, and for any belief system as an expression of human nature.

It is good to remember that beliefs in themselves can seldom, if ever, be described as constituting either a belief system or a religion. For these terms to apply, beliefs must be coupled with actions; these actions usually are repeated and themselves become endowed with a certain weight of sacredness. In short, religious systems, no matter how simple, are made up not only of what people think but what they do, under certain circumstances. Ritual activity may be enormously complex and require the participation of an entire society, or it may be carried out only by the initiated priests or magicians—or it may be some special, simple act known and practiced by everyone.

A Washo Indian who has successfully stalked and wounded a deer will seek out out a few drops of blood and quickly mix them with his own saliva. Then he starts a fire and in it heats a stone. When the stone is hot, he will put the mixture of blood and saliva on it and watch it boil and bubble away. Only then will he set out in pursuit of the wounded beast, certain that with this ritual act he has killed the animal. As often as not he will soon find the dead creature with a froth of blood and saliva on its lips. The cynic can point out that it is always best not to pursue a wounded animal too closely. If not pressed, it will lie down and, if wounded severely, stiffen and die. If pressed hard, it will run and perhaps escape before the wound kills it. But that means nothing to the Washo. Nor do similar rational explanations of comforting rituals mean much to the people who practice them. Human beings do respond to regular, expected, familiar acts or circumstances. They provide a feeling of certainty and continuity. Some of these comfortable and regular acts are linked to systems of belief and become in themselves special, evoking a particular feeling and requiring a particular response.

Mana

Almost all peoples have some view of a generalized and impersonal force or power that affects human fortune and can be "tapped" for specific purposes. For some societies—particularly for small, simply organized, hunting and gathering groups—this concept of power is central and constitutes most of what we would call their religion. In other societies—larger, more complex ones, our own included— this power concept has been ruled out of formal religion but it remains nonetheless. We call it "luck," and even if our churches and divinity schools ignore it, luck plays an important role in our lives.

This idea of impersonal power has come to be known in anthropology as *mana*, the term used in Polynesia where it played a central role in a complex and sophisticated religious system. It is also singularly important in North America, where we often hear of it spoken of as "medicine." In essence, *mana* is conceived of as something like electricity. That is it is a force found in everything, sometimes in amounts dangerous to handle if one is not properly insulated. In chapter thirteen of First Chronicles, we read of a man's being struck dead while attempting to steady the sacred ark of the Hebrews as it was about to fall. The writings and rewritings of the Bible, overlayed with all the development of Judeo-Christian thought since that time, have attributed this to a seemingly quick-tempered and ungrateful God. However, it seems more likely that it represents a time when the concept of *mana* was an important part of Judaism. The ark was simply charged with too much power for a normal person and, like a man attempting to set right a broken power line, Uzza died. Only the Levites, whose charge it was to take care of the ark, were endowed with the special insulation necessary to protect them.

It was something like this which supported the practice of incestuous marriage among the ancient Hawaiian royalty (see Chapter Five). The king was felt to have inherited such a large amount of *mana* that he was dangerous to other mortals. Wherever he walked, the land was so charged with his force that it was no longer safe for

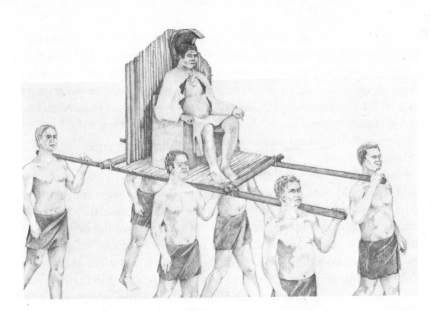

Figure 82. Kings in ancient Hawaii were believed to possess so much *mana* that they would "charge" the land and make it unsafe for commoners if they walked on it.

ordinary mortals, and so he was carried from place to place. Inasmuch as only a person of his social standing was equally resistant to the power of *mana*, it followed that he could marry only a person from his own family.

Among many peoples it is felt that it is possible to attract and hold more than a normal amount of power in order to accomplish certain tasks more effectively. The Washo Indians, for instance, hold that exceptional or regular success in any undertaking is a consequence of a person's having special power in that sphere of activity: medicine, as they say. A man reputed to be a successful bear hunter is thought to have a special bear medicine that permits him to bewilder, confuse, or attract bears. Now his success may be a product of exceptional skill. But how does one acquire skill? By application and practice, most certainly—but other men also practice and apply themselves, and some are simply better than others. In our culture, we would say that a man has a special talent for bear hunting, and when talent is coupled with application and practice the result is a superior performer. Yes indeed, but what is talent? Think about that before you answer. *Talent* is a word we use in some instances when other people would speak of medicine or *mana*.

No one can tell what the ingredients of talent are, or whether it is inherited, learned, or acquired in some other way. The fact that some people learn to sing well and quickly, and some who try just as hard never learn at all, is attributed to the presence or absence of talent. The Washo would also say that a man who regularly picked the winning horse at races also had medicine, and they would not be surprised if the person in question carried with him a stone or other talisman, or even a sack full of odd objects felt to attract or hold medicine. Now, we would view the same person as being very lucky, and we would not be very surprised if he wore the same hat, coat, or pair of shoes every time he went to the races because they were his "lucky" hat, coat, or shoes. Oddly enough, we would describe the belief of the Washo in his medicine under the rubric of religion, but probably not mention the luck of the horse player or the talent of a skilled pianist if asked to explain our own religious practices.

On the Great Plains of the United States and Canada, the pursuit of this impersonal power was the focus of much religious activity. It has been said that there was no one religion on the Great Plains, but rather that each man practiced his own religion. This is less than true, but at the same time does convey the spirit of the peoples of that region. Success in life, itself, the skills of the hunter, good fortune in war or love, ritual knowledge, wealth—all were attributed to the fact that a man had acquired enough personal power or medicine to shift the odds in his favor in some field of human endeavor.

Obtaining this power was the primary concern of the Sioux and Cheyenne, the Arikira and the Crow, and the other tribes of the high plains where the vast herds of buffalo were to be found. To obtain power required effort and search. The most usual means was for a young man to set out by himself to some remote spot. Once there, naked and without food or water or weapon, he would begin his vigil. Chanting sacred songs, staring at the sun until he could no longer stand it, slashing himself so that he would bleed, weak from hunger and tortured by thirst, the seeker waited. Often his songs called on the unseen powers to take pity on him and give him power. And, as often as not, he would find what he sought: a vision. The form of the vision tended to be patterned, in the sense that many people reported substantially the same sorts of experiences—a white buffalo or some other animal, an old man or woman, a bird, or even a speaking tree, would appear to tell him what he must do to obtain some special power. For instance, Roman Nose, the great warrior of the Cheyenne, was shown a particular style of warbonnet he must wear, and was cautioned never to eat or drink from an iron vessel. In return, he was given the power to avoid enemy arrows and bullets. Interestingly, Roman Nose died at the battle of Peach Tree Creek, the day after he had inadvertently taken dinner from an iron pot.

The Problem of Death

Man's capacity to believe enables him to consider the idea of death, and to ask and answer the question: *What happens when a person dies?* Our earliest evidence of a religious impulse in man is to be found in specially prepared graves marking the death of a man at least a hundred thousand years ago. All cultural systems since that time at least appear to have some explanation for death and what happens to the individual personality when a person dies.

The variety of these beliefs is too great to outline in detail. However, the range itself is interesting. Among many peoples—the Washo and Navajo Indians with whom I have worked, for instance— the spirit of a dead person, no matter how benign he was in life, is a malevolent and fearsome thing. Jealous and capricious, the ghost is presumed to linger around the scenes of his life and to interfere frequently with the lives of those he left behind. In such cultures, a funeral ceremony is simple, hurried, and fearful. The aim is to distract the shade of the departed.

Among the Washo, even at a Christian funeral ceremony, an older, respected person is called upon to address the dead person, pointing out that his life is over and he must go on and not harass those left behind. The spirit is assured that the funeral is not being held because the living disliked the dead person, but that it is simply necessary. In the past, the house in which a person died was abandoned by his family and a new one constructed. As houses came to be made of wood and were therefore much more costly, an obviously sick person was sometimes moved to a brush shelter in the backyard so that if he died his spirit would not remain in the permanent house.

The Navajo have a similar feeling, and also abandon the hogan in which a person has died. Both of these peoples and many others who share this belief have responded positively to the introduction of hospitals because these institutions could house the dying more comfortably until the end and would be the focus of any anger felt by the spirit. On the other hand, use of the hospital by those not dying was restricted because of the fear of the multitudes of ghosts which haunted the place. The traders and missionaries who came into the Navajo country often found themselves welcomed by the Navajo because they were willing to undertake the dangerous business of burying a corpse, a job willingly left to them.

In other societies, the dead are viewed as kindly entities who watch over the welfare of their descendants. In Melanesia, it is a common practice to keep the skulls and bones of ancestors in the house where they can be close to their family and watch over them. The ancestors play an important role in traditional Chinese, Korean, and Japanese religions. Their anger at having been slighted in family ceremonies is often given as the cause of family misfortune; on the other hand, they can often assist a family if they are properly respected, their graves tended and their names not forgotten. This contrasts sharply with the practices of people like the Navajo and Washo, who even try to avoid using the name of a dead person. Among the Washo, this often goes to the extreme of dropping a word from the vocabulary if it is the same or very similar to a dead man's name. Among the Hurok, Yurok, and Hupa of northwestern California, it was considered a grave breach of etiquette punishable by fine to mention the name of a dead man in the presence of his relatives and descendants.

Where the dead go after death is another question for which man has developed many answers. Even peoples who believe that the dead can remain in the same world with the living often have their

Figure 83. What attitude toward the dead is revealed by our elaborate cemeteries such as Forest Lawn?

versions of heaven or afterlife—which are usually, but not always, happy. On the other hand, a great number of the world's people believe that the individual personality or soul continues to exist on earth, and is reborn in new bodies time after time. The condition of each life is dependent on the behavior of the person in the previous life.

For many Buddhists, not only can one be reincarnated as another person, animal, or other living thing, but one can also be reincarnated in hell before continuing in the cycle of rebirths on earth. Eventually one can hope to be reborn as a *bodhisattva,* a person who in fact has a choice of whether to end the cycle of birth and rebirth, passing on to the blessed nothingness of *nirvana,* or to remain and help other humans achieve *nirvana.* The belief in reincarnation gives rise, for Westerners, to bewildering complications in identifying particular historical or mythological figures. The three hundred or more divine figures of Tibetan Buddhism represent various aspects of the reincarnated Gautama Buddha who was himself, in his historical existence, a reincarnated being. Religious systems which believe in reincarnation—Hinduism is another—contrast sharply with the Christian and Muslim view of a single soul with an individual and linear destiny progressing through various planes of existence: life and heaven, purgatory, or hell.

RELIGIOUS PRACTITIONERS

Whatever the specific mix of beliefs about supernatural power, death, and the human soul, every culture recognizes that there are differences in the ways individuals relate to such matters. Some people are better able to manipulate power, or communicate with the nonliving—be they ghosts, spirits, gods, or devils. Such people we can speak of in general as religious practitioners; in specific cases we think of priests, medicine, men, shamans, witches, warlocks, and magicians. Although we can make neat classifications for the purpose of study, we should remember that human life does not always yield to scholarly needs. It is hard to show that a given culture has shamans, and another priests—or even that magic and religion can be as neatly distinguished in practice as in theory.

Shamans and Magicians
On a worldwide level it does seem that the simplest expression of social differentiation in religion is the role of the shaman. In essence,

a shaman is a person who is unusually available to the nonhuman powers. His body can be used by them to benefit other people. Most frequently this occurs in terms of healing and curing, but people known to be subject to supernatural seizures and possession by spirits

For various approaches to the subjects of religion, magic, witchcraft, and related questions, the following books are excellent sources:

Emile Durkheim, *The Elementary Forms of Religious Life*, translated by S. W. Swain (The Free Press, 1954).

William Howells, *The Heathens: Primitive Man and His Religions* (Natural History, 1948).

Clyde Kluckhohn, *Navajo Witchcraft* (Beacon Press, 1962).

J. G. Frazer, *The Golden Bough* (Macmillan, 1922).

John Middleton (editor), *Magic, Witchcraft, and Curing* (The Natural History Press, 1967).

are, in various cultural systems, also employed to foretell the future, find lost articles, diagnose social and physical illnesses, and perform a host of other services. Among the Washo Indians and the Bushman of the Kalahari, the person subject to seizure by supernatural powers is simply an ordinary person with this special ability. He must continue to earn his living by hunting just as other men. In later times, among the Washo, a person with this power might well earn most of his living as a practitioner because of the introduction of the idea of money. In other cultures (in Siberia, for instance) the entire religious structure rests on the person of the shaman, who may be set apart from other men and become a full-time specialist. It should be remembered that possession by spirits is not always the attribute of a single person, exclusively, but when it is experienced by a person not specially suited to such seizures, it is dangerous and calls for the intervention of the specialist.

In many cases, particularly among American Indians, the shaman is also a magician with great powers for performing miracles— making objects move, appear, and disappear, eliciting voices from animals and material objects, knocking down sticks at great distances, and so on. Westerners would often describe these feats as simple sleight-of-hand tricks, no matter how skillful. Most people who are shamans or who believe in them, will describe how a person is carefully trained to do these things—but they will attribute his or her (because many shamans are women) ability to perform such tricks to his special powers. Magical ability is not limited entirely to unlettered tribesmen. Much of the mythology surrounding the spread of Buddhism in Asia includes episodes wherein a Buddhist teacher like Padmasampahva in Tibet overcomes pagan magicians by invoking the power of Buddha to assist him in performing tricks—or, if you prefer, miracles.

Many students of religion draw a sharp distinction between the magician, shaman, medicine man, and witch doctor, on the one hand, and the priest on the other. One, they say, manipulates the supernatural; the other communicates with it and entreats it, but does not pretend to control it. This contrast is useful in theory but less so in practice. I have called a Catholic priest to my house to perform special ritual that would drive away a reputed evil spirit so that my housekeeper would feel comfortable. She was a Catholic, but had she been a Japanese Buddhist I could have called on the priest of another religion to do the job.

Malinowski implied that magic is a precursor of science, inasmuch as it is based on assumptions of cause and effect and man's ability to directly influence natural phenomena. He also argued that magical formulae are most commonly employed to deal with high risk or uncertain situations. See his *Science of Culture and Other Essays* (University of North Carolina Press, 1944).

It is worth taking a moment to define magic, which is often considered separately from religion but in fact is a part of most religions in some sense, and certainly a part of most cultural systems. Magic assumes that there is a basic order to the universe, and that when one understands that order he can make certain things happen. A person who knows the proper spells or rituals can make rain fall or not, cause crops to grow, make an enemy sick or protect a friend from someone else who is trying to make him sick, and so on.

In short, magic is purely technical business. One does not have to have divine powers, only the proper knowledge and skills and ingredients. Malinowski suggested that magic was a precursor to science because they shared much the same set of assumptions. Many have argued with him about this, but there remains, I think, an interesting kernel of truth.

One should not think that magic is restricted only to simple or primitive societies. The priest who came to my home to drive out the evil spirit was performing a prescribed ritual that, according to the beliefs of his church, would drive away a malevolent spirit if performed properly. For those few moments at least he was being, even if he would deny it, a magician. A simple means of differentiating between a priest and a magician is to remember that a magician compels things to happen. If he has worked his spells correctly there is no other possible outcome. A priest can only entreat some higher level of existence; he cannot compel. But remember that while these are useful distinctions few religious systems can be neatly categorized as all one or all the other.

Curing

One of the most common forms of magic is curing. The magician, with the power of spells and incantations—sometimes in a shamanisitic state of seizure, sometimes not—can extract evil objects from the patient or otherwise compel the sickness to go away. The link between religious systems and curing is virtually universal. In modern Christianity we have passed much of the curing function of religion to the medical professional, but we still pray for the recovery of the ill, and practice faith healing, even via radio and television; the shrine at Lourdes in France is still the goal of millions of pilgrims seeking miraculous cures.

Religion for most men provides even more than a curing function. In fact, it explains the existence of disease and death in the most important way by answering the question, *Why me?* For most people in the world, the primary question one asks when stricken with illness is not, *What happened?* but *Why did it happen to me?* Our own medical science does not really provide any answer to that question. If one discovers that he has tuberculosis and asks why he, rather than his neighbor or his brother, got it, a modern physician can offer little information. He can tell a person *how* he got the disease—in general or often in specific—but to explain *why* fate singled that person out and passed over others is not the province of a physician.

It is, however, the province of most religious medical practitioners, who offer not only the cure but the reason for the illness. Such explanations are varied in detail but tend to fall into two categories. Often, one has become ill because in some way he has violated the order of the universe, done something which he should not do. For the Navajo it might be that he has killed a person, or even been too near a dead person or a place frequented by a ghost, or it could be that he has spoken to and looked directly at his mother-in-law. These and hundreds of other acts can cause illness, accident, or bad luck. The other common explanation of sickness is that some person possessed of evil power may be directing his power at the patient.

Once the proper cause is determined, one must seek out a practitioner. Among the Navajo this is a person who knows the ritual suited to the situation. Persons who set broken bones or provide herbal medicines (as well as American physicians who dispense pills or surgery) rank rather low on the Navajo scale of curers. The Navajo practitioner is not possessed of special power, but does have special knowledge. To learn the proper rituals, varying from one to nine nights in length, a young Navajo must apprentice himself to an older man and pay for his lessons with money, goods, or personal service. When he has been judged qualified, he can establish his own practice.

Figure 84. This is a copy of an engraving showing an ancient shamanistic ceremony in Virginia. The medicine man leads the ceremony to deal with some particular sickness or problem. In many cultures today, the services of a witch doctor, or *curandero*, are valued instead of—or along with—those of a medical doctor.

Such practitioners, unlike the shaman, are not seized by supernatural spirits. They are technicians of the supernatural. Of course the very term, *supernatural*, does not fit the situation. The Navajo and many other people do not draw a distinction between the natural and the supernatural—only between degrees of power and knowledge. So it is among the Trobriand islanders, for whom gardening is a sequence of clearing and breaking the soil, planting, and subjecting the garden to a magic ritual known to certain practitioners—some of whom can also control the weather.

Such power in the hands of a few individuals can give them a great deal of political authority. If the livelihood of a people is dependent on the exercise of power, the possessor of that power can demand a great deal in exchange. Perhaps—as some authorities believe to be the case—the institutions of government began with such a situation. In many tribes, and even in more complex societies, the chief or king is also the chief priest, his ritual knowledge being used for the welfare of the entire people. Such persons become exceedingly precious; their welfare is not infrequently symbolic of the welfare of the nation. Thus, early priest-kings of the Near East symbolically acted out plowing and planting, tending and harvesting crops—as does the secluded Emperor of Japan today.

THE SACRED AND THE PROFANE

However, the religions with which we are familiar, the religious practitioners—minister, priest, preacher, monk, rabbi, guru, and the like—are not in themselves sacred. The relics, books, and objects they handle, and the texts and prayers they recite may be sacred, but the practitioners are men, although perhaps specially called. We draw a sharp line between our religious servants on one hand, and prophets, saints, and truly divine beings on the other.

This brings us to what may be the central question of religion, the difference between the sacred and profane—between the common and the special, the mundane and the mysterious. Although a Navajo may not draw a distinction between the natural and the supernatural, he knows that under certain circumstances corn pollen has the power to protect him from witches or evil influences. He feels a special awe in certain holy places, realizes he must take special pains in certain situations. A Hopi, although an ordinary man, believes that he takes on the sacred personality of the holy personage he represents in the Kachina dances staged by his village each summer.

This particular human response is the basis of the human religions, and its roots lie in the human psychological make-up. The response is not random and idiosyncratic. A truly religious experience involves a sharing, an agreement between people that certain events, sounds, objects, or people are sacred. Responses generated under different circumstances will not be defined by the culture as religious. Thus, a Navajo can express his fear of a dog seen in the evening and invoke the protective power of the corn pollen he carries; such behavior would be considered normal. If he demonstrates the same behavior when confronted with a prairie dog, he is simply foolish. Similarly, an American Catholic may venerate a sacred relic and be considered a devout person, but if he treats a rabbit's foot in the same way he is considered superstitious. So it is also with ritual. A devout person may attend mass every day of the year and be considered a normal person. The regular and repeated acts of the mass are part of an accepted system of belief and behavior. If the same person insists that he must wash his hands every hour, he is considered a neurotic.

Emile Durkheim, the French sociologist, long ago pointed to the relationship between society and religion. It is, he argued, the collective belief and the collective acting-out of ritual that gives a specific object or act its sacred quality. We have, all of us, experienced a thrill of excitement or of awe in collective situations—singing a national anthem or a school song, or participating in a demonstration. None of these situations is defined as religious, but the response is of the same quality. A special exhilaration or otherwise unique experience can be induced, as we have seen among the Indians of the plains, by exposure, fasting, loss of blood, and chanting. Such experiences can also be brought on by alcohol, marijuana, peyote, red beans, certain mushrooms, and other substances. However, whether one is drunk or stoned or having a religious experience is determined not by the experience itself but rather by the social agreement as to what experience can mean.

Emile Durkheim, *The Elementary Forms of Religious Life*, translated by J. W. Swain (The Free Press, 1954).

Society, said Emile Durkheim, in fact does what we usually attribute to God, the spirits, or the external order: it provides protection, rewards good behavior, sets standards of morality. In the beliefs shared by a society and the regular coming together of people on ceremonial occasions to reconfirm their shared beliefs and interdependence, there is religion. Some authorities, perhaps those who like mysteries and complication have claimed that Durkheim has said society was God. In a sense, that *is* what he said, and it is, in a sense, true.

One must remember that anthropologists do not, or should not, search for truth or falsity in the religious beliefs and practices of the world. The existence or nonexistence of the soul, or God, or spirits is not in question in this chapter. The many systems of belief and ritual are an expression of a universal human characteristic channeled and shaped by a specific social and cultural heritage.

ANTHROPOLOGICAL RESEARCH

17

PROBLEMS WITH EARLY FIELD WORK

From its beginnings, when anthropology was a science devoted to the physical aspects of man (as it is still in Europe) and cultural anthropology was still spoken of as ethnology or ethnography, the research methods of the anthropologist and ethnographer differed from those of other social scientists. To learn about racial variation, physical anthropologists had to travel to where people of different races lived. And increasingly, to uncover cultural facts, the ethnologist went directly among the people he studied.

For the social scientist this was a dramatic departure. The natural historian, the botanist, geologist, geographer, and zoologist, of course, went into the field to find and report on the phenomena of these developing sciences.

The historian and political economist and sociologist, on the other hand, tended to deal with books and records, historical materials that had the sanctity we give to things printed. Few of the early theoreticians of the human sciences went out to look at the people they so freely used as illustrations. Karl Marx did his research in the British Museum, ranging through books to find facts to illustrate and support his theories. Emile Durkheim, a towering figure in the development of social science, developed his theory of religion drawing on reports of savage peoples he had never seen—and so it was with many others.

Travelers' accounts, military reports, administrative reports, and the like, provided almost all the information about primitive peoples accessible to scholars. Even Lewis Henry Morgan, one of the few early ethnologists who actually asked questions directly of his subjects, was a lawyer and businessman and had little time to spend in the field. Rather, on vacations and short periods stolen from business hours, he talked to knowledgeable Indians. This was much the style for many years. As ethnology and anthropology found their way to academic respectability and men of these persuasions became faculty members, the school year became a pattern for research. During the summers, anthropologists scattered among the Indians of North America or dashed off to other places accessible by the modes of travel then available to them. In the brief vacation months they located key informants and questioned them, often in great detail, about their lives and the lives of their ancestors.

There were two weaknesses to this kind of work. Anthropologists were most frequently interested in the aboriginal forms of culture, rather than the attenuated versions practiced in the late 1880's and early 1900's. The more closely the subject peoples approached aboriginal life, the better. In some parts of the West, for instance, some Indians were still not far removed from the old life; Samuel Barret went among the Washo in 1905 and found many of them still making stone arrowheads and living a life very little different from what it must have been before the white man began to poke into western Nevada. A. L. Kroeber, on the other hand, did his first field work among the Arapaho in the late 1890's, making the trip by train and stage coach. The Aprapaho, however, had, for many years, been contained on reservations—the buffalo gone, the wars gone, the horses and adventure of the free high plains gone. To capture the vanished culture Kroeber had to depend on the memories of the oldest people in the tribe, who in some cases had been only children in the great days of the past.

Thus, the first problem was determining the validity of the information so collected. How reliable was the memory of an old man telling you about tribal events and ceremonies he had only seen as a small boy and not really taken part in as an adult? Could one believe the word of an old woman recounting stories told by her mother about the days before the white men came? In fact, tribal peoples and illiterate peoples do maintain oral traditions and speak familiarly of many things we would relegate to the library. For them, the memories of their children are the only history a tribe will have, and so they tell the children much and tell them frequently.

Nevertheless, one could seldom obtain all the details of a culture in this way. Informants were usually good in describing the overt pattern—that is, telling an interviewer the way things should have been done (like the Washo who said the ceremony lasted four days). And they often could recount in detail many things about material culture, or about things of major importance to the tribal tradition. Thus, a Sioux who had not been old enough to fight even in the final tragic wars against the whites knew in great detail how the wars were conducted, and famous incidents of war. But when asked seemingly simpler questions about who gathered firewood, for instance, or how much was used, memory did not serve. Nor did memory serve to describe the covert variations on the overt themes of the old structure.

Nontheless, anthropologists became quite skillful in eliciting information from old informants. Sometimes they worked long enough with the same people to learn the language and question them directly. In most cases, summer field trips did not allow time for language study, so interpreters were utilized. In one case A. L. Kroeber and Edward Gifford interviewed an ancient Cocopah who spoke no English or Spanish by directing their questions to another Indian who spoke English and Spanish, who related them to yet another who spoke Spanish and Yuman, who in turn asked the old man. (It was fortunate that the informant also spoke Yuman, since there was no one remaining who spoke his childhood tongue.) Under Franz Boas' guidance, field workers learned to train native speakers of the language to write their own language in phonetic symbols and take down dictated texts—myths, stories, and reminiscences—to be translated line for line and used later as sources of data.

One can criticize these field methods, but we must remember there was a shortage of money. Research in the social sciences was not often well funded until very recently. When it was, it was likely to be the archaeologist, who might bring home boatloads of statues and museum pieces, who got the money. Philanthropists seldom saw the advantage of paying for a man to come home with nothing more than a notebook full of notes. There was a shortage of workers. Few schools had chairs in ethnology or anthropology, and thus few full-time professionals could be trained unless they could expect to find some other means of support. So a few men had to carry the load and recover much information.

There was also an urgent race against time. Soon the old ones would be dead and the evidence in their memories would be forever lost. At that point in time the facts rather than the processes of culture were important to ethnographers. The idea of diffusion encouraged investigators to seek information about tribes before their heritage became contaminated by white goods or ideas. And oddly enough, so did evolutionary thought: how was one to know if a tribe had really invented—that is, evolved—something, or simply borrowed it from the white man? This became a great issue when a small group of Shoshone living on the eastern slope of the Sierra Nevada were reported to have irrigated wild plants. To the evolutionist, this presented a rare and wonderful example of a transition, an evolutionary step taking place; to the diffusionist it was simply another example of borrowing. Neither one of these schools seemed to see that the new irrigation was important in and of itself—whether borrowed or invented—as a facet useful in understanding the process of cultural adjustment and development.

When anthropologists were able to go into the field for longer periods, it was usually to explore areas from which there had been few reports. Again, limitations on time and money usually meant hurried attempts to ask questions of many peoples, not long-term visits with a single people. Robert H. Lowie, one of the greatest of ethnologists, gives us the tone of anthropological research in the early 1900's when he recounts his early trips into Canada by train, wagon, and canoe in order to ask a single question about a certain dance ritual among several tribes.

Robert H. Lowie, Ethnologist: A Personal Record (University of California Press, 1959); this is his autobiographical account.

COMPENSATING STRENGTHS

The seniors of the science were not as jealous of the research privilege as they appear to be today. A bright undergraduate might be singled out and sent into the field with little more than a pat on the back. An intelligent and well-read secretary could be dispatched to a tribe without misgivings. And often they did very good jobs and added from their nonprofessional backgrounds insights that advanced the science. For most of the past two or three decades, field research has been reserved for the most advanced graduate students and professionals. No one who was not properly prepared was given the imprimatur as being ready for the field. Even students entering anthropology with long and sometimes unique experience in foreign cultures were politely given to understand that until they had been properly trained, what they knew was really of little value. Today one feels that we may be returning to a time when we realized that a lively curiosity and a clear, observant eye are more important than four years of reading old monographs—and perhaps more useful in developing new and insightful, rather than redundant and boring, research accounts.

In general we might say that early field work was fact-oriented rather than problem-oriented, although for men like Kroeber there was never any reluctance to build theory. His Ph.D. dissertation, primarily given over to descriptions of the development of Arapaho parfleche designs, concluded with an elegant summary of the processes of cultural change in general.

This is another aspect of early anthropological research that has luckily survived. There has always been the need to illustrate generalizations with specific facts. Now by this, I do not mean to seek out facts to support a theory but rather, by examination of manageable subjects, to establish principles for investigating wider areas. One reason for studying simple tribal cultures is that processes of culture were often easier to isolate in that context than in complex modern societies.

I do not mean to imply that all the early anthropologists did was collect lists of unrelated facts. Many of them made shrewd and meaningful analyses and built the foundations for modern theory. Nor is there anything easy or slapdash about the interview method of research. It is a tiring and frustrating job to keep asking questions sometimes for days at a time. One of the reasons for the Culture Element Distribution Lists (Chapter Twelve) was that they provided a framework for an interviewer to work with. It is amazing how quickly one runs out of questions, otherwise. The collection of genealogies was another method which gave the investigator a consistent line of questions to ask while eliciting other valuable information at the same time. An investigator could also give himself a framework by taking inventories of material items in a household or a camp, and by getting detailed histories of these items along with descriptions of how they were made. Where possible, anthropologists took informants onto familiar ground and let the old scenes bring forth forgotten memories. In one case, the last remaining member of his tribe, Ishi—

a southern Yana from the Feather River Country in California—took Kroeber and others on a long camping trip while recalling the details of his tribe's life, and death.

> The story of Ishi has been movingly told by Theodora Kroeber in her book, *Ishi in Two Worlds: A Biography of the Last Wild Indian in North America* (University of California Press, 1961).

Many of the major concepts of social anthropology were developed by men who used these methods. The lineage and a number of other descent systems were identified. The development of the concept of classificatory kinship systems was another contribution.

It would be foolhardy to say unequivocally exactly where and when the field research pattern changed. Certainly the experience of Bronislaw Malinowski played an important part in developing a new approach. Malinowski was a Pole living in England at the outbreak of World War I. As an alien he was subject to interment but instead chose to go on a research trip to the Trobriand islands, a small cluster not far off the coast of New Guinea. Everyone, Malinowski included, thought the war would be over shortly and his visit was evidently expected to be brief, like other field trips of the day. However, the war lasted four years, and its confused aftermath left little time for people to be greatly concerned about odd scholars stranded in the tropics. Malinowski remained on his islands until 1920. In those long years he had studied the Trobriand islanders, as perhaps no other tribal people had ever been studied.

> In addition to *Magic, Science & Religion & Other Essays* and *Argonauts of the Western Pacific* (cited earlier), **Malinowski's** field work in the Trobriands also produced *The Sexual Life of Savages in Northwestern Melanesia* (Harcourt Brace).

Malinowski's work included voluminous details of housing, diet, material culture, ceremonial life, subsistence agriculture, religion, and crafts—but it went beyond the mere collection of obvious data. He saw much of the system *behind* the surface behavior, and explored areas

Figure 85. In the Trobriand islands near New Guinea, men go on trading journeys between the islands, exchanging shell bracelets and necklaces of traditional design and fixed value, as well as all kinds of foodstuffs and other materials.

as no field worker before him had done. He collected details about the sex life of the Trobriand islands that shocked even the scholarly world (one doubts that the behavior itself was very shocking, but that a respected scholar would take note of it, was). Malinowski's work on the Trobriands became a kind of model for field research. First, he set the style of observing a society *in situ* for a long period. This made it possible to check the verbal response of an informant against observed behavior, making for much more accurate data collection. Moreover, Malinowski had not devoted all his time to a study of how things were "in the old days." He accepted Trobriand culture for what it was, with whatever borrowings it may have made, and went on to study it as a living, on-going system. This, too, became increasingly the style. Investigators began to look at the life of reservation Indians as examples of social and cultural systems in and of themselves, irrespective of what might have existed before. The search for the old and aboriginal very slowly (and often reluctantly) gave way to a study of the modern—although the modern was always the modern Pacific islander, Indian, New Guinean, or African. The focus remained on the simple, tribal peoples.

NEW APPROACHES

However, by the 1920's there remained very few simple tribal peoples who had not been studied. Communication and trade, imperialism and colonialism, industrialization, and all the other forces of the modern world left few peoples untouched. First, anthropologists had feared that the primitives would disappear before they could all be studied—and then some feared that once they had, anthropologists would have nothing to do. However, by the twenties, anthropologists had already begun to study the effects of intercultural contacts, the exchange of cultural elements from one society to another. Diffusion studies had aimed simply at determining a distribution and then drawing historical inferences from that distribution. *Acculturation* studies, the name given to the later investigations, were more and more directed toward a discovery of process.

What were the factors that led one culture to accept European patterns of living and another to reject them? What features of social life, status and role, social control, and religious structure encouraged or prevented the spread of one culture into another? These were questions older investigators had not asked, and a new generation went back into the field to ask them. Seldom now did one hear that it was useless to think of doing field work among the XX or the YY because Jones or Smith had already "done" them. As expert as he might be, Jones or Smith could hardly think of all the possible approaches to a single culture, even if he lived long enough to ask all the questions. For instance, the Navajo had been studied almost continuously for fifty years before I made my first field trip into northern Arizona, and yet I found an entire area of Navajo life that was largely unexplored. This is not to criticize those who went before. They simply asked different questions. In order to do my own work, I had to ignore many questions they felt were important.

By the 1930's, the nature of the questions being asked had altered dramatically—toward acculturation and a wide range of other subjects as well. There were special studies of such matters as the potters's role in Pueblo society, for instance. Asking whether all teen-age girls go through the same psychological stresses as girls in Europe and America, Margaret Mead, working in Samoa, produced one of the first comparative studies that intentionally used the United States as a subject culture.

Margaret Mead, *Coming of Age in Samoa* (Apollo); this famous book has also been reprinted in paperback by Dell Books.

Comparison of cultures had long been a part of anthropology. If you review what you have read thus far, you can see how often we have compared cultures in order to reach a conclusion. It is impossible to set up experiments in a laboratory, so one has to try to identify natural situations and compare them. However, to this comparative method was now added the detailed, problem-oriented question explored in depth with a single people. All during the 1930's, excellent monographs were developed using this principle.

This was particularly true of the British, many of whom limited themselves to studies of social relationships and structures and came to be called *social anthropologists.* This self-limitation narrowed the scope of their studies. Often they scarcely mentioned material culture, religious ceremonies, or many of the other categories usually found in ethnographic reports. However, this narrowness of focus permitted an exploration of social structures in great depth, and taught us much about things we had never considered before. Today, the division

Raymond Firth's book *Elements of Social Organization* (Beacon Press, 1963) is an excellent introduction to the British or social anthropological point of view. An imaginative and entertaining comparison of American and British anthropology can be found in R. Murphy's *The Dialectics of Social Life: Alarms & Excursions in Anthropological Theory* (Basic Books, 1971).

between social and cultural anthropology in America is long since closed and all of us are both, to one degree or another.

Anthony F. C. Wallace discusses culture and personality in his book of that title, published by Random House in 1961.

In the 1930's and 1940's we also saw the development of what has come to be called the *culture-and-personality* study—that is, an attempt to relate the individual and his development to his cultural context. This had been one of the aims of Malinowski, who tested some of the ideas of Freud about the relationship of a growing boy to his father in a matrilineal society instead of a patrilineal one like that of Europe. This basic approach attempted to combine the insights of two sciences, anthropology and psychology, into an understanding of how the individual related to his culture. Like most new ideas in the social sciences, culture-and-personality promised more than it has delivered. Nonetheless, important contributions were made to both sciences. Anthropological postgraduate training today almost always includes a culture-and-personality component, and courses in this area are offered in many undergraduate programs. Some psychologists have became increasingly aware of the influence of culture on the psychological and emotional patterns of the individual. We are more sensitive today to the fact that mental instability, emotional upset, and insanity exist as defined by the culture in which they occur, as much as they are caused by the psychobiological makeup of the individual.

The general pattern today is for field work to take a long time—usually a year, sometimes longer. It is hoped that this will allow an observer to see an entire seasonal cycle of social life and report on it. For some kinds of studies, shorter periods are acceptable, but for others, much longer periods or repeated trips must be made. Another aspect of field work has changed: more and more anthropologists try to do their field work in the native language. Longer field trips make language study more feasible. Training in linguistics, which has always been part of the anthropological tradition, provides techniques for learning. It would be less than candid to assert that all field work is now done in the native language. Good interpreters are as much in demand as they ever were. But much work is done in the native language, and even in the study of the language, the field worker gains insight into the culture he is exploring. These changes are important, yet the basic theme of anthropological field research has remained the same: in order to study man, one must go among men and speak to them. The day-to-day life and the words of people are the necessary data of cultural anthropology.

FIELD WORK TODAY

Malinowski's books were published during the 1920's and 1930's. It is perhaps well for the science that his diary was not published until twenty-five years after his death in 1942. Had his colleagues been able to read in 1920 what they were able to read in 1967, many might have rejected the new style of field work. In this revealing document we see the terrible price of prolonged field work in a strange culture. The loneliness and the dislocation of being constantly in a strange situation (we call that *culture shock* today), the despair at not having companions of one's own kind to share things with, the physical illness and psychological traumas of long-term field work are all revealed there.

See Bronislaw Malinowski, *A Diary in the Strict Sense of the Term*, translated by N. Guterman (Harcourt Brace Jovanovich). Another account of an anthropological field worker's personal problems has been published under the pseudonym of Elenore Smith Bowen: *Return to Laughter* (Natural History). A more systematic discussion can be found in G. Berreman's *Behind Many Masks: Ethnography and Impression Management in a Himalayan Village* (Society for Applied Anthropology Monograph Series, No. 4, 1967).

Each field worker goes into the field for the first time and discovers these things for himself. Only in the past decade have the trials of extended field research begun to be a subject in themselves. But once a researcher has survived the experience, and no matter how certain he is that the negative aspects will be repeated, although perhaps not quite as severely, elsewhere, there seems to be a constant magnet drawing him back to the field. The experience of being among a foreign people and seeking out their ways and thoughts and patterns, and finally being accepted as at least something of a human being, is a bit of a narcotic.

To achieve this reward, anthropologists have herded sheep in Arizona, reindeer in Lapland, and water buffalo in India. They have grown peanuts and yams in Africa, and risked their lives fishing in the South Pacific. Not one of them can afford to take the germ theory of disease too seriously—if they did they would never go into the field in the first place, or eat what they must eat, or live the way many of them have to live. Some of them have died in the field, and many will never shake off some plaguey disease.

Anthropologists need not always be heroes in a physical sense. I did field work in India while living in the summer house of a maharajah who needed the rent money, with servants and a radio and electric lights and—miracle of miracles—a hot water heater. Discomfort is not a precondition of field work. If one can avoid it, one should. No biologist would pound his microscope with a hammer and then use it, just to boast how tough things were. The anthropologist's own mind and body are the only instruments of observation he has, and he should not abuse them unnecessarily.

This is perhaps less an issue today than it was in the past. Increasingly, in the 1930's, anthropologists began to study peasant peoples, not simply remote tribes. These studies in many cases took investigators into cities as well. The phenomenon of urbanization that was sweeping the world also directed scholarly attention to cities. World War II forced us to think about the anthropological concepts we could apply to understanding both our allies and our enemies. The increasingly obvious domestic problems in the United States have increased our interest in scenes familiar and very close indeed. But the principle remains the same: to find out about man, you must go among men. There is no other way. It is perhaps the most important contribution anthropology has made to science, this simple idea.

To many scientists, including many anthropologists themselves, anthropological research in the field is singularly unscientific. The absence of controls such as are available in laboratory experiments, and the lack of valid statistical statements to support conclusions, have often engendered criticism of anthropology's claim to being scientific.

From one point of view, many of these criticisms are reasonable. However, in my opinion they are founded largely on a misconception of the problem at hand. Ideally, a field worker should choose his field situation to suit the phenomenon to be investigated; for instance, the village he lives in should be typical of the people he is studying. Some studies spend a great deal of time explaining, from this point of view, why the field worker went where he went. All too often, however, the thing that dictates the location of field work is some element entirely separate from scientific considerations. One cannot work in a village, no matter how typical it may be, if there is no place for him to live, or if the people of the village choose not to be studied. The modern sociologist can determine statistically that a given town or neighborhood is typical in terms of the factors he wishes to examine, and thus set up a very systematic project. For most anthropologists, however, the basic data on which the sociologist bases such a choice are simply not available. As Professor John H. Rowe once said, "If we knew what a typical village was, we wouldn't need to go there in the first place." In short, the business of studying cultures as they occur is guided entirely by the nature of the phenomenon, not by the methodological needs of the science. Although perhaps not so obviously, this is true in other sciences as well. The astronomer cannot use the tools of the biologist. His subject matter is in the sky, and he must find the place best suited to study it, and use the tools best suited to help him. He cannot make the planets and stars respond to the theoretical and methodological needs of the scientist. Nor can the anthropologist.

Seldom do the investigations of a field worker follow the neat outlines of his original proposal. His subjects, people, are too independent and interested in their own affairs. And he, as a human, must survive in human terms—that is, he must live and have shelter and minimal comforts to allow him to keep his mind on his business, rather than on his survival. The field worker who is reeling from fever, no matter how heroic and romantic he may seem, is seldom a good observer. The arrogant field worker who feels that the villager or peasant or tribesman should inconvenience himself to aid in the investigation is probably a worse observer because he is not dealing with his informants as human beings at all.

The physical scientists, and many of the social scientists, derive information from artificial situations—in laboratories, psychiatric clinics, and other experimental situations. For their purposes, this is fine. The information they seek can be obtained that way—perhaps only in that way. The anthropologist, however, has set himself a different task: observing culture in the natural state with as little distortion as possible brought about by the investigator. The anthropologist must depend on his own objectivity to the extent of understanding his personal bias and making it clear to those who will read his findings. He must not carry the standards of his culture into the

Figure 86.   Current methods of collecting anthropological data.

field as a yardstick by which to measure other peoples. He must report all he sees and make his conclusions clear. To that degree he is a scientist. If being a scientist means wearing a white coat, or having to support every statement statistically, then he is not a scientist—and many anthropologists are happy about it.

EPILOGUE: THE CONCEPT OF CULTURE

The concept of culture gives us a foundation for talking about differences in behavior and belief and attitude between different populations. But having found an explanation not rooted in genetics or psychology or superstitions, we are now faced with the problems of unraveling the processes and history of culture itself.

As we have seen, the term *culture* can be applied in many different ways: as a set of categories, or a study of patterns and style, or as a set of relationships between a group of people and their environment. Each of these applications, in a sense, is a specific example of cultural process. The ethnoscientist is perhaps the most aware of this, and he says, "The theory here is not so much a *theory of culture* as it is *theories of cultures,* or a theory of descriptions."

For example, the ethnoscientist who seeks categories and classifications used by different peoples realizes that his work is partially self-limiting because he does not seek universals to be found in all societies and cultures, but rather the accurate description of the specifics of a single society. And yet, he does have a theory of culture. Culture is to him a series of categories, taught by one generation to the next, which is shared by all the members of the group in question. The universal here is the existence of the categories themselves—the fact that men do organize their experience and define it in special ways.

What other anthropologists have discovered over the past century, is that there are certain preconditions for categorization. That is, in order to establish classifications for things as man does, a creature must possess certain attributes.

Human culture is dependent in part on the human body and its potentials. Perhaps the most important of these potentials, and one we have spoken about least, is *language*: the ability to speak to other men, to convey to them experiences which they have not had and will never have. Language allows men to create gods and spirits and devils and angels, although no one has ever agreed as to how these creatures look. Language allows one to establish a flag as an object worth fighting for. And language, to a degree, shapes the way we look at the world around us.

Yet the basis for culture is not language, for language itself is based on yet another human ability. Man makes symbols. Language is a system of symbols. Human life is inconceivable without language, and thus without the ability to make symbols. Man's ability to make symbols goes far beyond language, as we have seen. One cannot speak of patterns or categories without assuming that man has the ability to abstract to the degree necessary to include a number of individual objects or phenomena in a single classification.

The basic mental ability to make symbols and use language would appear to be a genetic inheritance. But precisely what symbols and what language we use is founded on our ability to learn, combined with the accident of our birth. The human being requires a long period during which other human beings must care for him and teach him before he can begin to take part in the human world. What he learns, for the most part, are the preconceptions—that is, the categories or patterns—of the culture into which he is born. Precisely how all the lessons of culture are conveyed is one of the mysteries of human life. Some aspects of a culture are implanted in the human mind so deeply and firmly that they seem virtually impossible to unlearn. Many are unconscious, and these are sometimes the most tenacious. Our culture is conveyed not only to our brains as conscious memory but also to our muscles and nerves and organs, so that we often walk, sit, bend over, defecate, and get sick according to patterns established for our own culture.

Culture also defines our reality for us. What is beautiful or ugly, valuable or worthless, admirable or despicable—even what is there or not there—is defined by the culture in which we live. To an American, whether he be a lumberman or a conservationist, a tree is a tree. The dispute between them is only in terms of what to do with the tree. But both of them would be a bit taken aback when confronted with an Indian peasant who may well think the trees, or at least certain trees, are living creatures like himself with needs and emotions to be served.

It is shortsighted to simply brush aside such beliefs as superstition, something to be swept away by Western education and the light of reason. For one thing, if you spend time in an Indian village, associating with the villagers as human beings, appreciating their individual talents, wisdoms, and idiosyncracies, you will soon find yourself believing that certain trees have special qualities. That is, you will begin to act as if they did because all the perfectly reasonable people around you act as if they did. Nor does a counterargument from another cultural context really have much impact.

In one Southeast Asian country many people are not deeply influenced by their belief in evil spirits being abroad, but this is not a triumph of reason over unreason. Rather, the very hard-headed and practical people of that country have assumed that with the increase of automobiles, most of the evil spirits have been run over and destroyed. A friend of mine working in the rural Philippines, while talking to a well-educated school teacher, mentioned the possibility of evil spirits inhabiting a certain grove of bamboo. The teacher laughed at the idea. My friend assumed that his amusement was a product of education and Western thought—our way of thinking had been transferred to him. He changed his mind when the teacher said, "We don't worry about that sort here anymore. A priest came out and drove all the spirits out of those woods."

The concept of culture has proven useful because it gives us a way of explaining human behavior without resort to biological or other kinds of explanations. We know so much about man today that it would be impossible to attribute much of what we know to biology. That is, to try to equate all the variations of human behavior with inherited differences would require reworking all we know about genetics. We have seen how an entire population can and does modify its culture, even abandon one and take up another, and change its language and social organization in the process. We have seen how a tribe can split into two parts and in a relatively short time learn that each of the new tribes has developed special patterns of culture and language and special social structures of its own. The rate of this kind of change is simply too fast to be accounted for biologically.

> In *Theory of the Leisure Class* (Kelley), Thorsten Veblen pointed out that conspicuous consumption of goods and services has social, not economic foundations. Many ethnographers have noted similar behavior in non-Western societies, both simple and complex.

The concept of culture frees us from dependence on any single line of explanation. We can look beyond economic structures, for instance, to help explain behavior which economics alone simply can't explain. There are those who would attempt to explain all of man's history in economic terms. The more closely they adhere to that rule the sillier their arguments become.

Even economic behavior itself is affected by cultural perceptions of reality. Veblen long ago pointed out that often man buys and consumes, not in the attempt to exert the least effort for the largest profit, but rather to remind himself and his fellows what a fine guy he is. I once asked a farmer in upstate New York why he had purchased a tractor. He obviously didn't like the machine and was uncomfortable with it. On the other hand, he loved his plow horses and loved working with them. His farm was of a size that made the horses practical, and the added expense of the tractor in terms of gasoline, oil, and spare parts was economically questionable. He pondered the question for a while, as if he had thought about it a great deal himself, and finally said, "My boys were embarrassed at school because their old man still used horses and all the rest of the kids' fathers had tractors—so I bought the damn'd thing." Thus it is with man. The opinion of his neighbors and their children is often more important than the economic facts which according to many, are supposed to guide us all. Rather than economics shaping culture, in this instance culture—that is, the expectations and attitudes of a rural community—shaped economics.

For many years, probably because they worked with simpler tribal peoples, anthropologists treasured the idea that each culture was a perfectly balanced whole. Any part of the cultural pattern could be analytically related to any other part if one studied hard enough, and a change in any part would affect all other parts. As we become involved in examining modern complex societies, and societies in a state of rapid change, we have become less certain of this. Man actually seems to be able to support a number of totally contradictory categories or patterns at one time without feeling too uncomfortable about it. This is not to say that cultures are a hodgepodge of customs and practices without relationship. We have learned too much already to accept that. But at the same time we also can see how change can be accommodated by individual societies without unduly upsetting them. This is partly accounted for by a general habit on the part of mankind to accept what *is* as what *always has been*, just as people accept the environment they see as the static and unchanging aspect of their lives. However, the rate of change in the world today is so rapid that man's ability to support a number of contradictory ideas and behavior patterns, each one carefully compartmentalized and trotted out when needed, is being challenged.

Culture has provided man with a way of dealing with his environment, and deal with it he has. Even the simplest and smallest band of hunters and gatherers has affected the world in which they live. So deeply have we involved ourselves in the processes of nature, utilizing them or ignoring them to the benefit of man, that we find that we seem to be threatening our own future. The life scientists, and many of the social scientists and humanists, who speak about the future, are exceedingly gloomy because they do not think in cultural terms. Or if they do, they think of culture as static and unchanging and therefore they give up hope that man can reverse his directions. Yet the history of the human race suggests that we can, because of our cultural potential, change very dramatically if it suits our purposes. We can, as have many people in the past, completely redefine our reality in order to continue to live. We may be in the process of doing that now. Thus, the concept of culture is an optimistic one.

If man were a totally biological creature, the only way we could change our behavior would be to kill off those we deemed "unfit." In fact, that is precisely what Nazi Germany tried to do; the entire Nazi philosophy was a biological philosophy, as is the racist philosophy that permeates our culture. Nor do economic or environmental explanations provide much more hope. Economic systems do seem to resist change, in and of themselves, but if man can change his expectations, assumptions, and definitions, then economic systems will alter to conform. We know that by examining many many different economic systems in many different cultures.

To understand culture has required that we first understand and accept the natural variation in the human behavior we see. That is, before we ask why men are different, we must accept the fact that they *are* different, and that this is to be expected and respected as the natural order of things. We must be willing to look objectively at all the things men do, as valid expressions of the human experience. Once we have accepted that notion, it is possible to examine the bewildering variety of human expressions and seek the generalizations and universals which are *human nature*. When we understand that each man is a creature of his own culture, but that he is physically no different than ourselves, and that the differences between us exist because we have responded to the same processes and stimuli, we can then see all men as indeed being human beings worthy of respect and trust as human beings. We cannot go half way. That is, we cannot assume that all men are capable of learning our culture and strive for *that* goal on the basis that *then* we could understand each other better. Rather, we must accept the variation between peoples as natural, and respect each man's culture as we say we wish to respect each man. It is unlikely that there would be much future for mankind if all of us spoke the same language, shared the same set of perceptions, and had the same goals. From whom would we learn anything or from which direction would new alternatives come?

Culture, then, is in fact *human nature*. The abilities and potentials of a culture-bearing creature create precisely the points of difference that exist between man and animals. In the past, culture has not infrequently been something of a prison as well as a protection. Many, perhaps many millions, of creative people in all cultures have been prevented from fully developing their own potentials. In large part that was because men did not understand the concept of culture and attributed "the way things are" to God or the Devil or some other dogma, secular or theological. If we understand the concept of culture, we can use that understanding to improve the human lot in both material and spiritual terms. A failure to grasp this basic concept will probably mean that man will never understand his own nature, and thus will follow wrong roads into the future—roads that could lead to his extinction.

INDEX

A

Acculturation, 44, 318–319
Acephalous societies, 110
Adult roles and childbearing, 125–126
Age-area hypothesis, 232–234
Animals, social behavior of, 80–81
Anthropological research, 311–324
    fieldwork, 311–314
    scientific method, 205–207
Anthropology
    classifications, vii
    cognitive, 203–206
    cultural—*see* Cultural anthropology;
        Culture
    defined, vii–viii
    history, 2–11
    social, 319
Anthropomorphism, 194
Arensberg, Conrad, 212
Avunculocality, 173

B

Behavior
    and kinship, 111–113
    patterned, 215–226
Beliefs and believing, 293–310 (*see also*
    Religion)
    effect on fieldwork, 294–295
    power of, 293–296, 327
Benedict, Ruth, 216–217, 219–220
Biological explanations of cultural
    variation, 13–37
Biological foundations of culture, 39–46
Black Americans
    and caste in the United States, 155–158
    contributions, 31–32
    prejudice, 30–31

Boas, Franz, 230, 313
Brahman caste (*varna*), 158–161
Brain and head of man, 42–43, 47–48
Bride price, 146–148
    Hupa Indians, 147–148
Burakumin, 161

C

Caste, 153–161 (*see also* Classes)
    defined, 154–155
    structure in: India, 157, 158–161;
        Japan, 161; United States,
        155–158
Caucasoid, definition of, 17
Childbearing and adult roles, 125–126
    Island of Yap, 125–127
Child-rearing and mating, 43–46
Civilization, variety of, 21–27 (*see also*
    Anthropology; Culture)
Clans, 106–110
    lineages, 108–110
    Navajo, 107–108
Classes
    military, 183–184
    social, 162–170
        and kinship, 169
        differences and conflicts, 168–170
        in China, 165–167; in Japan,
            162–165; in United States,
            167–168
        mobility of, 166–168
Classification
    racial, 16–20
    systems, 207–214
Classificatory kinship, 113–114
Cognitive anthropology, 203–206
Conklin, Harold C., 206

Personality and culture, 320
Phonemes defined, 51–52
Physical characteristics, human, 16, 19
  hands and feet, 40–42
  head and brain, 42–43
  primitive traits, 20–21
Political units, 171–190
Polyandry, 135–137
Polygamy, 130–135
Polygyny, 130–137
Power, transfer of, 188–190
  United States, 189–190
Prejudice, American, 30–32
Priests, 303, 305, 308
Primitive traits, 20–21
Primogeniture, 102
Psychological testing, 27–29

R

Race
  classifications, 16–21
    Caucasoid, 17
    Mongoloid, 17
    Negroid, 17
    Oceanic Negroid, 17
  definition, 13–14
  physical features, 20–21
  study of—see also Ethnology
Racism
  and science, 15–17
  foundation for caste, 153–158
Reality: structured by language, 55–57
Reincarnation, 303
Religion (see also Magic; Mana)
  belief and, 293–310
  curing function, 306
  defined, 296–297
  drug induced experiences, 309
  practitioners of, 303–308
  problem of death, 301
  sacred and profane, 308–310
  society and, 309
Republic, 180
Residence and marriage, 172–174
Roles, human: determined by society, 81

Romance in America, 141–145
Rowe, John Howland, 8

S

Samurai, 163–165
Sapir, Edward, 55–57
Scholarship, history of, 3–6
Science and racism, 15–17
Seligman, Brenda, 65–66
Sequoya, 201
Sex and marriage, 126–127
Sexuality
  human and animal compared, 43–44
  incest taboo: society's foundation,
    59–73
Shamans, 303–305
Shockley, William, 34
Shogun, 162–163
Sibling rivalry, 66–67
Slavery: as racism, 15–16
Social behavior
  animal, 80–81
  human, 76–190, 194, 255–256
Social stratification—see Caste; Classes,
  social
Social structure, 81–82 (see also Caste,
  Classes, social)
  hunting and gathering societies, 24–25
Societal controls, 120 (see also Kinship)
  and use of force, 176–177
Societies (see also Caste; Classes, social)
  acephalous, 110
  and kinship, 105–121
  and social behavior, 76–190
  based on incest taboo, 59–73
  defined, 60
  varieties, 7–8, 10
Sororate, 130
State (the), 178–182
Status, 82
Steward, Julian, 245–246, 287–288
Superstition, 309
Symbols
  and categories, 199–203
  and language, 47–58, 201